OPERATION AUTONOMOUS

OPERATION AUTONOMOUS

—

WITH S.O.E. IN WARTIME ROMANIA

—

Ivor Porter

CHATTO & WINDUS
LONDON

Published in 1989 by
Chatto & Windus Ltd
30 Bedford Square
London WC1B 3SG

A CIP catalogue record for this book
is available from the British Library

ISBN 0 7011 3170 5

Maps by John Flower

Typeset by Opus, Oxford

Printed in Great Britain by
Mackays of Chatham PLC, Kent

For Katerina

Contents

Illustrations

Maps

Acknowledgements

Elisabeth Barker encouraged me to undertake this work and, had she lived to look at the draft, it would undoubtedly have been a better book.

I am grateful to Professor Ghita Ionescu, Dr Dennis Deletant, Sir Denis Wright, who also lent me his diaries, Sir William Deakin, Mircea Ionniţiu, Kim and Sheila Fergurson and the late Horia Georgescu and his wife, Paddy, for their comments on the draft and to Baron Mocsony-Styrcea, Dr Maurice Pearton, Clare Hollingworth and Dr Harry Hanak for their advice on specific points.

I am particularly grateful to King Michael for letting me have his photograph.

I am greatly indebted to Caroline Dawnay of A.D. Peters for making the book possible, to Elaine Robson Scott for helping me with official German documents, to Prince Matei Ghica for giving me the pilot's angle, to Baron George Serdici for enriching my Romanian library, to Mircea Ionniţiu for clearing up points about the coup from his first-hand experience, to Annie Samuelli for reminding me of events which I had forgotten, to Olympia Zamfirescu for letting me see her memoirs in draft, and to friends who have lent me photographs of the period.

To two people I feel an especial gratitude – Rica Georgescu and Jeremy Lewis of Chatto & Windus. When the book was running late Jeremy Lewis applied no pressure, only kindness, encouragement and pertinent suggestions. Rica Georgescu has not only paid several visits to London to discuss the events of 1944, he has also, and for the first time, described his own and his wife Lygia's experiences in detail. My great debt to him is apparent throughout the book.

Although I did not have access to the SOE archives, Christopher Woods, the SOE Adviser to the Foreign Office, has gone to great trouble to provide fully documented answers to my questions. I should also like to thank the Romanian Embassy for the very useful collection of Documents in *23 August 1944: Documente, 1939–1944*, the officials of the Public Record Office where most of my research was done and the librarians at the Royal Institute of International Affairs, the British Library, the London Library and the library of the Imperial War Museum; also the Royal Geographical Society for their help with maps.

Finally, a word of thanks to my family for putting up with it all so cheerfully.

The poem on page 134 is reprinted by kind permission of Shepheard-Walwyn Ltd.

List of Romanian Names

Note: As Romanian names are so unfamiliar to the English reader the list below is given for reference. The accented vowels and consonants are pronounced roughly as follows:

ă as the 'u' in 'cut'; â as the 'u' in 'cull'; ţ as the 'ts' in 'tsar'; and ş as the 's' in 'sugar'

Antonescu, General Ion	Became pro-German dictator of Romania September 1940. Executed 1946.
Antonescu, Mihai (Ica)	No relation. Minister of Justice and later Premier and Foreign Minister under Antonescu. Executed 1946.
Balan	Electrical engineer. Member of the Popovici network.
Beza, Jean	W/T operator. Member of the Popovici network.
Bodnăraş, Emil	(Code-name *Ceauşu*). Influential member of the Romanian Communist Party. Minister of Defence 1947.
Brătianu, Constantin (Dinu)	Suceeded Duca as head of the Romanian Liberal Party in 1933. During the war worked closely with Maniu in support of the Allies. Died in prison.
Brătianu, Gheorghe	Pro-German Professor of History. Ostracised for a time by his family for collaborating with King Carol. Friend of Mihai Antonescu. Died in prison.
Brătianu, Ion	1821–91. Liberal Leader. In 1866 invited Prince Charles of Hohenzollern-Sigmaringen (later

	King Carol I) to be prince of Moldavia and Wallachia.
Brătianu, Ionel	1864–1927. Son of Ion Brătianu. Prime Minister during the First World War. Largely responsible for Romania's agrarian and electoral reforms.
Brătianu, Vintila	1867–1930. Engineer. Succeeded his brother Ionel as head of the Liberal Party.
Brauner, Harry	Distinguished folklorist.
Călinescu, Armand	Wallachian lawyer. Minister of the Interior February 1938, Prime Minister March 1939, assassinated by the Iron Guard September 1939.
Codreanu, Corneliu Zelea	Founder of the pro-German Iron Guard. Executed by King Carol in 1938.
Cretzianu, Alexander	One of Maniu's collaborators. Appointed Romanian Minister to Turkey in September 1943 and kept in touch with SOE during and after the armistice negotiations of March–April 1944.
Cristea, Miron	Romanian Patriarch. Prime Minister February 1938–March 1939.
Cristescu, Eugen	Head of the Romanian Security and Secret Service under Marshal Antonescu.
Davidescu, Colonel Radu	Head of Marshal Antonescu's military cabinet.
Davidescu, Ştefan	Member of the Foreign Ministry.
Dobrojan, Captain	Prison duty officer.
Duca, Georghe	Ion Duca's son. Appointed Counsellor at the Romanian Legation in Stockholm August 1943 with a brief from Maniu.
Duca, Ion	Leader of the Liberal Party after Vintila Brătianu's death. Formed a government under King Carol, November 1933. Assassinated by the Iron Guard, December 1933.
Duţa, Captain	Prison duty officer.

Fărcășanu, Mihai — Leader of the Young Liberals. Publisher of the newspaper *Viitorul*.

Filderman, Dr W. — Leader of the Jewish community during the Second World War. Friend of Marshal Antonescu.

Gafencu, Grigore — Pro-Allied Foreign Minister under King Carol December 1938–May 1940. He was then appointed Romanian Minister in Moscow and remained abroad for the duration of the war.

Georgescu, Lygia — *Née* Bocu. Married to Rica Georgescu. An active member of the Romanian Resistance.

Georgescu, Rica — Code-name *Jockey*. Managing Director of Romana Americana before the war. Arrested for pro-Allied activities. Ran a network of agents from prison and helped re-establish Maniu's communications with the Allies. Under-Secretary of State for Finance and Economy in the post-*coup* government.

Georgescu, Teohari — An influential member of the Romanian Communist Party. Minister of the Interior, 1947. Purged 1952.

Gheorghiu — Managing Director of Creditul Minier. In 1943 he contacted de Chastelain in Istanbul on behalf of Maniu and Georgescu.

Gheorghiu Dej, Gheorghe — Railway worker and member of the Romanian Communist Party. First Secretary of the Party and Minister of Communications, 1944. Head of State, 1961.

Ghica, Prince Matei — Pilot. Worked with the Romanian Resistance.

Gigurtu, Ion — Headed a pro-German government after the loss of Bessarabia in June 1940.

Groza, Petru — 1884–1958. Leader of the Ploughman's Front affiliated to the

	Communist Party. Prime Minister 1945, President 1952.
Ionescu, Captain	Prison duty officer.
Ionescu, Alecu	Rica Georgescu's assistant at Romana Americana and later a key man in his SOE network.
Ionescu, Colonel Emilian	Officer in charge of the Palace Guard during King Michael's *coup d'état*.
Ionescu, Colonel Radu	Governor of the prison in Calea Plevnei from where Georgescu operated.
Ionnițiu, Mircea	King Michael's Secretary.
Lupescu, Elena	Mistress of King Carol II.
Madgearu, Virgil	Economist. Secretary General of the National Peasant Party. Murdered by the Iron Guard 1940.
Maniu, Juliu	1873–1953. Led the Transylvanian National Party and later the Romanian National Peasant Party. Democrat and constitutionalist. Sworn enemy of King Carol II. Leader of the anti-German resistance during the Second World War and one of the prime movers of the *coup* which took Romania into the Allied camp. Died in prison February 1953.
Manoilescu, Mihai	Gigurtu's pro-German Foreign Minister. Signed the Vienna Diktat on 30 August, 1940.
Manolescu, General	Head of the Royal Domain at Bușteni. Lygia Georgescu's uncle.
Mihalache, Ion	Born 1882. Teacher. Leader of the Wallachian Peasant Party which in 1928 united with the Transylvanian National Party to form the National Peasant Party. Maniu's close collaborator.
Mocsony-Styrcea, Baron Ion	King Michael's Marshal of the Palace.
Mugur, Costica	Accountant. Worked with Georgescu and later with author.
Nanu, Frederick	Romanian Minister to Sweden during the armistice negotiations of 1944.

Nasta, Liviu	Distinguished Romanian journalist. Died in prison.
Nasta, Pussy	Daughter of Liviu. Broadcast back to Romania from the Middle East.
Niculescu-Buzeşti, Grigore	Head of Communications Department of the Foreign Ministry during the war. Foreign Minister in first post-*coup* government.
Pantazi, General Constantin	Marshal Antonescu's Minister of War.
Pătrăşcanu, Lucreţiu	Communist Party link with the traditional parties. Minister of Justice in the first post-*coup* government.
Pauker, Anna	Influential member of the Soviet wing of the Romanian Communist Party. Minister of Foreign Affairs, 1947. Purged, 1952.
Petrescu, Titel	Born 1888. Leader of the Social Democratic Party. Died in prison.
Pogoneanu, Victor	Head of cypher section of the MFA.
Popovici	Engineer. De Chastelain's assistant at Unirea. In 1940 set up SOE network in Romania.
Rădescu, General	Prime Minister, December 1944 to February 1945.
Rădulescu, (Pichi)	Collaborated with Buzeşti, Maniu and the King during the war. Died in prison.
Samuelli, Annie	Annie and Bobsie Samuelli were friends of the Legation. After the *coup* Annie joined the author's office.
Sănătescu, General Constantin	Head of King Michael's Military Household. Prime Minister of first two post-*coup* governments.
Sima, Horia	Succeeded Codreanu as head of the Iron Guard in 1938.
Ştefanescu, Alecu	Coates representative in Romania. Friend of Marshal Antonescu. Provided financial facilities for Georgescu's network. Died in prison.
Şteflea, General	Marshal Antonescu's Chief of Staff.

Ştirbey, Prince Barbu	Close adviser to Queen Marie. Maniu's emissary to the armistice talks of 1944.
Stiubey, Sandy	Member of the Romanian Navy. Worked with SOE.
Tătărescu, George	Dissident Liberal. Brătianu and Maniu never forgave him for collaborating with King Carol. Groza's Foreign Minister, 1945–7.
Titulescu, Nicolae	Distinguished Foreign Minister and president of the League of Nations during the Thirties.
Tobescu, General	Head of the Romanian Gendarmerie.
Turcanu, Nicolae	Code-named *Reginald*. Wireless operator working with Captain Russell and subsequently first with Georgescu and then with author.
Ungur, Captain	Prison Duty Officer.
Vasiliu, General 'Piki'	Marshal Antonescu's Under-Secretary at the Ministry of the Interior and Inspector General of the Gendarmerie.
Vişoianu, Constantin	Diplomat. Protégé of Titulescu and Maniu's close collaborator. Took part in Cairo armistice negotiations. Foreign Minister, November 1944–March 1945. Escaped to the USA.
Zamfirescu, Olympia	A friend of the Legation.

Foreword

In the summer of 1943 Albert Speer, Hitler's Minister of Arms Production, forecast that the war would end ten months after the Balkans were lost to Germany.

On 23 August 1944, a group of Romanian leaders carried out a *coup d'état* against the Germans. This narrative is about that *coup*, the events leading up to it, and its consequences.

It proved Speer right. It cleared the way for the Red Army to cross the narrow gap between the Carpathian mountains and the Black Sea: one of the best defensive positions in Europe. Within weeks the Balkans were lost to Germany and the war in Europe ended nine months later. Many American, British, German and Russian lives were saved, yet not one in a million has heard of this event.

By chance, the war caught me in Romania. I left with the Legation in February 1941, returned as part of an SOE mission in December 1943 and took part in the *coup* the following August.

PART ONE

———

March 1939–February 1941

Chapter 1

A Puritan's Guide to Bucharest

I took up a British Council lectureship at Bucharest University in March 1939, the month Hitler's troops occupied Prague and Mr Chamberlain was finally convinced that war was inevitable. Without fully realising it I had become a small cog in our belated attempt to stop the spread of German influence in Eastern Europe.

My recollection of that first journey to Romania is now spasmodic. The Channel crossing is a complete blank, the farewells at Victoria perhaps too painful. Yet I remember boarding the hushed Simplon Orient express at the Gare du Nord. I remember the national cuisines, the food becoming less familiar as each new dining car was attached to the train, and waking very early to gaze out at the great wheatplains of the Banat. I remember, too, the wagon-lit attendant in his brown uniform, an oldish man, wise in the ways of frontier officials and international crooks, and have still not forgotten the anxiety of trying to estimate his protection money.

At Ljubljana, in Yugoslavia, the main portion of the train headed south-east for Constantinople while the rest of us continued steadily eastwards. In those days the countries we crossed – Switzerland, Yugoslavia, Romania, even Mussolini's Italy – still recognised Britain and France as the world's leading nations. It was a comforting thought for a young Englishman travelling to a place which he knew might soon be pincered between Hitler's *Drang nach Osten* and Stalin's determination to restore tsarist frontiers.

The Gara de Nord at Bucharest was even livelier than the Gare du Nord – the crowd more Latin, 'swarthy' (a term applied in those more outspoken days to any European whose complexion was a little less pink than our own), perhaps shorter, the men blue-chinned, the women a mite frilly, the peasants dressed like peasants, the one Englishman on the platform dressed like an Englishman. This was, undoubtedly, Professor Burbank, his small glance swinging anxiously from one second-class sleeping compartment to the next, wondering what kind of an assistant they had sent him.

We shook hands and made English noises, both probably aware of what was left of my northern accent. He asked me questions about my journey; I

gave him the expected answers casually, concealing my excitement. He
selected porters and then, in the station courtyard, I saw my first horse
cabs, *trăsuri*, Burbank called them – their owners tall in their dark robes,
brightly coloured sashes round their bulky stomachs, peaked caps against
the sun. Eunuchs of the Skoptzi sect, Burbank informed me, and hurried
me and my small stuff into a regular taxi; the heavy luggage had been
registered through from Victoria and could be picked up later. On the way
he spoke of the quirks of an East European educational system based on
the French, and while I am sure I replied respectfully, turning to face him,
my eyes were really on the churches with hexagonal towers instead of
steeples, the small stuccoed houses each with its garden, minute domed
churches down side streets, the prosperous heavily built shady houses, the
skyscrapers, the tree-lined boulevard. There were Paris buses, single-
decker trams trailing second-class carriages, tramlines built too high so that
we bumped over them. At one crossing an armed policeman reversed his
stop-go sign with such a casual swing of the handle that our driver was
nearly caught napping, a whistle already shrieking as we shot past. In a side
street, stuck behind an ox cart, I had my first whiff of the Orient – a
mixture of raw sheepskin, rough wool, herbs, sun-baked manure. This was
Wallachia, a gateway to the East through which Romanians would always
look westwards.

Perhaps I spent that first night with the Burbanks, perhaps at an hotel.
Either way I soon moved to Madame Arditti's flat in Strada Spătarului. I
can no longer see her rooms though I feel them to have been spacious,
heavily furnished, *gemütlich*.

Madame Arditti looked after a covey of English. There were May
Hartley, secretary to Archie Gibson, the *Times* correspondent, Gertie
Gellender who worked with Desmond Doran, head of the passport office
at the Legation, John and Mary Campbell,* American graduates writing a
thesis on Nicolae Iorga, the Romanian historian. Alexander Miller and
Mary Vischer were with Astra Română, the biggest of the oil companies.
In June we were joined by David Walker, the *Daily Mirror* correspondent,
who, though a serious political observer, never missed a good body-in-the-
bath story.

I realised after a while that May Hartley and Alexander Miller had put
down roots in the country. They laughed with the rest of us about
Romanian inefficiency and backwardness, and warned me about corruption and a touch of brutishness, but nothing could alter their affection for
the people. Later I was to understand that feeling myself – not yet. I spent
the best part of one morning on a post office bench waiting for a parcel

*   He became Director of Studies on the US Council of Foreign Relations, which
publishes *Foreign Affairs*.

which I could have had in five minutes by slipping the underpaid clerk his bakhshish. Never forget that you are representing Britain, the chairman of the British Council had told me; but this kind of priggish behaviour was presumably not what he had had in mind.

In Bucharest I formed a lifelong habit of getting to know a town by walking its streets on Sundays. It was March, the garden restaurants on the broad boulevard were just opening, and I passed a rapturous hour drinking the local plum alcohol, called *ţuica*, from a bulbous glass with a long spout, breathing the spring air which touches Bucharest briefly between the snows and the continental heat, delighted with my few words of Romanian and my handling of the money.

I strolled along the three kilometres of Calea Victoriei, one of Bucharest's oldest streets which runs from the Piaţa Victoriei to the river Dâmboviţa, and commemorates the victory over the Turks in 1878 after more than four hundred years of Ottoman rule. Here Romanians shopped for anything special, had their hair done, met friends, hoped to meet friends, drank coffee at pavement tables, paraded in the evening, very occasionally demonstrated in the morning, and did all the things one would expect of a Latin people. It was a mixture of charming single-storey houses, which had stood in their shady courtyards since the last century, cafés, restaurants, Greek Orthodox churches – Romanians crossed themselves as they passed them – the pseudo-classical Royal Academy, the National Theatre, the concert hall, the new, long, low Royal Palace, and ministries – easily identified by policemen in pillboxes outside, though I was told at the Ardittis that any important family could hire a policeman to stand at their gate. Here, too, was the American telephone building, which was said to have high-speed lifts.

I enjoyed being part of it all, a foreigner at ease among such unfamiliar architecture and so many beautiful women, among officers in cardboard-stiffened épaulettes and shiny boots, people dawdling, others eager to get somewhere, peasants in their white smocks, their shirts outside their trousers – the sign of an honest man – the brown, unwashed breasts of the flower girls and, in the evening, the hungry smell of corn-on-the-cob cooking over the street braziers.

Among these people were some businessmen, civil servants and academics, but fewer of the established middle class than one would have found in Regent Street. Many were the children or grandchildren of peasants, a *petite bourgeoisie* which had only existed for twenty years, relying on their hair-dos, their contempt for village life and a smattering of French to distance themselves from their past.

I watched women carrying hods of bricks up rickety ladders, and men working on wooden scaffolding which we would have condemned in Britain. Some sat on the ground, eating slices of garlic and white cheese on a cold corn polenta called *mămăligă*.

On the Piaţa Brătianu, the gypsies looked as colourful in their skirts and kerchiefs as the large, flat baskets of blossom beside them. At first I startled them by paying what they asked. Later, when I had more Romanian words, I learned to haggle until we got down to a price which was only about double what they had expected.

I heard street cries of a kind that had almost disappeared from London. The paraffin man carried two drums on a shoulder harness and called *gāzu* with a long, long 'ā', while the man who sold glass carried it on his back in a wooden frame shouting *geamgiu*, which sounded like 'jāāām-jew'. Yoghurt was sold from a tray in small pots. And eggs – *ouă* – were carried in a basket, and sold to the melancholy sound of 'wōwā'.

One Sunday morning I walked to the outskirts of the town – to peasant houses, small factories, warehouses, and glimpses of the surrounding plains. Here the asphalt gave way to thick white dust, which must have been kinder to bare feet than town shoes. I approached two young women leaning on a fence, the next moment, one of them had pointed her breast and was squirting milk at me and both were in fits of laughter. I walked on, dumbfounded. For the rest of the day I kept asking myself whether this had been a gesture of high spirits or an unfriendly act directed against a Western intruder. I invented a great deal of political and moral gobbledegook to sooth my wounded puritanical soul.

From my window at Spătarului, I once witnessed another kind of violence: a man shot down, a touch of red blood in the snow. On a Saturday afternoon an old man would tramp along the street with an ancient hurdy-gurdy strapped to his shoulder; when some of us borrowed it for half an hour we collected a small fortune for him.

And sometimes, probably not as often as I felt I should, I sat down and wrote home about my experiences. My parents lived in Barrow-in-Furness, a clean, well-planned shipbuilding town on the edge of the Lake District with a beautiful bird-island called Walney alongside it. My father was a frustrated poet with an interest, like many other people of his time, in comparative religion. My mother came from the Lake District, where my brother Eric and I had spent our holidays playing tennis and croquet, swimming in the estuary, and walking in the hills. My mother was a cockney of the mountains, always cheerful, often nagging my father whom she really adored for having his head in the clouds. Both yearned for a bigger world and it was not difficult to convey to them the strangeness of the land where I was now living.

I had come to Bucharest for two reasons. After eight hungry months of freelance teaching, I badly needed a regular job. And my lectureship would combine my love of literature with a growing curiosity about Eastern Europe. Mr Chamberlain had described Czechoslovakia, for which we were now digging trenches in Hyde Park, as a faraway country about which we knew nothing. Romania was another of those faraway countries for which we might well go to war, and I wanted to know something about it.

At British Council headquarters in Davies Street, I had been briefed about the job and given a clothing allowance, a little of which I spent on clothes. About Romania itself, I knew little. An atlas showed me that it lay north of the lower reaches of the Danube between Hungary and Russia and was made up of three main provinces grouped around the central mountain ranges. Wallachia stretched from the Transylvanian Alps southward to the Danube and eastwards to the Black Sea. Moldavia, including Bessarabia and Bukovina, stretched eastwards from the Carpathians to the Russian steppes. Transylvania, the once wooded province where the story of Dracula was set, lay between the mountain ranges and the Hungarian frontier. I read that the language was basically Latin, but contained many Slav and some Turkish words. It was a comparatively rich country – 'the breadbasket of the Balkans' – with large British investment in oil and a community of British engineers and their families living in the Ploeşti region. Some leader writers thought that Romania had benefited unduly from the post-war collapse of the Russian and Central European powers, and that since these had now been resurrected as the USSR and the Third Reich it was in danger of losing Bessarabia to Russia and at least part of Transylvania to Hungary. I knew that Romanians were loyal supporters of the League of Nations. I had heard of dadaism, not knowing that it was Romanian in origin, and of Elvira Popescu, the most popular Paris comedienne of her day. In the popular press I had read about King Carol's love affair with the attractive red-head, Elena Lupescu. Although in the flurry of getting away, I had had no time to read any serious books on the region, I was not entirely ignorant of the country I was going to.

In 1930 the Treasury informed the Foreign Office that an annual grant of £2,300 would be available for Britain's cultural activities abroad. In 1935–6 the total grant to the British Council was £5,000, at a time when the French, Germans and Italians were spending as many millions.

It would have seemed absurd to a government as commercially minded as Mr Chamberlain's to spend money on propaganda in a country like Romania where students clamoured to learn our language and governments to increase their trade with us, and where we already had more friends than in any other East European country except possibly Greece. When Lord Lloyd, the Chairman of the British Council, requested £275,000 for worldwide cultural activities in the financial year 1939–40, the year we went to war and needed to keep and win friends, he referred, half apologetically and half ironically, to the Council's activities in

Romania: 'In Bucharest it was pressure of impatient students which forced us to open the Institute of English Studies before we were really ready.'[1] At King Carol's request, the mayor of Bucharest had offered the Council land 'for a building similar to the French and Italian'. Since then Lord Lloyd had obtained a professorship and a lectureship at the university, which were filled by Burbank and myself.

While adoring archaic uniforms and ceremony, the British disliked the idea of self-advertisement. Had a professional propagandist offered himself for my job he would almost certainly have been turned down. Britain preferred the amateur, and in me it certainly had one. At the time, I had probably never used the phrase 'political warfare'. More than most people, I shied away from ideological tags. The blues of the Thirties were, for me, apolitical – the blues of jazz and of Mr Eliot's *Waste Land*.

Chapter 2

Conversations and Bears

An old Greek vagabond of the Krivara district told Patrick Leigh Fermor that in his day – before the First World War – beggars would always head north of the Danube: 'Romanians were more prosperous and more open-handed, the place teemed with cattle and fowl and livestock of every kind, even buffaloes that the Romanians used for ploughing.'[1]

In 1939, when I arrived, well-to-do East Europeans would make shopping expeditions to Bucharest – 'the Paris of the Balkans', with one of the best native cuisines in Europe, and shops and restaurants known to connoisseurs as far away as London. In the country there were still plenty of cattle, buffaloes, pigs, and fowl. Romanian gypsy women had a little trick which they would never have confided to a Greek vagrant: as they passed a peasant farm they made a low purring sound, hardly noticeable to the human ear but all the turkeys, cocks, hens and chickens would immediately march out of the yard and follow them.

Never again would I see a country of such contrast and contradiction – of plains and mountains, the waters of the Danube and a thousand chattering trout streams. Lagondas, Hispano-Suizas and Packards sped along the national highway, but had to swerve to avoid ox carts or brake suddenly at night before a ring of gypsies cooking over the burning tar. Houses in Transylvania were not unlike houses in Austria or Switzerland, yet the monasteries further east could only have been built under the influence of Byzantium.

One Friday afternoon in May Ada, a Romanian girl, took me out of the Bucharest heat and up to the mountains for a weekend with her parents. Since I had no car this was my first drive to Ploeşti, through the Prahova valley, past oil rigs that stood against the sky like men in a Dali painting. The peasants, Ada said, could bring up a bucket of oil, like water, out of a well.

As we climbed into the Carpathians the smell of firs and pines took over from that of the oily plain. We flattened out for a moment in Sinaia, past the small railway station, elegant tea shops and an inelegant, white stucco casino which Ada said was run by an Englishman – a captain who had flown arms into Spain during the civil war, though she did not know to which side. I caught a glimpse of handsome villas dotting the hillside and the King's summer palace, the castle of Peles – a mixture of Gothic, Renaissance and Byzantine architecture which somehow did not look out of place up here; a kind of Balmoral for the Romanian royal family.

Her wolfhound, Fiţă, stood on the back seat, her nose stuck out of the window – she often caught a cold, it seemed, when driving to the hills. The Foreign Minister once rode for five kilometres with Fiţă's tail in his mouth, Ada said. She would never be properly trained and in the country could be taken for a wolf and shot. Ada cornered fast – Fiţă bracing at every bend – making what we called in those days a racing change; showing off a bit, but a good driver. Twenty minutes after leaving Sinaia we had climbed to Predeal on the pre-war Austro-Hungarian frontier and half an hour later to Timişul de Sus on the western ridge of the mountain range. Before the road dropped to Timişul de Jos we turned right, down a lane to the villa. The view was breathtaking. The Carpathian peaks stood behind us. Before us the Transylvanian plain stretched out into the haze of Central Europe.

Ada's father was very like her, but without her youthful fizz – dark hair, brown eyes, well built, courteous yet very direct. Like all Romanians he relied for communication on a warmer personal relationship than we English find necessary. Her mother, herself a Transylvanian, had already been at the villa for several weeks. I felt that to prepare for my visit she had got out of her working shoes, changed her dress, put away her book but that on Monday she would again become someone who – at a distance at least – could be taken for one of the locals.

When I had been introduced, Ada promised to be back for dinner and took me and Fiţă to the ridge of the Făgărasi mountains. The climb was hard, the going at the top easy on the rich, soft ground. We came upon primeval groves, and clearings where Ada showed me the holes left by bears digging for a succulent root. Yes, she said, there were plenty of brown Carpathian bears up here – they were quite friendly unless someone like Fiţă annoyed them.

The village girls climbed the mountain at four in the morning to fill their bucket-shaped baskets – *doniţe* – with wild strawberries, raspberries and blackberries. The bears were in competition for the fruit. If they heard a bear they would lie down with their skirts over their heads so that it would know they were women and not attack them.

'I don't believe it,' I said.

'Well you should. It has probably been happening since pagan times.'

Before we turned back we sat for a while on the edge of the ridge looking down at the meadows of harebells, campanulas, gentian, and marguerites, the high grass rustling and shimmering in the late afternoon light. Far down the valley was a cluster of houses and the slow movement of a peasant cart. It was, I told myself, only a grander version of something I had often seen from the Langdales, yet it had a very different effect on me.

'What do the peasant girls do with their fruit?' I asked.

She laughed. 'They run down to Predeal in time to catch the Bucharest express and sell it through the carriage windows in cornets, which they twist out of leaves.'

Since Ada's father was a historian, I hoped at some point to get him to talk about Romanians. I already knew something about their turbulent history – the barbarian invasions sweeping up the Danube valley, Romanians taking refuge in these mountains and emerging a thousand years later looking as Latin as ever and speaking the language of their Daco-Roman ancestors, the fall of Constantinople in 1453 after which they became a buffer between the Turks, Russians and Austrians. But that did not tell me why, for instance, they disliked the Russians more than the Germans, or preferred the French to the British. Those were the kind of questions I wanted to put to Ada's father.

Next morning I had my chance. The three of us had been practising iron shots on the slope in front of the house, and when Ada went in to help with lunch, we gave up chipping at golf balls and sat down in the grass, knees up, staring down at Transylvania.

After a while he said 'I love all this.' He raised his club a few inches to include the mountains behind us. 'I probably love it more than any other part of the country.'

'And will you be able to hold on to it if Eastern Europe goes back into the melting pot?'

He hesitated. 'We can handle the Hungarians. The Wehrmacht, I don't know. We rely on you and the French . . .' He let the thought hang between us, knowing I was no more in the confidence of my government than he was.

Under Austro-Hungarian rule, the Romanians of Transylvania had become an underprivileged majority: their Orthodox religion was not recognised, while their women wore only black giving their children names that could not be magyarised. 'The idea that Romanians never revolt is ridiculous,' he said. 'Our history is full of revolt.' He had the unselfconscious way of handing out information which a professional lecturer displays even in ordinary conversation. Romanians had massacred hundreds of their Hungarian landlords in 1784, and their leaders had been broken on the wheel. 'It was probably a class as much as an ethnic oppression in those days,' he said: 'Yet a hundred years later Transylvania had become one of Europe's great nationalist issues.' Then he fell silent, as if suddenly aware of being on the verge of contemporary history.

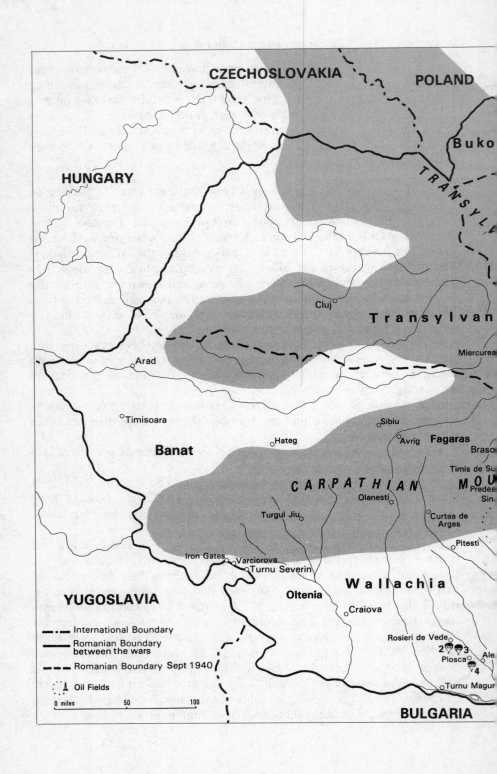

CZECHOSLOVAKIA

POLAND

Buko

HUNGARY

TRANSYLV

Cluj

Transylvan

Arad

Miercurea

Timisoara

Sibiu

Banat

Hateg

Avrig   Fagaras

Braso

Timis de Su

CARPATHIAN   MOU

Olanesti   Predea

Sin

Turgul Jiu

Curtea de
Arges

Pitesti

Iron Gates   Varciorova
Turnu Severin

Wallachia

Oltenia

YUGOSLAVIA

Craiova

Rosieri de Vede

2 ⚑ 3

Plosca   Ale

4

─·─ International Boundary
─── Romanian Boundary
    between the wars
─ ─ Romanian Boundary Sept 1940

⚑ Oil Fields

Turnu Magur

0 miles   50   100

BULGARIA

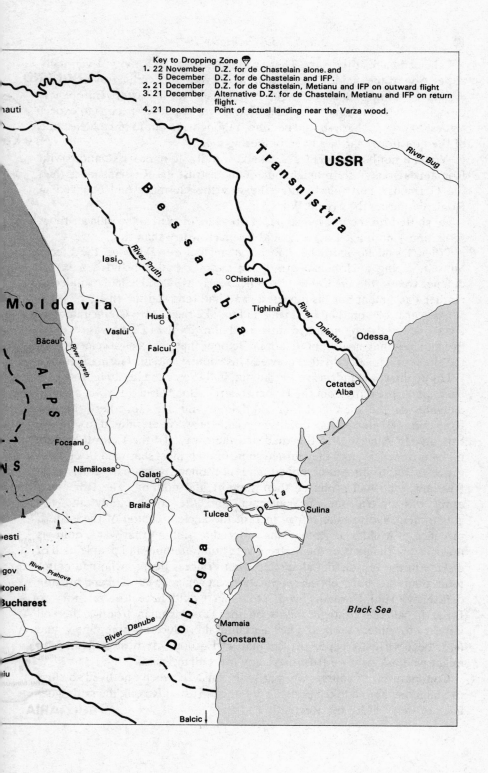

Key to Dropping Zone 🎈
1. 22 November   D.Z. for de Chastelain alone. and
   5 December   D.Z. for de Chastelain and IFP.
2. 21 December   D.Z. for de Chastelain, Metianu and IFP on outward flight
3. 21 December   Alternative D.Z. for de Chastelain, Metianu and IFP on return flight.
4. 21 December   Point of actual landing near the Varza wood.

USSR

Transnistria

River Bug

Bessarabia

hauti

River Pruth

Iasi

Chisinau

Tighina

River Dniester

Odessa

Moldavia

Husi

Vaslui

River Sereth

Bǎcau

Falcui

Cetatea Alba

ALPS

Focsani

Nǎmǎloasa

Galati

Braila

Tulcea

Delta

Sulina

N S

esti

River Prahova

gov

topeni

Bucharest

River Danube

Dobrogea

Mamaia

Constanta

Black Sea

iu

Balcic ↓

I glanced back at the villa. There was still no sign of activity. Eventually either Ada or the maid would appear on the verandah with a tray of drinks and olives, white goat cheese, squares of bread – for in Eastern Europe it is thought unwise to drink on an empty stomach, and discourteous to expect a guest to do so. There should be time, I thought, to put to him at least one of the questions that had been bothering me.

Would it not be a good idea, I asked carefully, to improve relations with Romania's great eastern neighbour? Why distrust the Russians more than the Germans? Particularly after the way the Germans had behaved in Romania during the World War?

He shifted on the uneven slope. 'Two years of systematic pillage, rape, spoliation – nothing, I agree, could be much worse than that.'

When I said no more he glanced at me before taking up the theme himself. Being a Hohenzollern, King Carol I had concluded a secret defence treaty with the Central Powers as early as 1883. He had confided in neither Parliament nor his ministers, and had renewed the treaty in 1913. When war broke out and he finally had to take the Crown Council into his confidence, only one man had supported him. By then Carol was seventy-five and in failing health; his death in October that year was accelerated by the stress of a loyalty divided between his country and his German family.

His nephew, the indecisive Ferdinand, had succeeded him. He, too, had been under pressure from the Hohenzollerns. But Marie, his wife, was the daughter of the then Duke of Edinburgh and she, together with the Romanian people and most of his government, was determined to join the Entente. In August 1916 they had had their way. To the Central Powers this was treachery, and they turned some of their most seasoned troops and generals on to the ill-equipped and ill-trained Romanian army. The Russians, who had promised their support, did nothing. The Romanian army was driven out of Wallachia, and the royal family and the government had to take refuge in Iaşi, the ancient capital of the eastern province of Moldavia. Romanians suffered terribly in that war – quite as much as the Belgians or the Serbs. Three hundred thousand people died of disease in the Iaşi district alone and even Princess Ileana, who had better food than the bulk of the population, never recovered from vitamin deficiency. Had Germany won, Romania would have lost territory to Bulgaria, all the strategic points on the Transylvanian frontier, her oil industry for ninety years and her agricultural produce for nine. She would have been virtually wiped off the map of Europe. My host smiled. 'You might well ask why we trust Germany more than Russia.'

Communism, of course, was partly the answer; when one lived so close to Stalin one had to take notice. 'Yet our mistrust of Russia,' he said, 'goes back to long before the Revolution.'

For instance, Catherine the Great had proclaimed that she would liberate her Romanian coreligionists from the Turk. But once over the frontier she established a protectorate which lasted for two generations. A century later Prince Charles of Romania had joined the last of the Russo-Turkish wars on the Tsar's side; in 1877 he personally had led the joint Romanian-Russian forces to victory at the decisive battle of Plevna. Yet at the peace settlement – the Congress of Berlin – Russia intrigued with Britain to take southern Bessarabia, a part of Moldavia, away from her ally who did not have a seat at the congress. Gladstone in opposition was outraged; Joseph Chamberlain in government tried to keep the British public in the dark about his part in the deal for as long as possible.

Nor had St Petersburg lifted a finger to help her Romanian ally against the Austro-German forces during the World War. Once again they had designs on Moldavia. This time Britain protested; the French described Russia's behaviour as 'military treason'; Queen Marie was about to go to St Petersburg to plead with her cousin the Tsar when news reached Iaşi of Rasputin's murder. 'The fact that the Russians have almost always pillaged us not as enemies but while pretending to be our allies – that, I think, is what we cannot forgive.'

He fell silent again, but then went on: 'We Romanians have strong loyalties and hatreds which to you will not always seem rational. We often see conspiracy where it possibly does not exist. Invasion and occupation may toughen but, believe me, they also corrupt.' He turned to me. 'If Romanians had today to choose between the Allies and Germany, ninety per cent would choose the Allies. You've been here long enough to see that. But if ever they had to choose between the Russians and the Germans, ninety per cent would choose the latter. We're hoping, of course' – we were already scrambling to our feet because Ada was calling us – 'not to have to make that choice.'

When we were all seated on the verandah, I steadied Fiţă's tail with my left hand, raised my glass a few inches above the table and said, 'To Romania.'

"To a democratic Romania,' my host replied and Ada and her mother, who had heard it all before, started to tell me about Braşov, where we were going that afternoon, and what there was to be seen there.

I asked my second question – about France – towards the end of a long Romanian lunch with a journalist friend. I can still see his room – the curtained glass doors with squeaking handles, an ancient wireless sitting primly on a piece of lace on an eighteenth-century cupboard. The wood-burning, upright stove was throwing out a great deal of heat, so it must have been during the winter of 1939. There were several of us, mostly British and American newspapermen, and our host had just gone to the kitchen to have a word with his wife and bring another bottle of wine – clean wine from her village, he said, which we could drink all afternoon without risk of a headache. While he was drawing the cork I asked him why Romanians were so pro-French. What could the French do for them that the British could not? 'Nothing,' he replied, 'but we feel they are more likely to try,'

Then he told me that in the mid-nineteenth century, when Wallachia and Moldavia wished to unite, only France had supported them. Austria, Britain and Turkey were against union. The plebiscite was so rigged by Turkish officials that only eleven per cent of the electorate could vote, and naturally the anti-unionists won. The Austrian Consul was directly implicated in the fraud; even the British observer, a First Secretary from the Turkophile Embassy in Constantinople, reported that though 'not altogether free from reproach', the elections 'were conducted with general regularity and propriety'.[2]

Feelings ran high over these elections. Napoleon III persuaded Queen Victoria that the Sultan should hold a fairer plebiscite on condition that the Romanians would be permitted not outright unity, but only similar institutions, in each province. Relatively free elections followed: the unionists won hands down, and with typical Romanian astuteness, the parliaments in Iaşi and Bucharest each elected the same ruler, Prince Alexander Cuza, who turned out to be one of Romania's great reformers. His progressive ideas together with his unconventional private life led to a palace revolution and his expulsion seven years later. Ion Brătianu, the leader of the ruling Liberal Party, then invited Prince Charles of Hohenzollern-Sigmaringen, a cousin of Napoleon III, to become prince of the united provinces. Romania became independent in 1878, and in 1881 Prince Charles was proclaimed King Carol I.

Then again, when the Romanian army had been beaten back to the Russian border in 1917, it was a Frenchman, General Berthelot, the head of the French military mission, who re-equipped and turned it, in the words of the US Ambassador, into 'one of the best fighting organisations in Europe'.[3] At the battle of Maraseşti, with the Russians capitulating on their flanks, the Romanians held the combined Austrian and German forces for a week, and saved Odessa and probably Moscow[4]. Even Lloyd George – who did not know where Transylvania was – promised that the Allies would never forget how brilliantly Romania had carried out her duty to the common cause. Under the peace settlement the accession of Transylvania, part of the Banat (the rich wheatlands to the south-west of Transylvania), Bessarabia and North Bukovina (both originally parts of Moldavia), and the Dobruja on the Bulgarian border, gave Romanians more territory than they had had since the days of Michael the Brave in the seventeenth century. They felt that, without the French, this Greater Romania would never have come into being.

Because they were Latin and so close to France, and so individualistic, talented and enterprising, I expected Romanians to be more westernised than they were. I had forgotten that traumatic split in the middle of the eleventh century when, unlike other Latins, they had turned to the Byzantine Church, which never imposed the same inhibitions as the Church of Rome. Romanians had an uninhibited attitude to sex which most British were not to acquire until the Sixties: one morning, walking along the beach at Mamaia on the Black Sea coast, I was introduced to a lady sunbathing in nothing but a large floppy hat, and, since we had met at a dinner party only a few days before, she seemed surprised that I did not immediately recognise her. When a couple of nuns swinging a basket of washing down the street giggled at my outlandish Anthony Eden hat I was slightly taken aback.

The Phanariot influence, too, had had its effect on Romania. In the eighteenth century the Turks, feeling more threatened than ever by Austria and Russia, decided to strengthen their hold on Wallachia and Moldavia, north of the Danube. They did not trust the Romanian princes and replaced them by these so-called Greek Phanariots – a very mixed lot. A few were genuine descendants of the Byzantine emperors; some were said to have been cooks whose dishes had pleased the Sultan; many were rich merchants who had acquired a privileged position with both the Ottoman and the Greek Orthodox authorities. They had already proved to be effective go-betweens with other Orthodox peoples, and the Porte urged them to buy governorships in Moldavia and Wallachia and to recover the cost by what amounted to extortion of the Romanian people. In 1821, after a great nationalist uprising led by Tudor Vladimirescu, rule by Romanian princes had been restored.

The Phanariots had heightened the intrigue and corruption that was already a part of Romania's Byzantine and Ottoman heritage, and in 1939 corruption was still more widely accepted in Romania than in most West European countries; slush funds were distributed more democratically – to the postman and engine driver as well as to the management. Yet the Phanariots had had a civilising as well as a corrosive influence on eighteenth-century Romania. They had introduced Greek and French culture to the often illiterate Romanian *boiar* or nobleman. Voltaire, Rousseau and the Encyclopaedists were widely read, and by the end of the century, Bucharest and Iaşi both contained highly cultured Graeco-Romanian societies. Sacheverell Sitwell, drawing from a fashionable newspaper of the period, describes the luxurious social life of Bucharest after Independence in the 1880s – a gala night at the opera every week; magnificent balls and suppers; a man and a woman dressed in the height of fashion, walking down the Calea Victoriei next to a half-naked gypsy; Russian, Armenian, Turkish, Jewish, Greek merchants in their distinctive costumes; coaches as magnificent as any in Europe galloping down the Boulevard Kiselev.[5]

Although the Bucharest of 1939 was, of course, less exotic than this, there was still an ostentatious, almost oriental, disregard for the poor. There was still a love of colour and ceremony – of capes, uniforms, sports cars, hearses with horses swathed in black and wearing jet-black plumes. Sometimes the vestiges of Byzantium were more delicately displayed. When lunching with Princess Bibescu, a descendent of the Phanariots and well known for her political opportunism, I saw letters signed 'Winston' and 'Ramsay' on an occasional table, and knew that others from equally distinguished Germans were, for the time being, locked away. After a delicious meal and a conversation which, for her at least, seemed to have no cultural frontiers, we opened the French windows; and as we walked out on to the terrace, the peacocks turned and fanned out their magnificent tails for us.

Chapter 3

Royal Dictatorship

I was lecturing in English language and literature. For the history of the language I relied on such authorities as Jesperson, but was more involved with the literature and often caught myself still rehearsing a lecture before being brought back to earth by the flower girls on the steps of the University. Afterwards, I used to slip out to the grocer Dragomir Niculescu – one of the best in Europe – for a glass of dry, white pelin and one of his wonderful hot meat and mushroom patties. I was still suffering from mid-morning hunger. The French educational system, mentioned by Burbank, had indeed left its mark. Students were sometimes more familiar with French culture than their own. The staff were respected to the point of adulation so that I had to talk utter nonsense before I could get anyone at my seminars to argue with me. When, at the start of a lecture, I admitted to being no specialist in fifteenth-century English literature, I was told by my superiors that students expected members of the faculty to know everything about their subject; when I lectured sympathetically on Byron, I was reminded that the man was immoral; and when I made friends with the students, the German professor whispered that I must be an English spy.

At first I was most interested in the sons and daughters of the new bourgeoisie. A few were the products of the post-war land reform – the most radical in Europe outside the Soviet Union – and the universal suffrage that had accompanied it. I found the male students among them easier to get on with: the girls had been brought up to be genteel and this, together with their anxiety to please, made them less attractive than, for their looks alone, they should have been. I remember painful sessions at an elegant tea shop in Calea Victoriei, with a girl student looking embarrassed while her mother paraded her literary clichés – she was the kind of woman who, in the stage satires of the Romanian playwright Caragiale, would have always referred to knickers as *indispensabili*.

The students were the usual mix. A few loved their subject, but most saw it as a way to a better job or a husband with a better job. The bright ones, being only a little younger than I was, kept me on my toes. Most of them were likeable enough – even the mother-ridden girls, once they had dropped their affectations. When, later, I was working at the Legation, half a dozen of them came to ask whether they could join the British army; a big bonus on top of the pleasure I had had in teaching them.

Romanians who, unlike the Poles and Hungarians, had carried through major agrarian and electoral reforms after the war; had resisted royal dictatorship longer than any of their neighbours; and had particularly close relations with France, liked to think of themselves as a part of democratic Europe. Most – including most of my students – felt that Juliu Maniu, the Transylvanian leader, was the only man capable of lifting the country out of the demoralisation which by 1939 seemed to be infecting all the democracies. Maniu might not be as colourful as the two dictators, King Carol and the recently murdered Zelea Codreanu – but his integrity, and his total commitment to the interests of his country and to constitutional government were prized more highly by most people. I used to sit outside cafés with Hugh Seton-Watson,* who had been sent out to the Balkans on a roving mission, discussing how best to bring about King Carol's downfall and, in our youthful way, criticising the British Government for not backing Maniu openly against him. When Olivia Manning's David Boyd, who in some ways is very like Hugh, says 'We lost this country . . . through a damn fool policy of supporting Carol . . . Maniu and the other liberals would have been with us but we had no use for them,'[1] he was speaking for those of us who did not accept that our government had to deal with the man in charge, and that this was undoubtedly King Carol.

Maniu will be a dominant figure throughout this narrative, and it is time to introduce him properly. He was one of the least flamboyant heroes any country has ever produced – honest, prudent, too often right and completely lacking the fashionable bombast of war. Slightly built, with mild, intelligent eyes, rather formally dressed, he had the air of a provincial notary rather than the popular idea of a wartime resistance leader. He must have been sixty-eight in 1939, but looked younger.

He had made his reputation in Transylvania while it was still a Hungarian province. When, in the 1880s, the whole executive committee of the Transylvanian Romanian National Party had been jailed and their party dissolved for addressing a memorandum of grievances to the Emperor Francis Joseph, Juliu Maniu was working for a doctorate in law at Budapest University. At student meetings he called for Transylvanian autonomy and the revival of a more active National Party, so the authorities already had him in their sights. Later he was co-opted on to the

---

* Later, Professor Hugh Seton-Watson of the School of Slavonic and East European Studies at London University. He was the son of Professor R.W. Seton-Watson, author of the definitive *A History of the Roumanians*.

new party's committee and elected to the Hungarian parliament, where he attacked and publicised Budapest's racial policies. His lifelong commitment to parliamentary government dates from this period.

Maniu was drafted into the Austro-Hungarian artillery in 1914 – an attempt to curb his political activities which failed. In the autumn of 1918 the middle-aged Lieutenant Maniu found himself in a near-chaotic Vienna, in which Austrian regiments and police were virtually out of control while, characteristically, Romanian units seemed untouched by 'Bolshevism'. With his neat moustache, straight shoulders and bright eyes, he had little military authority, but he had won the respect of all Transylvanian Romanians; and he took control of the sixty thousand Romanian troops in the Vienna area. He then talked the authorities into letting him operate from the Ministry of War; and with its facilities he transferred to Transylvania not only the Romanian soldiers around Vienna, but others from the Prague region. These troops formed the vanguard of the army which, in 1919, overthrew Bela Khun's Communist government in Hungary and occupied Budapest. By then Transylvanians had opted for union with Romania; and Maniu and his National Party were henceforth to become involved in the politics of Wallachia.

Until the First World War the politics of the Old Kingdom (Wallachia and Moldavia) had been dominated by two parties – the Conservative Party, representing the large landowners, and the Liberal Party, representing the banking and professional classes. Economically, Romania had been the most successful of the emerging East European states. By 1900 two thousand miles of railway had been built and the Iron Gates blasted to make the Danube navigable for large steamers. Her grainland doubled and half her wheat and about forty per cent of her corn was exported. Food-processing was the first main industry but by the turn of the century her oil was being exploited. International financial circles had such confidence in her that before the First World War Romanian governments could borrow at just over 4 per cent. However, in their drive for industrial expansion governments overlooked the peasant's standard of living which eventually slumped and in 1907 there was a peasant revolt on the same scale as that of Tudor Vladimirescu's of 1821. After the war the Conservative Party was destroyed by the Liberal Party's land and electoral reforms: the latter, by enfranchising the vast peasant electorate, eventually weakening the Liberal Party itself, and bringing Maniu to power.

The Liberal Party had been created in the 1880s, at about the same time as the Transylvanian National Party. Romanian Liberalism had always been associated with the Brătianu family. As far back as 1848 a Dumitru Brătianu had been one of a group that had forced the Prince of Wallachia to agree to a package of human rights which would be considered too radical by some European governments even today. Ion Brătianu had

persuaded Prince Charles of Hohenzollern-Sigmaringen to become the first
Prince of Romania; his son, Ionel, had led the country throughout the First
World War, working closely with King Ferdinand and Queen Marie. For a
decade after the war Ionel Brătianu was still the most influential man in
Romanian politics.

Maniu, now in opposition, worked closely with the radical Peasant Party
led by Ion Mihalache. Mihalache, who described his party as 'the will of
those who died in the trenches',[2] looked the part of a peasant leader: he
was usually dressed in a kind of smock, his black hair was brushed straight
back, he wore a thick moustache but, unlike the average peasant's, his eyes
were contemplative rather than acquisitive. In 1926 he and Maniu joined
forces to form the National Peasant Party under Maniu's leadership. In
July 1927 King Ferdinand died, to be followed four months later by the
fiery Ionel Brătianu. Brătianu was replaced as leader of the Liberal Party
by his brother Vintila, a man of integrity but not of Ionel's calibre. The
Liberals appeared to be running out of steam. Peasants demonstrated in
favour of the National Peasant Party, and in 1928 Maniu was finally
entrusted with the formation of a government. His elections – considered
to be the freest in the whole interwar period – gave him 77.76 per cent of
the vote.

From the start he set himself and his party high standards of conduct.
Measures were taken to prevent anti-semitic demonstrations. He encouraged foreign investment, and although some of his colleagues undoubtedly lined their pockets the idea of Maniu himself taking a bribe of any
kind was inconceivable. He and his close collaborators – men like Ion
Mihalache and the economist Madgearu – were among the most
distinguished Romanians of the century.

Yet his government did not come up to expectations; a year after he
took office the Great Depression set in, and he was able to do very little
even for the better-off peasant. Nor did the disparate nature of his party
help. Mihalache was interested primarily in the economic and social
welfare of the peasant; Maniu's heart remained in Transylvania, and he
handled Wallachian politics far less astutely than he had those of the
trans-Carpathian province where his reputation had been made under the
Austro-Hungarian Empire.

Many of the younger members of the Romanian electorate had become
disillusioned long before Maniu came to power. King Ferdinand had kept
the promise he had given his peasant soldiers in 1917 when they were
holding out in Moldavia against the Central Powers and resisting the
revolutionary propaganda of their Russian allies: land reforms, which
included the royal domains, were implemented immediately after the war.
But they were not given the necessary economic and educational support.
Peasant cooperatives were not encouraged. The sons of rich peasants went

to university and became teachers, lawyers or civil servants, rather than agronomists. Competition from highly capitalised North American grain had a disastrous effect on Romanian agriculture; and when the peasant looked for part-time work in industry, he was exploited in order to keep down industrial wages. Lack of skilled and educated workers made free trade unions almost impossible to organise. The peasant electorate was easily manipulated; and since prime ministers were appointed by the King before they held an election to confirm their appointment, it was rare for a premier to be dismissed by popular vote.

In many countries post-war disillusionment drove young people towards Communism, but Communism had never established itself in Romania. Romanians were individualists, proud of their national culture and unlikely to vote for a group – many of them 'foreigners' – which advocated the return of Bessarabia to Russia and took its instructions from a neighbour whom Romanians had always feared. The Romanian Communist Party was made illegal four years after it had been founded in 1920. Its members were hounded by the police as a 'bolshevik conspiracy', while Moscow taunted them with practising 'only a kind of Sunday underground' and suffering from 'legalist delusions'.[3] The first two decades of the party were, in the words of the BBC commentator George Schöpflin, 'a somewhat uninspired affair',[4] and in 1939 its membership was still only around 800. This is not, however, to belittle the great courage of individual Romanian Communists who, however ineffective their party, ran the risk of very rough treatment at the hands of the police, followed by imprisonment or execution.

Many of the disgruntled young – including some of my students – turned instead to the Iron Guard, with its nationalistic, pseudo-religious, anti-semitic, anti-corruption appeal and its charismatic leader, Corneliu Zelea Codreanu.

Codreanu – who had been executed four months before my arrival – was already a legend. Later I was to read his own account of his life. He had been born in Iaşi, the ancient capital of Moldavia. In his teens he had been greatly influenced by Professor A.C. Cuza, a friend of his father who was advocating a simplistic anti-semitism. Codreanu's own father, too, saw in such propaganda a chance to make a name for himself. Codreanu had been brought up in an atmosphere of anti-semitic theorising and, being by nature receptive rather than critical, had absorbed the ideas of his elders without their cynicism.

At the Iaşi School of Arts and Crafts he had come under the influence of the Guardians of the National Conscience, led by a police *agent provocateur* with an anti-semitic and anti-Communist brief. From him he learnt subversive techniques and how to manipulate the masses. When the Guardians became so powerful locally that Manciu, the Prefect of Police, decided to suppress them, Codreanu's fanaticism erupted. On the morning of 2 October 1924, he entered a courtroom and, surrounded by law students and police, shot and killed Manciu and two other officials. At the door, according to his own account, he saw 'thousands of Jews with hands raised and fingers twitching with hatred'[5] waiting to lynch him. He forced his way through, brandishing his pistol, but was immediately arrested and sent to the military prison of Galata.

The authorities decided to hold his trial at Turnu Severin, some 350 miles away, hoping that it would be less susceptible than Iaşi to Codreanu's charisma. Even so, the courtroom was packed with his supporters. The public prosecutor was frequently interrupted, and beaten up on his way home. Codreanu was released, and he and his followers were seen off on a special train by a crowd of cheering and flower-throwing students.

In 1927 Codreanu created his Legion of the Archangel Michael, pledged to destroy Jews, Communists and the parliamentary system of government. Many Legionaries, who considered themselves to be deeply religious people, found mystical satisfaction in the movement. 'It is not a programme we have to create, but men – new men.'[6] The Legion was organised on classic subversive lines, with cells, verbal orders, little red tape and an élite of killers. An outer circle of sympathisers included the Transylvanian Dr Vaida Voevod, the Interior Minister in Maniu's government. When Codreanu came under particular pressure from local authorities Vaida Voevod allowed him to recreate the Legion under the new name of the Iron Guard, though its members were still often referred to as Legionaries or Green Shirts after the colour of their uniform. Vaida Voevod was forced by the press to resign because of his association with Codreanu. His successor, Ion Mihalache, suppressed the movement which then went underground. In May 1933 suicide squads were formed with such names as Decemviri, the Ten Men, or Nicadori, coined from the names of the three men who made up the squad.

As Professor Ghiţa Ionescu has pointed out, Codreanu's fascist organisation would have remained on the lunatic fringe of Romanian politics in normal times. In the Thirties, however, the German Nazi Party saw in it a potential fifth column. Vaida Voevod, who had played such a distinguished part in the liberation of Romanian Transylvania, should have known better than to encourage it. Even Maniu may have felt some sympathy for youngsters who, in the early days of the movement, had hoped to root out political corruption. King Carol was himself trying to take over Romanian youth and destroy a pluralistic system of government, and his relations with the Iron Guard were at first equivocal.

In her semi-autobiographical Balkan Trilogy, Olivia Manning gives my university job to Harriet Pringle's husband, Guy. Olivia's own husband,

Reggie Smith, was number two at the British Institute, the British Council's greatest investment in Romania. In 1937, the Council had sent out John Amery as Director of Studies. He had had seven teachers and 1,600 students when he started and two years later the numbers had doubled. As the shadow of war lengthened, Romanians, many of them Jews, flocked to the Institute to learn or brush up their English.

Like Guy Pringle, Reggie Smith was a warm, easy-going, left-wing character who stood by Russia even after the Russo-German pact. Though I saw quite a lot of the Smiths I found him a little too woolly, Olivia a little too severe. She and I would sit together in Bucharest cafés, surrounded by Reggie's crowd of which I was one, but she never really joined in. If a few of us called at the Smiths after a party, Reggie was always welcoming, ready for a discussion about anything under the sun. But Olivia made you feel that the moment you had sense enough to leave she would like to go to bed.

I now realise that she must have been very alone, living on the edge of the Romanian scene, knowing, apart from some of the British colony, only those small-minded, pushy women whom I had met in the mothers of some of my students, and the dissolute hangers-on one finds in every capital city. If the Romanian officers I knew had borne anything but a superficial resemblance to her Ruritanian officers, they would not have survived twenty-four hours on the eastern front two years later. Sir Reginald Hoare, the British Minister in Bucharest, once warned London never to forget when sending out speakers that the Romanians were a highly intelligent people: yet Olivia does not seem to have found a single ordinary Romanian friend and she tends to adapt history to suit her mood.

Unless you are Romanian, perhaps none of this really matters; her brilliant satirical stories justify the means. Her selective observation probably had less to do with Romania than with Reggie Smith who, when he returned, married, to Bucharest continued to sleep around as if nothing had changed. Her dislike for Romania reflected her vulnerability and her resentment. Cut off from her own country with war approaching, without friends or even the language to help her, she watched her young marriage breaking up, seemed incapable or unwilling to do anything about it, and hated the place where it was happening.

My own reaction to Bucharest was rather different. I was a bachelor, free, a hunter of new experience, stimulated rather than repelled by affronts to English prejudice. Of course I was irritated by the parochial and snobbish ways of the small bourgeoisie but with none of Olivia's bitterness. Unlike her, I was lucky enough to get to know Romanians who had no reason to covet an Englishman's passport. Since I had no introductions, this had to be a spontaneous process, which took rather longer than discovering bistros in which one could eat delicious Romanian food

untouched by the French cuisine, but not as long as learning the language –
which was relatively easy to read in the newspapers, where Latin and
foreign words predominated but was difficult to speak with any of the
subtlety or humour of a cultivated Romanian.

For me, there was an exuberance in the air, a welcome absence of
inhibition. I worked hard and long at the University and, later, even
harder and longer at the Legation. But after work one could ride in a
trăsură, with scarlet ribbons on the harness to keep off the evil eye, down
ill-lit cobbled streets and broad scintillating boulevards, flirting, or talking
politics, or, sometimes serious, probing the deeper problems of life,
making one's clippity-cloppity way to a restaurant where, arriving at nine
in the evening, one could find the place just beginning to fill, or could eat at
one in the morning. With the summer as hot as India's, the siesta was
respected: those of us who played golf or tennis in the early afternoon only
did so because we had not been in the country long enough for the heat to
enter our bones, or to know the pleasure of a long siesta with the right
person.

King Carol was probably the most widely discussed individual in
Bucharest. He was imaginative, well-read, and a man of initiative. During
the Thirties he had constructed a string of lakes to drain the marshes
around Bucharest. Instead of sending his son to Eton, he formed a class of
twelve boys drawn from all levels of Romanian society – a kind of
tailor-made comprehensive. In a rather simplistic way, he was genuinely
interested in the peasantry, encouraging them to vary their diet of corn
with meat and vegetables instead of selling them all for cash – an excellent
idea if the peasant had not needed every penny he could lay hands on to
buy his cooking oil, farm equipment and *ţuica*. When Carol arranged for
mobile baths to travel from village to village, Bucharestians smiled but saw
no harm in it.

But it was his private life that intrigued the middle class and shocked the
peasants with their lingering belief in divine right. It was said, for instance,
that he owned the factories providing cloth for the uniforms worn by
government officials and that, when short of cash, he simply ordered a
sartorial modification. When I arrived he had for many years been
estranged from his wife, Queen Helen, who had moved to Florence. He
was living with his mistress, Elena Lupescu, the daughter of a chemist
called Wolf who had become a Christian and changed his name to Lupescu
('lupu' being wolf in Romanian) in order to be able to practise his
profession. Like her mother, Elena was a Roman Catholic; but after
contriving to meet Prince Carol at Bistriţa in Transylvania, she quietly
divorced her young Romanian husband and became Carol's lifelong
companion.

Since they could not live openly together, she had a villa on the edge of town and would meet him in the Casa Nouǎ, a four-roomed house he had built in the Palace gardens. His irregular domestic life meant that there could be no normal court, and he was soon surrounded by a dubious coterie which isolated him from his people, his aristocracy and many Romanian statesmen.

Elena Lupescu was said to be both circumspect and faithful to Carol, and she and the King were happy together. One of the more innocent stories Romanians told about her concerned a row between the King and his brother which resulted in his receiving a black eye. 'Daughter, daughter,' old man Lupescu remonstrated, 'what kind of a family are you getting mixed up with?'

At a more serious level, King Carol has been held largely responsible for the erosion of parliamentary democracy in Romania, resulting – eighteen months after my arrival – in a pro-German military dictatorship.

Carol was temperamentally unsuited to constitutional monarchy: his personal ambition became ever more unscrupulous, and by 1927 his mother had noted in her diary that 'I have lost all belief in Carol . . . he does not know the difference . . . between right and wrong, honour and dishonour, truth & lies.'[7]

The flaws in his character had been aggravated by the frustrations he had suffered as Crown Prince. He was in his early twenties during the First World War, but was given no real responsibility. His mother was allowed closer to the front line than he was, and she – rather than Carol or his father – became the army's hero. Constitutionally he could only marry a foreign princess, but none was available in war-ravaged Romania. Not surprisingly, he fell in love with a girl of good Romanian family called Zizi Lambrino; in September 1918 he eloped with her and married in Odessa.

This came as a blow to the royal family, which was by then exiled in Iaşi and under attack from both the Central Powers and the Russians. The former urged King Ferdinand to abdicate, disown Carol and appoint a pro-German regency for Carol's younger brother Nicolas. Supported by his wife and the wise and experienced Prince Ştirbey,* Ferdinand survived the onslaught. He sentenced Carol to two and a half months' imprisonment in a mountain monastery for deserting his army post, and Carol never forgave him. Carol's marriage was dissolved, and the throne saved; but the following spring Carol asked to be allowed to renounce the succession and remarry his pregnant wife. This was refused. When the King asked him to

---

* Prince Barbu Ştirbey came from one of the great ruling families of Wallachia. He studied law at the Sorbonne, advocated agrarian reform and his model farm was recognised for the exceptional quality of its products. He not only recognised Queen Marie's ability, they fell in love and he became her intimate life-long adviser.

join a mission to the Far East he shot himself in the leg: and when his regiment was posted to Hungary to fight Bela Khun he at first refused to leave unless he was allowed to remarry beforehand. Finally he was persuaded to take a trip round the world. When he returned he met Princess Helen of Greece, a suitable bride, and they were married in March 1921. It soon became clear, however, that they had little in common. Helen had a particularly difficult time at the birth of Prince Michael and took her baby to her family in Athens for four months. When she returned Carol had lost interest in her. He had met Elena Lupescu.

Carol appeared with his wife in public for the last time on 7 November 1925. He represented his parents at Queen Alexandra's funeral in England on the 27th but then, instead of escorting his sister Ileana home from school, he joined Elena Lupescu in Paris and went with her to Milan. From there he wrote to his family, again renouncing the throne, and this time his request was accepted. Both the Palace and Ionel Brătianu were convinced that he would never make a constitutional monarch. After King Ferdinand's death in 1926 a regency was set up for Prince Michael, consisting of Prince Nicolas – who protested about having to give up his career in the British Navy – the aged Patriarch, Miron Cristea, and the Chief Justice, the only effective member of the trimvirate.

In 1930, Prince Carol asked to return. Maniu, by then Prime Minister, welcomed an opportunity of replacing Nicolas, who was not interested in his role of Prince Regent with his more intelligent brother. He sent envoys to Paris to see Carol. One of these, Sever Bocu, told his daughter, Lygia Georgescu – who will return to this narrative – how he negotiated with Carol in a small Paris flat, the bedroom door always ajar so that Madame Lupescu could hear every word. The Prince finally agreed to Maniu's terms: that he should return only as Prince Regent, leaving his son Michael as titular King; that he should be reconciled to Princess Helen; and that Madame Lupescu should never return to Romania.

Carol landed in Bucharest on 7 July 1930 and immediately informed Maniu that he wished to become King, with the legal proviso that he had reigned since his father's death. Maniu gave way. Maniu also recognised that reconciliation with his wife could take some time, since Princess Helen was no keener on it than Carol. But when a certain 'Madame Manoilescu' arrived in Bucharest, travelling as the wife of a close friend of Carol's, and moved into a house in a fashionable quarter, Maniu immediately challenged the King. Carol told him that he must be mistaken. Maniu insisted; his security people had not only assured him that the lady was Madame Lupescu, but that the King had seen her during the last forty-eight hours. When King Carol replied that he knew nothing of all this, Maniu rose to his feet. 'You have deceived me and your country,' he said;

he then handed the King his resignation, bowed but did not shake hands, and left. Once Carol had refused to admit the truth there had been no more hesitation on Maniu's part. There were two things Maniu could not stand, and his aversion to them will crop up time and again in this story. One was violence. The other was deceit, and the King·had lied to his face.

Those who did not fawn on the King were considered his enemies. He cut off the allowance his father had willed to his mother. His agents spied on her, and whenever she crossed the frontier her luggage was sent to the Palace for inspection. He persecuted his wife until she fled the country. Prince Ştirbey was expelled. Carol also exiled his brother Nicolas who had welcomed his return. In a letter written in July 1932, Queen Marie told her cousin George that 'Lately I have been living in a world I no more understand & which has become very lonely'. Replying from Cowes, King George V commented, 'I cannot help thinking he is mad'[8].

Maniu's self-reproach for having allowed Prince Carol back must have inflamed his hatred for the King. For the rest of the decade he refused to work with a man who respected neither the constitution nor, he felt, the good name of the country. A deeply religious man – he was a Uniat, a Catholic following the Byzantine rite – Maniu was shocked by King Carol's relationship with this attractive intelligent red-head. Yet Maniu's own rectitude contributed to the downfall of Romanian parliamentary government. In a somewhat legalistic way, he stuck to his principles through thick and thin at a time when expediency was becoming the rule everywhere; accused of priggishness by the King and of being 'negative' by the British government he committed his party to sterile opposition at a time when it should have been heard. Maniu was blessed with neither the ruthlessness nor the opportunism needed to handle King Carol; Ionel Brătianu would have been a formidable opponent, but the new head of the Liberal Party, his brother Vintila, was not.

King Carol now set out with his considerable influence, ability and personality to intrigue and persuade the more ambitious members of the Peasant and Liberal parties to accept his short-cut to power. He brought into government men without any popular support; although some of them were very able, they all became dependent for their political careers on Carol rather than the electorate. The King used, for example, Professor Iorga, an historian of international repute but a vain man with political ambitions; and Vaida Voevod, who, while still a leading member of the National Peasant Party, had become estranged from Maniu. The King spread the rumour that Maniu was finished.

One of the King's ministers stood head and shoulders above the rest. Nicolae Titulescu had a solid international reputation; nor could he be dubbed a King's yes-man. He belonged to no political party. He had served in post-war governments as a brilliant Finance and Foreign Minister.

Holding the dual post of Minister of Plenipotentiary in London and Romanian representative to the League of Nations, he was the only President of the League to be elected two years running. For four years – from 1932 to 1936 – he was Foreign Minister under King Carol, and owing to his enlightened and far-sighted foreign policy the country enjoyed a European reputation which owed nothing to King Carol's manoeuverings at home.

Titulescu's defiance of Mussolini over Abyssinia and of Hitler over the reoccupation of the Ruhr won him the hatred of the Axis and the Iron Guard, and made the King nervous. On one occasion he refused to continue in office unless the King did something about the Iron Guard sympathies of the Palace coterie. He put his faith in collective security against the Axis. He strengthened the Little Entente of Romania, Czechoslovakia and Yugoslavia, and had already initialled an agreement with Litvinov whereby Moscow recognised Bessarabia as Romanian when the King, disturbed by his independent and idealistic political thinking, finally decided to relieve him of his post.

After Vintila Brătianu's death, Ion Duca, the new Liberal leader, made it clear that he mistrusted the King as much as had Ionel Brătianu. In the elections at the end of 1933 Duca obtained 51 per cent of the vote. Three weeks later he was assassinated on Sinaia railway station by the *Nicadori* – an Iron Guard suicide squad. Security seems to have been non-existent on the dark country station; the assassins pushed through the group of friends seeing the Prime Minister off, shot him, and disappeared into the forest. Codreanu, who had undoubtedly authorised Duca's murder, hid in a house belonging to Madame Lupescu's cousin until the dust had settled.[9] The King may have known nothing of this, but by now Romanians were prepared to believe almost anything of King Carol and his friends.

After Duca's death the King appointed as Prime Minister a dissident Liberal called George Tătărescu. Having split the National Peasant Party, he now split the Liberal Party between the constitutionalists led by Constantin (Dinu) Brătianu, Vintila's brother, and his own Tătărescu faction.

Still in his forties, clean-shaven, good-looking and ambitious, Tătărescu did much during his four years of office to prepare the way for King Carol's dictatorship. For this, he was never forgiven by Brătianu and Maniu. Tătărescu's official relationship with the King was well described by a member of the German Ministry of Economics in a letter to Göring* at the end of 1937:

> The King conceives of his government as an authoritarian leadership
> whereby he consciously pits the permanent institutions of the

*   Göring was in charge of the Reich's Four Year Plan

monarchy against the political life of the Rumanian parties. In the case of the Tatarescu government it is actually not a question of a government by the so-called Liberal Party together with friendly party groups but of a government which carries out the intentions of the King.[10]

The elections of November 1937 marked the penultimate stage in the abolition of Romanian parliamentary government. Believing that the King and his puppet, Tătărescu, were a bigger threat than the Iron Guard to constitutional government and the country's future independence, Maniu made a tactical electoral pact with Codreanu with the object of defeating Tătărescu so badly that he could not remain in power. Again, King Carol outmanoeuvred him. Although Tătărescu failed to obtain the 40 per cent necessary to stay in office, the King then offered the premiership not to Maniu but to the Transylvanian poet, Octavian Goga, with only 9 per cent of the vote.

Goga collaborated with Professor A.C. Cuza, Codreanu's anti-semitic mentor, and for the next six weeks his blundering policies brought the country to the edge of civil war, aroused international Jewry and even hit the headlines in Britain. The British Minister, Sir Reginald Hoare, reported to London on 24 January 1938 that 'It is becoming daily more certain in my mind that the only possible solution of the present situation is the suspension of parliamentary life.'[11]

In February, King Carol dismissed Goga and a new constitution which suppressed all political parties except his own National Renaissance Front was submitted at short notice to a plebiscite without secret ballot, and approved almost unanimously. 'Most remarkable', according to a German Foreign Office circular of 9 March, 'is the provision under which the judges whose duty it is to enforce this regulation are to be called to account if by intention or neglect they arrive at acquittals . . . Romania, therefore, is now under a barely veiled royal dictatorship.'[12]

Having achieved direct rule, the King appointed as dummy Prime Minister the aged Patriarch, Miron Cristea. Tătărescu became Foreign Minister while for the Ministry of the Interior the King chose a tough one-eyed Wallachian lawyer – Armand Călinescu – who was to be the scourge of the Iron Guard. For now that he had taken personal control of the country, King Carol saw the German-backed Iron Guard as a potential threat to his dictatorship. Codreanu was arrested and given six months, imprisonment. Then in May he was suddenly charged with high treason and in spite of influential defence witnesses, condemned to ten years, hard labour which, in Romania, could mean death in the salt mines. A few months later, without explanation, he was moved from the salt mines to a prison near Bucharest.

   The King's personal dictatorship seemed acceptable to both London and Berlin. As a member of the Foreign Office minuted on the telegram Sir Reginald Hoare had sent on 24 January, 'If Carol decides on this course, we shall hardly be worse off than we were as a result of similar steps in Greece and Yugoslavia – in fact better thanks to the particular affection of H.M. for this country and its government.'[13] Hector Bolitho, who visited Romania for ten days the month I arrived, wrote that 'He has given them their Magna Carta'[14] while George Martelli of the *Daily Despatch* reminded his readers that 'democracy as practised in Romania bore little resemblance to democracy at home'.[15]

   Despite the King's attitude to the Iron Guard, Berlin, too, was satisfied. The King assured the Germans that his intention remained to draw closer to Germany 'slowly and systematically'.[16] King Carol detested Hitler, but as the prospect of effective Allied help against German expansion seemed to become more remote with each new German diplomatic victory, he prudently, though without enthusiasm, kept open the door to an understanding with the Third Reich.

Chapter 4

Hitler and Romania

Although Hitler's decisions were often impulsive or expedient, the two most important ambitions outlined in *Mein Kampf* were pursued consistently: the German Reich would establish a pan-German racial state; this state would be protected by the acquisition of *Lebensraum* in Eastern Europe – more particularly at Russia's expense. It is this second ambition – Hitler's *Ostpolitik* – that concerns us here.

Two conditions seemed to him essential for its success. Since Germany could not take on the two continental powers simultaneously, France had to be knocked out before the invasion of Russia; and since German military tactics depended on mobility – the rapid pincer movement of panzer divisions backed up by devastating air power – an ample supply of oil was essential.

In 1933 Germany was importing a total of 370,000 tons of oil from the Dutch West Indies, the USA and Mexico – all sources that could dry up in wartime.[1] Hydrogenation from coal provided just over 100,000 tons, and another 100,000 were imported from Romania. Hitler knew that his annual requirement would increase tenfold in wartime and that, although the hydrogenation process, which involved no foreign exchange, could be stepped up – German aircraft were already being designed for it – he would depend largely on Romania to make up his shortfall.[2] Romania had to be taken 'alive': Hitler could not risk oil sabotage by the Allies, as had happened in the First World War. Nor must Russian, Hungarian or Bulgarian revisionist claims be solved by armed conflict. Romanian oil must be protected at all costs; as he was to tell his generals early in 1941,'the life of the Axis depends on those oil fields.'[3]

As a result, Hitler pursued a tailormade policy towards Romania. He knew that to pacify her without disrupting her valuable grain and oil resources would not be easy. A Hohenzollern monarchy had not prevented her going to war against Germany in 1916. Her intelligentsia were francophile almost to a man. Since military invasion had to be avoided, he had to embark on a more protracted, trickier policy which involved undermining Romania's confidence in the Western Powers; destabilising her political and social structure from within; securing economic and then political control; and finally, when Romanian resistance was at a sufficiently low ebb, exerting sufficient influence on the country's policies without actual occupation or military disruption. Neither the Romanians nor the Allies seemed fully to grasp Hitler's logic. The Anglo-French guarantee of spring 1939 was given on the assumption that Germany might well invade Romania along with Poland; Allied plans to sabotage the oil fields were geared to a military invasion. What the Allies did not foresee was that whereas Hitler's troops would enter Warsaw in tanks, they would arrive in Bucharest by train or car, often in mufti.

Between 1933 and 1939 three factors worked in favour of Hitler's Romanian policy. His two internal assets were, as we have seen, the Iron Guard and King Carol. When the time came for Hitler to turn Romania into a military base, he had no need to incur the odium of destroying Romania's parliamentary system – it had already been done for him.

But his greatest asset was Allied military and moral weakness, an inclination to give way to his Central and East European ambitions in the hope of buying peace, on a piecemeal basis. Britain's unilateral disarmament during the Twenties and France's demoralisation in the Thirties did more harm to Europe than anything any East European German satellite was capable of during the war. The Romanians, who had acquired more territory at the end of the Great War than they were used to administering, held out against German diplomatic and military successes, seemingly backed by the Western Powers, for a surprisingly long time. For as long as Titulescu was Foreign Minister Romania was committed to collective security against the Axis. After his removal in August 1936, the King adopted a more even-handed policy between the Central and Western European Powers.

1938 was a particularly good year for Hitler's Romanian policy. Democratic leaders had been reduced to voices in the wilderness. Although the royal dictator continued to appoint pro-Allied ministers, he was realistic enough not to close the German option. His February constitution finally cut him off from any popular control, criticism or support; he was on his own with his mistress, his army, his flamboyant capes and uniforms, his police and his political yes-men, and was unlikely to prove a match for the oil-hungry corporal.

In April 1938, the German State Secretary Weizsäcker – father of today's President of the German Federal Republic – had commented that, without taking any special measures to improve relations with Romania 'we intend to let the actual development of commercial relations between our two countries work for us.'[4] After Munich, Fabricius, the German Minister Plenopotentiary in Bucharest, reported a growing interest by those close to the King in a rapprochement with Germany. They argued that, as the Munich Agreement must have created friendlier relations between England, France and the Reich, it would now be 'much easier for the King of Romania to bring about the friendship with Germany he has always desired'.[5] Fabricius told them 'how wrong it was for Romanian economic policy to try again and again to assume every other orientation except that towards Germany!'[6] The British Government certainly seemed unwilling to respond to Romanian approaches or to put any obstacle in the way of Hitler's economic ambitions in Romania. When Carol visited London two months after Munich, still hoping to sell Romanian oil and wheat to Britain rather than Germany, he was met with a purely commercial response. A Foreign Office memorandum of 8 June 1938 referred to the increase of German influence in Eastern Europe after the Anschluss, and to steps which might 'provide for certain countries in this part of the world a *point d'appui* other than Berlin'.[7] Romania was one such country, and an invitation to King Carol to pay his first official visit to London in November was renewed after being postponed from March at the request of the King, who had feared a German invasion after the Anschluss.

By the summer Romania seemed more settled, and without Goga anti-semitism had become less strident. During the next few months the British press was steered away from Carol's private life. 'What matters now,' Britain's chargé d'affaires in Bucharest commented, 'is that he does his job well and works hard at it.'[8] There was a tricky moment when Maniu gave an interview to a visiting *Daily Express* correspondent and spoke so violently against the King that Lord Halifax, the Foreign Secretary, had to intervene personally with Lord Beaverbrook to suppress the piece. In the end the visit went smoothly enough, while doing nothing to encourage Romanian resistance to economic dependence on Berlin.

When the King saw Chamberlain on 16 November, he tactfully suggested that, after Munich, Hitler's ambitions in Europe would be economic rather than territorial. Yet these might open the door to political influences, perhaps 'in a measure greater than was desirable'. 'What,' the King then asked, 'was, in this connexion, the degree of our interest in the economic side?'[9]

Chamberlain replied that natural forces made it inevitable that Germany would enjoy a preponderant economic position, which did not mean that Britain was not interested in the practical possibilities of trade with Romania. Halifax explained that the British Government could not take up a commercial or trade proposition unless it was economically sound. One of the main difficulties was the wide difference between Romania's internal prices and those on world markets, particularly for wheat and oil. King Carol was, in effect, being told that Romania was in Germany's economic orbit, and that although oil and wheat were her only source of foreign currency Britain was not ready to pay above world prices to deny them to the Führer. Lord Gage, who was attached to the royal party, reported that in the train down to Dover a senior Romanian official had expressed himself well pleased with the visit 'on the general, represen- tational and "moral" side, but *quant à la politique*' – and he had shrugged his shoulders suggesting that nothing had resulted. According to Lord Gage, Carol had said that 'other countries acted while we were still talking.'[10]

King Carol left England on 18 November. On his way home he visited France and Belgium before going on to Germany to visit his uncle, Prince Frederick of Hohenzollern-Sigmaringen. On the 24th he met Hitler for a political *tour d'horizon*. He was reassured about Hungary's claim to Transylvania and Russia's to Bessarabia. He complained about links between Germany and the Iron Guard, mentioning one German agent by name. The Führer promptly ordered his recall. With Göring, then Commissioner for the Reich's Four Year Plan, he had an even more substantial talk, covering a wide-ranging economic agreement, which went so well that in the end the King asked that Helmut Wohltat of the German Ministry of Economics should be sent in person to Bucharest for the negotiations.

On 11 November a member of the German Legation, reporting that the Romanians were being difficult about terms of trade, added that 'I assume that King Carol's visit to London will result in nothing new in the economic field and that the visit of the King to Germany may, on the other hand, create a more favourable atmosphere.'[11] Yet on his return to Romania Carol did something which, had Hitler not considered relations with Romania so vital, could well have upset the still fragile apple-cart. He was met at the frontier by Armand Călinescu, his Minister of the Interior. Călinescu reported a resurgence of Iron Guard terrorism, and without waiting to reach Bucharest the King signed Codreanu's death warrant. Within forty-eight hours Codreanu and thirteen others had been shot 'while trying to escape'. We can only guess at the King's reasons. Perhaps his decision had been prompted by resentment against Hitler, the feeling that as a result of Britain's apparent refusal to see trade in political terms, he had had to do a deal with Hitler, which could well lead to German economic domination of his country. Perhaps he had interpreted Hitler's readiness to withdraw his agent as a green light to suppress the Iron Guard. Whatever the explanation, he miscalculated German reaction badly. Berlin papers screamed about 'mass murder', 'disintegration of the country', 'victory for Jewry'. Germany's leaders even returned Romanian decorations and orders.[12]

Nevertheless, when certain trade agreements and protocols were signed in Bucharest ten days later, the German negotiator commented drily that the tensions over Codreanu had, if anything, helped because Romanians did not want economic relations to suffer on account of their political differences.[13] Wohltat's arrival was postponed until the following February, and the broad economic settlement, known as the Wohltat Agreement, which opened the way to considerable German control over Romania's economic and military establishments, was not signed until March 1939, the month I arrived in Romania.

The Patriarch had died that month and the tough, honest, black-monocled Armand Călinescu had succeeded him as Prime Minister. Hitler had just taken the rest of Czechoslovakia. Romania had supported her ally throughout the Sudeten crisis and we in Bucharest expected her, with Poland, to be next on Hitler's list. Our Romanian friends looked, in vain, to the British and French for concrete help. Later that year we suspected the truth about Britain's military weakness as we scoured Bucharest for binoculars and cameras to send back to London but in the spring I think we would have been astonished to learn that she had only two fully-equipped divisions and only one operational squadron of Spitfires. Lord Halifax had in fact admitted to Gafencu, the Romanian Foreign Minister, that while we were equipping our own forces we could not spare arms for Romania to replace those she had previously bought from Czech Skoda.[14] When Germany offered Romania the Skoda armament she needed in exchange for the oil Britain was unwilling to buy, she at first held her off but later accepted, as the only practical solution.

After the invasion of Czechoslovakia, Britain and France guaranteed Poland – a justifiable deterrent tactic. Britain guaranteed Greece, which, given Greece's geographical position and British naval power, also made sense. Under pressure from Paris, London then extended her cover to include Romania, which made no sense at all. Although Călinescu welcomed the Anglo-French guarantee at its face value, militarily it was meaningless. And in the economic field, where Britain could well have buttressed Romanian resistance to German encroachment, very little was done to help.

I was friendly with Maria, a Romanian girl in whose parents' French-style drawing room I had first tasted the rose jam called *şerbet* which, taken with ice-cold water, was even more refreshing than tea in a Romanian summer. She was fanatically pro-Western. Her older step-brother was a senior member of the Bank of Romania and a friend of Fabricius, the German Minister. One afternoon he told me of Romania's attempt to reach an effective economic agreement with London, and of how they had been palmed off with a five-million-pound credit with which to oppose Dr Schacht's enormous economic drive. Would we English, he asked, ever break out of our blinkered view of trade and realise that in Eastern Europe, at least, it was a highly political matter? Although I secretly agreed with him, at the time I put much of his outburst down to his pro-German inclinations. I now know that the leader of the British trade delegation to Romania had written to the Treasury in almost identical terms.[15]

In 1939, on Professor Burbank's initiative, a summer school was held at Sinaia under the auspices of the Universities of Bucharest and Cluj. Lectures on different aspects of British culture were attended by some seven hundred students. Phonetic specialists came up from the British Institute in Athens. Professor Grimm, the splendid, bearded scholar who had translated the poems of Robert Burns into Romanian, represented Cluj University. The brilliant Professor 'Tommy' Thompson of the Bucharest Institute was there. My main contribution was to persuade Professor Bonamy Dobrée to attend. Dobrée, who had rediscovered Restoration drama in the Thirties, had been my professor at Leeds and was to become a lifelong friend. As Richard Hoggart says, 'Each year Bonamy Dobrée seemed to pick one or perhaps two students to keep an eye on. We were . . . likely to be quirky and off-beat . . . Dobrée always had more time for the creatively untidy than for the steadily reliable.'[16] Bonamy, who lunched regularly with T.S. Eliot and Herbert Read, brought to our academic life in Romania a gust of fresh critical air. He got on well with the staff and students, sang Basque songs one evening, and was excited about the work of Harry Brauner who was already recording Romanian folk music. Having started life as a soldier, he was called back for military service before the summer school ended. I did not see him again until after the war.

For three weeks we held our summer school in Sinaia, with its seventeenth-century monastery, and a cake shop which sold jam made of those same wild raspberries which Ada's Carpathian bears were said to risk breaking their necks to pick. In Moscow the prospect of an Anglo-French agreement with Russia was breaking on the rocks of mutual suspicion while Molotov and Ribbentrop were tentatively building on a conversation about 'normalisation and even improvement' of relations which had taken place in Berlin on 30 May between a senior official of the German Foreign Ministry and the Soviet chargé d'affaires; the chargé had remarked that for all practical purposes their foreign policies and their domestic affairs could be kept apart.[17]

The fear of supping with the Soviet Union was widespread from Eastern Europe to the Atlantic but, as Titulescu had warned the House of Commons might happen, it was Hitler who first put expediency before his deep mistrust of the USSR. By the end of August a Russo-German non-aggression agreement had been signed, and in a secret protocol the Soviet Union had emphasised her interest and Germany her lack of interest in Bessarabia. Three days later Berlin, in a belated *esprit d'escalier*, instructed her embassy to ensure that any German official involved with this protocol should sign the pledge of secrecy.[18] A leak could have seriously upset Hitler's plans for Romania.

When the Reich invaded Poland and on 3 September Britain declared war, Berlin asked Bucharest to close the Polish frontier, intern refugees, and prevent arms shipments through Romania; yet the Romanians allowed the Polish President to go to Switzerland, accepted some 22,000 soldiers and 3,500 officers and civilians, set up centres for refugees, and helped military personnel to escape westwards. Even when Polish politicians, contrary to their undertakings, made political statements from Romanian territory, the Romanians, despite their own fears of a German invasion, continued to allow Poles of military age to go west to Britain and France. Denis Wright,* our Vice-Consul at Constanţa, noted in his diary on 15 September that seventy tons of Polish gold had been loaded with the Consulate's help on to a tanker skippered by a Captain Brett. This was the Polish gold reserve worth £20 million. Four days later, when the Germans asked for Romanian cooperation in seizing it, it was no longer in Romania.

On 21 September the Arditti household – where I had my digs – were about to start lunch when the music that preceded the radio news bulletin was suddenly interrupted and a voice announced that 'Prime Minister Călinescu has been killed. A group of the Iron Guard has executed him.'[19] David Walker leapt for the telephone. Driving home for lunch, the Prime Minister had been held up by an ox cart. Legionaries had driven alongside and shot him before proceeding to the broadcasting station, where they had wounded the porter and made their announcement.

They were caught immediately, taken to the scene of the murder and shot; their bodies were left on the road for thirty hours. The King now had a pretext for suppressing the movement, and ordered five Legionaries to be executed in each county. Rumour put the total killed at over 2,000. The German radio announced that Călinescu's murder had been carried out by Polish and British agents in order to compromise 'the good relations existing between Romania and Germany'[20] but the Romanian Government would not buy this. Next day they refuted the German allegations, confirmed that the murder had been the work of the Iron Guard, and decreed that university students would in future be obliged to join the King's Renaissance Front. Olivia Manning's account of the official Romanian reaction to the murder is amusing but somewhat distorted.[21]

Codreanu's execution had been revenged; Horia Sima, the fanatical Transylvanian school teacher who had succeeded Codreanu (though he was only a shadow of the *Capitan*), had proved himself. Călinescu and his

* Later Sir Denis Wright, HM Ambassador at Teheran.

family knew all along the great risk they ran. I was shocked by the decision to expose the murderers' bodies on the public highway but the shock of Călinescu's death was far greater. By then I knew enough about Romania to realise just how difficult he would be to replace. The King was never again to have such a strong-willed, pro-Allied premier; and after a short provisional government he turned back to his old friend George Tătărescu.

By then I knew people outside the academic world. I spent a weekend at Constantin Brătianu's model farm at Florica and remember the old man in his chair after lunch, his legs stretched out, children jumping over them, while he either watched or slept. While staying at the Racotta estate — they will come into this story later — I remember a very spruce old man, straight out of Chekhov, driving over in a trap one morning and eating a soft-boiled egg with a flat, silver knife which he produced from his pocket. A Romanian country house in 1939 was still like a Russian dacha before the Revolution. Three or four generations milled around including servants and villagers and their children. The house acted as a dispensary and citizens' advice bureau. Though there were undoubtedly bad and absentee landlords in Romania, the Brătianus and Racottas, like all the Romanian landowners I knew, expected to help a peasant financially if he had medical or legal problems, and would put him up at their house in Bucharest if he had to go to the city.

In Bucharest we played golf or tennis. In winter we skied, and in summer we swam. At all these sports the Romanians, including many of the girls, were better than I was. Some of us would cut our hands collecting mussels from the rocks on the Black Sea coast, and in the evening make *moules marinière* over a fire. We talked to Bessarabian fishermen whom I could not understand. There were weekend parties in a villa at Snagov, a lake with an island monastery, with rushes growing inland from the end of our pier. We swam from a rowing boat, putting on warmer clothes in the evening and having drinks on the terrace or in a room lined with Romanian, French, English and German books. We ate late and talked late. In those days people of Eastern and Western Europe seemed less classified than they are now; there was no absolute ideological divide, no Warsaw Pact or NATO or Comecon or Common Market; we felt ourselves to be all part of one great European hotchpotch, and were more inclined, I think, to see our differences as facets of the same culture.

Chapter 5

The Phoney War in Romania

The phoney war was even phonier in a neutral country where Allies and enemy milled around together. At the Athenée Palace Hotel bar Edith von Kohler, the blonde who was said to be Germany's top agent in Romania, sent us notes via Mitica, the barman who owned racehorses. British and German oil men followed each other out of the bar to exchange family news over the privacy of a pee. At a garden restaurant, a British Council visitor gave an unsolicited performance of English folk dancing; the Germans gaped, while the British wished he would stop and applauded loudly.

For me the phoney war included amateur attempts at intelligence gathering. When, for instance, I took ten days' leave in Transylvania the military attaché asked me to keep an eye open for Romanian military dispositions. I was luckier than John Davidson-Houston, the assistant military attaché, who had made a professional report the year before – no fleas, no effeminate men or emotional women, no arrest. But one morning, after a delicious breakfast in an inn garden of *oeufs au plat*, home-made bread, local honey and good coffee, I almost walked into a trench. The soldiers were suspicious, but friendly enough when they realised that I was English.

At Romanian government level the phoney war seemed to be characterised by a desperate hope that some *deus ex machina* could still intervene to prevent them ending up in the German camp. On 30 November, we heard Gafencu, the Foreign Minister, confirm in a wireless broadcast that Romania under Tătărescu's premiership would continue Călinescu's policy of non-intervention. He described the Wohltat Agreement as a genuine instrument of peace, referred warmly to the Anglo-French guarantee, and made friendly noises about Russia while knowing full well that she was only biding her time to take Bessarabia, and had invaded Finland that very day. We felt that he was whistling in the dark, trying to keep up his own spirits and those of the Romanian people.

A year before, Clodius* had referred to a profound change in Romania's

---

* Deputy Director, Economic Department of the German Foreign Ministry.

political attitude occasioned by the decline of France, her economic dependency on Germany and realisation that only Germany could provide effective protection against her most dangerous enemy, the Soviet Union. But he had then commented that 'the change is not due to sympathy for Germany but solely to realistic political considerations, often even to fear.'[1]

On 26 January 1940, Sir Reginald Hoare, our Minister in Bucharest, made much the same point in a despatch to Lord Halifax.

> The Roumanians will make promises to us, not really believing that they can keep them but hoping that something will turn up to enable them to do so, whereas they make promises to the Germans hoping that circumstances will break them for them or that in a month or two they will, themselves, dare to evade or break them.[2]

Given their circumstances and sympathies, it is difficult to see what else they could have done. Romanian soldiers were a hardy lot. They would have put up a good fight against the Hungarians or Bulgarians but, with their outdated leadership, training and equipment, could have done little against the German army. On the other hand, Romania's long experience as a buffer state had taught her the arts of compromise and subterfuge, and these were practised against Germany with great skill during the winter and spring of 1939–40. The British may not have been happy with Romania's behaviour, but the Germans were furious when they later discovered from documents captured in France the extent to which they had been deceived.

Tătărescu's domestic policy attempted two things: to unite the country, which proved impossible around King Carol, and to strengthen national control over the country's economy, particularly oil.

Oil had been developed in Romania since the 1880s. Germany had been the largest investor until the First World War in which she lost everything. By the late Thirties most of the major Western oil companies had established subsidiaries: Romano Americana was affiliated to Standard Oil of America, Astra Romănă to the Royal Dutch/Shell Oil Company, Unirea to the British Phoenix Oil and Transport Company and Concordia to Petrofina.

In November 1938 King Carol and Göring had laid the foundations for Germany's re-entry into the industry, and Wohltat and Clodius had then worked hard to set up German-Romanian companies to prospect, drill and refine Romanian oil. But after the Wohltat Agreement and the oil pact that followed, Tătărescu assumed exceptional powers over the oil industry. These were at first detrimental to Allied companies, but were later to prove as effective a brake on supplies to the Reich as was Allied bombing.

Britain's declaration of war removed a number of ambiguities. She could now wage economic if not military war in neutral Romania, and an all-out effort was made to direct her oil away from the Reich. The Treasury subsidised the gap between world and Romanian oil prices. Eric Berthoud* of the Ministry of Fuel and Power was sent out to coordinate government policy with British oil companies. The Goeland Transport and Trading Company, established and financed by the Ministry of Economic Warfare and headed by a huge and kindly chartered accountant called William Harris-Burland,† bought up or rented tugs, lighters and barges to deny river transport to the Germans.

By now the British naval blockade had closed the Mediterranean to German shipping. The Reich was left with only two channels for the import of Romanian oil – the Danube, frozen for at least two months in the year, and the railways, using the single-track line between Predeal and Braşov. Romania's oil exports to Britain and Germany (including Austria and Czechoslovakia) from the outbreak of war to the following June are indicated in the table below.[3] Quantities are in thousands of metric tons.

| | 1939 | | | | | | | | | 1940 | | |
	Aug	Sept	Oct	Nov	Dec	Jan	Feb	Mch	Apr	May	June
Britain	24	33	30	35	140	120	75	120	70	75	—
Germany	107	70	83	87	85	27	31	50	55	110	205

Production varied from month to month. Yet by December, Britain had built up her purchases from 24 to 140 thousand tons – and by then ice was beginning to close the Danube. Allied Romanian subsidiaries committed their export surpluses to their parent companies; when the parent companies in Western Europe finally fell into German hands, a direct struggle began between Germany and Romania for control of the subsidiaries.

Romanians permitted a maximum of six oil trains daily to Germany but in practice far fewer ran. Delivery schedules were lengthened so as to provide an official reason for delaying oil trains to the Reich.[4] Sabotage, usually inspired by British agents, included the dropping of sugar into gasoline and putting sand in the grease boxes of tank cars. Locomotives would break down all too often on the stretch of single line between Predeal and Braşov. Even when Clodius had persuaded the government to double this line, tank cars to Germany were delayed by Romanian troop movements.

* Later Sir Eric Berthoud, British Ambassador at Warsaw.
† Later a director of the British Railway Board.

To supplement overt economic warfare, London also authorised sabotage operations. These were on the whole unsuccessful and rather typical of our predilection for amateur status in the early stages of the war.

The first plan was to block the Iron Gates – the narrow Danube channel, with its bypass canal, through which all river craft going to Germany had to pass. The Goeland company amassed tugs, lighters and barges, to be crewed by members of the Royal and Royal Australian navies dressed in civilian clothes. On 24 March 1940 Denis Wright helped through customs seventeen 'merchant seamen', who had arrived from Egypt on the SS *Transilvania* en route to Braila to man the naval attaché's barges. They spent the day at the Constanţa consulate in their 'ill-fitting civvies' and left that night. The following week he steered a further nine naval ratings past the Romanian authorities. Meanwhile it was rumoured that a British merchantman, the SS *Ardinian*, had discharged at Sulina on the mouth of the Danube about sixty more naval ratings and six tons of gelignite, three pounders, grenades etc.[5]

The military stores were loaded on to the lighter *Tormonde* and declared as oil equipment en route for Budapest. This motley collection of river craft then set off up the Danube. However the sailors had been so indiscreet at Sulina that when they reached Giurgiu on 3 April the whole town knew that they were up to something. Some sailors who thought they had syphilis went to see a doctor, who turned out to be German. The port captain, a Germanophile, ordered a search, and although his men at first missed the *Tormonde* cargo, they found enough guns, uniforms and money to detain the vessels. Two days later, while the naval officer in charge was in Bucharest, port officials searched the *Tormonde* and confiscated the arms and explosives.[6]

On 8 April Denis Wright noted that, as a gesture to the Germans, the Romanians had expelled twelve seamen whom he had escorted on board a British tanker bound for Istanbul. He hoped that the eighty seamen left could still proceed with the operation once they had recovered their arms and explosives. Romanians, he said, 'seemed sincerely sorry and sympathetic at the turn of events and the expulsion'. By then, however, the secret was out. Our friends in the Romanian Government – including Gafencu the Foreign Minister – did what they could, but the Germans had the cooperation of the Romanian security services headed by General Moruzov and his obese but very able assistant, Eugen Cristescu. On 14 April Manfred von Killinger, a 'diplomat' with high Nazi connections, who had been sent to Eastern Europe to impede the 'enemy's secret operations', reported to Berlin the successful defeat of the Iron Gates operation.[7]

By then the German armies were advancing through Denmark and Norway. Berlin threatened to cut off arms supplies if the Romanians continued to assist the British. Yet our naval personnel were not interned;

they were expelled and allowed to return to their bases in Malta and Egypt unscathed. Denis Wright was filled with 'gloom at our bungling of the Danube affair – at the wasted money and effort, just because a lot of amateurs tried to do something in too slick a way without thinking it out properly'.[8]

Despite Romania's declared neutrality, she had agreed with the Allies just before war was declared that the oil installations should be destroyed in case of invasion and that this should be a joint operation by the British, French and Romanians. Engineers from the oil companies would provide the expertise; the actual demolition would be carried out by Royal Engineers from Egypt and French troops from Syria. As in the First World War, the Romanian army would keep the enemy – which was expected to invade from Poland – out of the Prahova valley until the operation was completed.

Major Davidson-Houston, the assistant military attaché, was a sapper. Commander Watson of the Royal Navy was sent out to coordinate the operation. Geoffrey Household arrived disguised as an insurance agent.[9] Our military attaché and his French colleague liaised with the Romanian chiefs of staff.

The sappers' equipment had been sent on ahead and, on 2 October 1939 Davidson-Houston went down to Galaţi to take charge of it. The SS *Fouadieh* had been ordered to come up the Danube secretly by night at top speed – as a result of which it had caused quite a stir by flooding riverside gardens. At the port, Davidson-Houston found some British-looking men in cloth caps shivering on board. They had been taken out of their khaki drill, put into cotton dungarees, given serially numbered passports and sent off as 'deck hands' with vehicles still yellow with desert sand. When Davidson-Houston suggested that they should be allowed into town to buy warmer clothes, the Romanian authorities refused in case of a 'scandale'.

The wells were to be destroyed by inserting an electrically fired rocket into the tubing; once the tubing had been cut the Germans would have to drill a new well. The rocket sent out from the War Office collapsed under pressure but the local oil men – who included Gwynn Elias and Gardyne de Chastelain – were not to be defeated. Working in a garage, they used the War Office model to make sturdier rockets, which the Russians later tried out in Baku and found to work perfectly. In Romania, however, they were never used. The invasion never took place, though Germans were arriving in fairly large numbers, smuggling in their weapons in empty tank cars. When the Germans took Paris in June 1940 they discovered French documents on the sabotage operation, which then had to be abandoned.

Even then, the British had a fallback plan to destroy Astra Română's high-pressure field at Boldeşti. It was at this point that I became involved –

and since I had no experience of oil or explosives, it must have been in a relatively minor capacity, probably to assist one of the engineers. Afterwards, I was to make for the Danube and try to cross into Bulgaria; had this desperate attempt succeeded, it could have seriously reduced Romania's oil production for a time. However the plan was leaked – and by now the friendly if tricky Tătărescu had been replaced by Gigurtu, a committed pro-German. Forty-eight hours before the oil wells were due to go up, the company guards, who would have cooperated with us, were replaced by Romanian troops – two to each well. As a result, even the fallback operation had to be abandoned.

By 1 May the Norwegians had surrendered. On 10 May, the day Churchill became Prime Minister, the Wehrmacht attacked the Low Countries and within three weeks Belgium had capitulated and British troops had evacuated Dunkirk. On 3 June, the pro-Allied Gafencu was replaced as Romanian Foreign Minister by the pro-German Gigurtu who within weeks was to become Prime Minister. Gafencu was packed off to head the Legation in Moscow, where he let it be known that Romanians still believed in an Allied victory.[10] On 10 June, Italy declared war on Britain and France, and on the 14th the Germans occupied Paris. On the 22nd the Franco-German armistice was signed at Compiègne; according to Denis Wright, the French Consul at Constanţa became an old man overnight.

Morale among our Romanian friends plummeted after Dunkirk. They were now certain that Romania would receive no help from the Allies for the foreseeable future. By July, the Romanian papers, wireless and newsreels were dominated by Deutsche Nachrichtenbüro (DNB), the official German news agency. British and American foreign correspondents kept their readers informed, but British propaganda in Romania was virtually non-existent. One of Lord Beaverbrook's people was appointed press attaché, but was not even given a proper office. The German Legation had an answer for every question put to them, while the British were often insufficiently well informed to be able to refute the most absurd German military claims. Even those Romanians who knew the British well enough to understand our attitude to propaganda were angry about our incompetence in this field. It is true that we circulated a news bulletin but since it was in English it reached mainly the already converted. We relied on the BBC to speak to Romanians in their own language. In those days the press was on the outer fringe of our diplomacy and even economic questions were given nothing like the priority they are today.

However, some effective private enterprise in the propaganda field was achieved by Denis Wright in Constanţa. The Germans posted a daily bulletin in the cinema's showcase. Iona Wright searched the town and found a key that would fit the padlock. Denis wrote a mock German communiqué and had it translated, and a young Romanian friend made the substitution. Then they retired to the restaurant opposite to await events. More people than usual gathered round the showcase, and the German Consul and his staff in the same restaurant looked pleased. Soon there was quite a crowd, and when they began to laugh the Germans went over to see why. Some hours passed before they could find the man with the key to open the case and for a few days the people of Constanța took courage from the fact that, with all Western Europe lost to the Nazis, the British had still not lost their sense of humour. This is what they had read:

Special German Communiqué

War in the Air

German planes attacked S.E. England and S. Wales. Out of 252 German planes only 10 returned to Germany.

War at Sea

On 20 August the aircraft carrier *Ark Royal* was sunk for the fourth time by a submarine commanded by Lieutenant Dr Goebbels.

The gallant Lt Goebbels has already sunk 10 of England's 7 aircraft carriers. It is expected that by the end of the week, the rest of the British fleet will have been sunk.

Total Blockade of the British Isles

As a result of the blockade Herr Hitler has cancelled his proposed summer holiday in England. He expects that Mr Churchill and Mr Eden will visit him in Berlin in 1942.[11]

After the fall of Western Europe I realised that I would probably be spending the war in the Balkans or more likely the Middle East. During the vacation I went for a few weeks to Transylvania spotting Romanian military units and then helped out with the Legation cyphering. The Legation asked me to stay on and since the British Council was a reserved occupation the Foreign Office arranged the transfer before the new academic year began in September. I had enjoyed university work but, with the phoney war over, was glad to be doing something more directly relevant to the national crisis. When the Diplomatic Mission left Romania I would join up.

The Legation was in Strada Jules Michelet, off the busy Boulevard Brătianu, in a private house which had been partially converted to offices, with the Minister's study a kind of no-man's-land between chancery, where we worked, and the residence. Colonel Geoffrey MacNab, the military attaché, Captain Despard, the naval attaché, Lord Forbes, the air attaché, and the Legation wireless operator had their offices in the stables. They were cramped, but had a wonderful view of the chestnut trees.

British diplomatic missions were, as now, meagrely staffed. The head of a Legation, a minister plenipotentiary, would have two or three diplomatic secretaries to help him with the political work, perhaps someone to look after the commercial side and, if he was lucky, a consul or two in the provinces. Cyphering in peacetime was done by whoever could spare the time – as late as July 1940 Sir Stafford Cripps complained that in his 'not unimportant embassy' in Moscow he had a typing and shorthand staff of one, and no cypher staff at all. Apart from his counsellor – Ian Le Rougetel who was later to come to Bucharest – his entire staff spent nine-tenths of their working day cyphering.[12]

The war had trebled cypher traffic in Bucharest so the Foreign Office sent out Francis Buckley – in peacetime a stockbroker and county cricketer – to take charge. He was later assisted by Denis Wright, until recently vice-consul at Constanţa, and myself. The discipline of cyphering, the humour and equanimity needed to handle the old book-cypher for hours on end helped, I am sure, to establish lifelong friendships amongst us.

Diplomatic telegrammes – as the word was then spelt – were not written in telegraphese. I admired their clarity, the power of persuasion that could occasionally change, however slightly, the course of international events. I knew that under existing regulations I was unlikely ever to be established in the administrative branch of the Foreign Service, but that had become my ambition. I knew now that members of the Service were among the most friendly, amusing, loyal and undevious people I was ever likely to meet; after the war I was lucky enough to join them, albeit through the back door.

Our Minister, Sir Reginald Hoare, had a difficult task. Whereas his German colleague, Wilhelm Fabricius, was navigating with the current, he had nothing going for him except the goodwill of the Romanian people. To the end, he defended British interests resolutely and, though conditions became very sticky indeed, with dignity and humour.

Lady Hoare was a warm-hearted eccentric whose eccentricities were entirely logical. Being rather vague, she carried an alarm clock in her hand bag which rang when it was time for her to say goodbye to her hostess. She flew a small aeroplane, using roads and railways as her only navigational aids, and was very put out when the RAF – who, as she rightly said, were short of aircraft – declined her offer to sell it to them.

When Poland fell, Robin Hankey* came to us as Head of Chancery from Warsaw, and spent much of his spare time at the Polski Dom for Polish refugees. There were two third secretaries, an archivist and his assistant and two shorthand secretaries, Frances Flanagan and Anne Windham – ladies in chancery, we called them. I used to go riding with Frances at an

---

* Later Sir Robert Hankey, HM Ambassador at Stockholm, now Lord Hankey.

Austrian riding school where the horses, even with me up, would do their high-school tricks. Once outside the *manège*, Frances would take a deep breath and we would ride Irish, and were in constant risk of being garrotted by the telephone lines the military strung across the paths.

Hugh Seton-Watson, whom I have already mentioned, was often in Romania. He spoke several East European languages and knew more about that part of the world than any other Englishman in Bucharest. He was a warm, likeable person and after our Romanian days we kept in touch.

Despite Allied failures on the western front and the increased German influence in Romania, the Legation still had many loyal Romanian friends. I cannot now remember the majority of them by name but among those we younger ones saw frequently were Pussy Nasta, daughter of the distinguished journalist, Liviu Nasta, who went to the Middle East, from where she broadcast back to Romania. There were Annie and Bobsie Samuelli, from one of the oldest Sephardic Jewish families. There was Olympia Zamfirescu and her brother – their father made the best chocolates in the Balkans. There was Maria whose pro-German step-brother had lectured me on Britain's blinkered view of trade and who, when John Davidson-Houston returned from discreetly meeting the SS *Fouadieh* at Galaţi and telephoned her, told him that she knew from her brother where he had been all day.[13]

In Western Europe the phoney war had ended in April 1940. In Romania it ended in June, by which time the whole of Western Europe except for Britain had been occupied.

Chapter 6

Dismemberment of Romania

Between June and September 1940 Romania was reduced in size by about one third. Those three months were among the worst of her whole turbulent history.

On 22 June, with Russia, Hungary and Bulgaria poised to go for her throat, Romania lost France, the only real friend she had among the Great Powers. When France fell Romanians wept openly in the street; the German Legation, if they had ever had any doubt, could now see for themselves where the country's sympathies lay.

Before we in Bucharest could recover from the disasters in Western Europe, Russia – lest her partner steal all the thunder – had occupied the Baltic states; and on 26 June the Russians told the Romanian Minister – Gafencu had not yet arrived in Moscow – that Romania had twenty-four hours to agree to the cession of Bessarabia and North Bukovina, the latter as compensation for twenty-two years of 'unlawful' Romanian occupation of Bessarabia. As Foreign Minister, Gafencu had tried in vain to discover whether, in August 1939, Ribbentrop and Molotov had discussed Russia's claim to Bessarabia; Fabricius had written to Berlin of 'the distress in which the Romanian Government finds itself', but had been instructed to tell them nothing.[1]

Next day the King, who had received the ultimatum without its accompanying map, called Fabricius to the Palace. In November 1938, he reminded him, the Führer had stressed that a rapprochement with Germany excluded one with the USSR. The King had followed this advice so could Germany now do nothing to help? Fabricius brazened it out, reminding the King that he had repeatedly advised him to take up the Bessarabian question directly with Moscow. The claim to northern Bukovina, he admitted, came as a surprise.

A member of the German Legation then interrupted to hand Fabricius an urgent personal message from Ribbentrop, despatched from Hitler's special train which at the King's request he read out. It advised Carol to cede the disputed territories to Russia. The King was dismayed, then furious, calling the Reich 'unreliable'. Romania, Fabricius replied, had only herself to blame. She had accepted the British guarantee enthusiastically, knowing full well that it was aimed at Germany, had since pursued a see-saw policy and missed the opportunity of a reasonable settlement with the USSR. He would now retire to give the King a chance to cool off and consult with his advisers.[2]

The Crown Council split. Three members, including Iorga the historian, called for resistance. Ministers were less confident. The chief of staff said the army was ready to fight, but with three fronts to defend against the Russians, Hungarians and Bulgarians it could not be expected to hold out for more than a month. The King, with Hitler's message in mind, was afraid of partition along Polish lines. After a long discussion, the Council decided to submit and keep the army intact for the defence of Transylvania.

Romanians were appalled. Moldavia had included Bessarabia for over four centuries until a weakened Turkey had ceded the province to Russia in 1812. At the Treaty of Paris in 1856, part of southern Bessarabia had been returned to Moldavia but this had been taken back by Russia twenty-two years later at the Congress of Berlin. For roughly a hundred years, St Petersburg had tried hard to russify the province – even the name 'Romanian' had been proscribed – but the Romanian peasant had a proverb *'Tata rus, mama rus, dar Ivan moldovan'* ('Father Russian, mother Russian, but Ivan is Moldavian', ie Romanian). Romania's administration of Bessarabia after its return to her in 1920 had not been brilliant – Maniu once described the civil servants Bucharest sent out to the province as 'satraps'. But during the winter of 1939 David Walker had seen peasant soldiers digging themselves in on the Romanian side of the river Prut, ready to take on the Russians. Only the King's personal appointees, who should never have been promoted anyhow, were quick to quit their army posts when they heard that the ultimatum had been accepted.[3]

Bukovina – 'The Beech Forest' – only came into existence as such in 1775 when it was granted to Austria. It had always previously been Moldavian territory and in 1920 was returned to Moldavia which was by then a part of Romania.

Bukovina had not been included in the bargain struck between Molotov and Ribbentrop in August 1939 and when, in addition to Bessarabia, Russia now claimed the whole of Bukovina, a province which had at no time belonged to her, Hitler insisted that the claim be limited to the northern part only, before he would advise Romania to yield.

After the loss of Bessarabia and northern Bukovina, Gigurtu became Prime Minister and was replaced at the Foreign Ministry by Manoilescu, another pro-German. Gigurtu announced that 'The direction of Romania's Foreign Policy within the framework of the Axis combination is now an accomplished fact.'[4] He pretended to have uncovered an Anglo-French plot to destroy the oil fields, knowing full well that it had been agreed with his predecessors. He then expelled forty British oil engineers and their families, people who had been in the country for most of their professional lives. I remember them milling around in the Legation garden, and the Minister meeting them, as a gesture of defiance, in the most public place in Bucharest, the Athenée Palace Hotel. Early in August a Legation messenger, a locally engaged teenage boy called Nelson Matthews, was arrested and maltreated because he refused to give the authorities a daily list of visitors to the Legation; we were particularly angry about this. A month later the entire staff of the British Institute, led by John Amery, was expelled. But there was worse to come.

By now the King was sending desperate messages to the Führer asking him to prevent Bulgaria and Hungary 'extending demands beyond the limits of national justice',[5] but Hitler had some sympathy for countries which, like Germany, had suffered from the post-war peace settlements.

At the Congress of Berlin in 1878, when Russia had taken southern Bessarabia away from Romania, Romania had been given as 'compensation' a piece of territory known as the Dobrugea to the south of the mouth of the Danube. It was the barren land to which Ovid had been exiled. Bulgaria, the other claimant to this territory, had been on the losing side in the First World War, so Romania had retained it. Talks with Sofia now opened on 19 August and the Craiova agreement was signed on 7 September 1940. When Bulgarian troops occupied southern Dobrugea Romanians regretted in particular the loss of Balçic where Queen Marie had had her favourite house and where at her request her heart now lay. But there was little resentment towards Bulgaria; Hungary was by far the greater enemy.

Hitler met Mussolini on 28 August, when the Romanian-Hungarian talks were about to collapse. The Führer admitted that Hungary's claim to Transylvania was confronted by an 'ethnographical case that was incontestable'. He warned his partner that Romanian oil to the Axis would cease at the first gunshot. Hungary could not be counted on to defeat Romania, and a protracted war would almost certainly bring Russia into the Balkans. If stability was to be restored, the Axis must arbitrate in Hungary's favour but guarantee what was left of Romania. Since Hungary might not accept arbitration unless she thought the way had been left open for a second bite at the Transylvanian cherry, only Romania should be told of the guarantee until the arbitration had been signed and sealed.[6]

The two foreign ministers were called to Vienna. Raoul Bossy, the Romanian Minister at Rome, described in his diary the meeting of the 29th which Ribbentrop, accompanied by Ciano, had with Manoilescu.[7] Ribbentrop referred angrily to Gafencu, who had been saying in Moscow that as soon as Britain was on top Romania would help Russia against Germany. He told Manoilescu that if Romania accepted arbitration (though she did not know what it involved) the Axis would guarantee the new Romanian frontiers against any threat. This, he said, would not be an 'English-type' guarantee but a real one. If she did not accept arbitration she would be considered an enemy of the Axis. Hungary and almost certainly Russia would attack her, the Axis would wash their hands of her, and she would cease to exist as a state. The pretence that Germany had no interest in Romania's future hardly tallies with the concern Hitler had shown over the fate of her oil only the day before when discussing the situation with Mussolini. Hitler in fact gave secret instructions for five armoured and three motorised divisions, preceded by parachute and airborne troops, to be ready to move in and protect the Ploeşti oil installations if negotiations broke down.[8]

On 30 August, the award, known in Romania as the Vienna Diktat, decreed that Romanian troops should evacuate northern Transylvania within two weeks and that civilians could opt for Hungarian citizenship within six months. The whole ceremony lasted under half an hour; Manoilescu fainted when he heard the terms, so he was passed over when the time came for him to make his brief, prepared speech. Germany and Italy gave the promised guarantee of Romania's 'integrity and inviolability', but at the time the Romanian delegation were too shocked by the terms of the arbitration itself to give the guarantee much attention. The Hungarian delegation, who had obtained advance copies of the new map of Transylvania, gleefully distributed them to the press the moment the ceremony was over.[9]

Many Romanians believed the Vienna arbitration to be the result of collusion between Berlin and Moscow. They were wrong; Molotov was not informed of the award until the 31st,[10] and considered the guarantee of Romania's new frontiers to be directed against Russia. Although at the time Romanians seemed less interested in the guarantee than in the loss of northern Transylvania the former was to become a prime element in the deterioration of Russo-German relations leading to the invasion of the USSR, which was to prove so disastrous for Romania. In a sense it is unfortunate for Romanians that they were at no point invaded militarily by the Reich. Even a short-lived resistance would have improved their wartime reputation with the Allies but, one has to accept, would have made no difference to their treatment after the war.

While the British in Bucharest were shocked by the Vienna Diktat we also felt a nagging anxiety about the future of our own country. Britain seemed to have had the best of the air battle in August, but the Luftwaffe attack on London had still to come. Shipping losses were serious and, as invasion threatened, we in Bucharest could only guess at Britain's unpreparedness. Sometimes I was irritated by Romanians, who seemed so preoccupied with their own problems while Britain alone was actually

fighting Hitler. Some of them asked why we were not already bombing
Bucharest, or at least the oil fields; whatever the immediate damage to
their country, they felt their only hope in the long run lay in an Allied
victory. They had no idea, of course, of the range or shortage of British
aircraft, or the low bombing priority the RAF would give to Romania.

The loss of so large a part of Transylvania without a shot being fired was
considered a national disgrace. According to my personal notes, even the
Iron Guard newspaper, *Buna Vestire*, declared that after being the vassals
of Paris, Romanians must not now become the vassals of Rome and Berlin.
People had openly accused Carol of cowardice after the Bessarabian crisis;
now they called for his abdication. I remember a snappy little verse that
was circulating in Bucharest:

> Ruşilor am dat un pic,
> Las pe Mama la Balçic,
> Ungurii sunt la Avrig,
> Nu-i nimic.
> Fie tronul cât de mic
> Eu nu abdic.

> I've given the Russians a bit,
> I've left Mama at Balçic,
> The Hungarians are at Avrig,*
> It's nothing.
> However small the throne may be
> I shall not abdicate.

In the summer Maniu had proposed a national government of all parties,
and if the King had taken this opportunity of sharing responsibility he
might have saved his throne. Transylvania was now on the point of
insurrection: several Romanian generals refused to obey the order to
withdraw, and Romanians looked to Maniu for leadership. London felt
that if a *coup* by Maniu led to German intervention this 'would in itself
serve our purpose since it would bring about a situation which might well
be conducive to a clash between Germany and Russia.'[11] Some of the
pressure would have been taken off Britain.

But – to quote Clare Hollingworth, then of the *Daily Express* – Maniu,
though a good democrat, an honest man and a friend of England, was 'the
last conceivable person to ride the whirlwind and direct the storm'.[12]
Twenty years before he had done just that against the Austro-Hungarian
Empire when working for Transylvanian independence. But now he was a

* Avrig is near Sibiu in Transylvania.

more prudent man, and in Wallachia he seemed somehow less sure of himself than he had been in his beloved Transylvania.

London had nevertheless decided that Maniu, with his powerful, organised opposition in Transylvania, was the man to support once diplomatic relations had been broken off, and during the summer of 1940 he was approached by representatives of the newly formed SOE. SOE, a purely wartime organisation, had an operational and an intelligence-gathering brief. Under Chamberlain, three small sections in the Foreign and War Offices had carried out provisional research into irregular warfare and anti-Nazi propaganda.[13] When Churchill became Prime Minister he combined these under Hugh Dalton with instructions to 'set Europe ablaze'. After a great deal of haggling the Political Warfare Executive (SO1) and the Combined Operations Section (SO2) were split. SO2 then became known as the Special Operations Executive, or the more familiar SOE. Its objective was to harass the enemy in occupied territory by identifying, encouraging and arming resistance movements of whatever political or ideological leaning. After a period of somewhat unruly independence, its political activities were put under broad Foreign Office supervision.

One of SOE's earliest recruits, with the symbol DH13, was an oil engineer called Gardyne de Chastelain. He was a friend of both Juliu Maniu and a Romanian called Rica Georgescu. Georgescu, who belonged to no political party but was devoted to Maniu, spoke perfect English. He had been at school in England and studied at Birmingham, then the only British university with a course in oil engineering.

When de Chastelain arrived in Romania in 1927, a young civil engineer employed by the British Unirea oil company, Georgescu had trained him in oil engineering and in the tough cowboy life then lived in the Prahova valley. Sharing a house, riding out day or night to deal with problems at the rigs, they became close friends.

When de Chastelain left Romania in the late summer of 1940 he was sales manager of Unirea, while Georgescu had become managing director of the American subsidiary, Romano Americana. Chas, as we called him, was married and had two children. From Romania he went to Istanbul to work under Colonel Bill Bailey, SOE's representative in Turkey, though he was to make several trips back to Romania before the British Diplomatic Mission finally left. His wife, Marion, spent most of the war in New York working with 'Little Bill' Stephenson,* the Canadian steel magnate who was in charge of all British secret activities in North America.

I knew Chas and Marion in Romania, though not particularly well; he was one of the key men in the plan to destroy the oil wells. A short, active

---

* Later Sir William Stephenson.

man with a large head and little hair, he was convinced that with Maniu and one or two other Romanians, notably Georgescu, he could bring Romania into the war on our side. Since he had lived in the country for thirteen years, he tended to see the Romanian, as well as the British, point of view, and was made unhappy by some aspects of British policy. He was an able and honest man who did not always recognise deviousness in others.

After the Vienna Diktat, de Chastelain made contact with Maniu in Georgescu's house. Maniu agreed to go to London, where he would form a Free Romanian Committee and conduct propaganda against the Germans. More especially, he guaranteed a Transylvanian uprising against the Germans when they had eventually to withdraw from the province. In return, Britain would do what she could to guarantee Romania's integrity and, in particular, to restore northern Transylvania. With characteristic prudence Maniu asked for confirmation from Churchill in person, and Georgescu recalls the meeting at which the telegram was produced. It was attended by Maniu, de Chastelain, the president of Romano Americana and the US Minister, Mott Gunter – the last two present at Georgescu's request, since he wanted his company and the still neutral US Government to know what he was up to. According to the telegram, the British Government would assist in financing Ardealul, Maniu's Transylvanian movement, and do what they could to guarantee Romania's integrity. The US Minister, who was notoriously pro-British, assured Maniu that it would not be long before the USA was in the war on Britain's side. Although this SOE telegram first notified Maniu of Churchill's undertaking, the actual letter from the Prime Minister to Maniu, which I have not yet traced, would normally be sent via the Foreign Office and Sir Reginald Hoare. According to Baron Styrcea, who later became Marshal of the Royal Court under King Michael, Maniu referred to this letter during an audience with His Majesty early in 1941. Georgescu tells me that as late as 1945 when Romania was already in the Soviet sphere of influence, Maniu still considered this 'personal undertaking', given to him as pro-Allied leader of the Romanian opposition, to be the key to his wartime activities.

Details of Britain's financial support for Ardealul were worked out later. The British Government would credit the British Phoenix Oil and Transport Company, Unirea's parent company. With the help of a Greek trader in Istanbul, de Chastelain was to transfer the money to an engineer called Popovici, who had been his assistant at Unirea. The chain would subsequently be Popovici, Georgescu, Maniu and, finally, Maniu's nephew Ionel Pop, who continued to live at Cluj, which was now in Hungary. Apart from Maniu, the only Romanian who knew all the details of this transaction was Georgescu.

While the British were preparing for subversive work after their diplomatic mission had left, the Germans were elaborating the last stage of their peaceful takeover of Romania.

Two years before, Fabricius had decided that General Ion Antonescu, the Minister of Defence in Goga's government, was someone worth cultivating. Stumpy, with a fair complexion and blue eyes, Antonescu was a proud man, a bit of a martinet but with a reputation for fairness and complete devotion to the army. He came from a modest military family: his father was a captain in army administration, his mother an intelligent, energetic and cultivated woman. He had trained as a cavalry officer in Romania and St Cyr, in the tradition of 'one's word is one's bond'. During the peasant uprising of 1907, when the Roşiu regiment was sent into Teleorman, Antonescu's was the only platoon to settle the trouble without opening fire. When in charge of a squadron at the officers' school at Târgoveşti, he refused the Palace's request for one of his cadets to be given three days' leave of absence to attend a court party on the grounds that the man in question 'is taking part in an exercise'.[14]

Quite early on there seems to have been a touch of fanaticism in his make-up. After the First World War a bad fall caused a brain haemorrhage which put him out of action for six months. Subsequently he was given less active duties as a military attaché in London and Paris. During an interview at the London Legation with Rica Georgescu and another student, Sandu Racotta – who will recur in this narrative – he reprimanded them for not knowing about an item in the *Monitorul Oficial*, the Romanian Official Gazette. Racotta had leapt to his feet – all two metres of him – leaned over the small colonel and told him: 'You're crazy if you think Cambridge undergraduates spend their time reading the *Monitorul Oficial*.' But Antonescu quite seriously had replied that even if they should find themselves at the North Pole it would still be their duty as Romanians to familiarise themselves with the *Monitorul Oficial*. He had meant it; and Georgescu and Racotta had had a glimpse of a single-mindedness which was to become mildly megalomaniac in later life.

When Fabricius first met him, Antonescu had been a great admirer of Britain and France. However, the Minister had talked Berlin into appointing a part-time German military attaché to Bucharest, whose main task would be to win Antonescu's confidence. That had been in 1938, and now Fabricius's foresight was to pay off.

Antonescu, who at no point in his life showed any sign of being over-awed by the monarchy, had once written to King Carol calling on him to abdicate, and had narrowly escaped being shot as a result. He had since spent much of his time in prison or under house arrest, where he was visited regularly by two friends, Professor Mihai Antonescu (no relation) and Alecu Ştefanescu, the Romanian representative for Coates, the British cotton firm. When Antonescu was released on 1 September, Ştefanescu brought him to Maniu's flat, where they were shortly joined by Dinu Brătianu. Although Antonescu had no party affiliation he had one thing in common with Maniu and Brătianu: none of them would serve under King Carol. The opposition leaders knew that the King would never abdicate at their request so they looked to Antonescu to try to obtain the abdication on behalf of all three. If he succeeded they would give him their full political support. Antonescu agreed. He promised to meet them again after his audience. On 4 September, the day Antonescu saw the King, Maniu and Rica Georgescu dined together. They waited up until after midnight, but the general did not appear.

The King had offered Antonescu the premiership and, instead of consulting the party leaders as promised, he had gone to see Fabricius, the German Minister. He was toying with the idea of forming a government with the Iron Guard – something that Maniu and Brătianu would never have countenanced. Fabricius had advised him to assume dictatorial powers, remove the 'universally hated entourage of the King',[15] and order ministers to stay at their posts until the question of abdication had been settled. Telegraphing a summary of this conversation to Berlin, the Minister commented: 'I believe we have found in him a man at the head of the Romanian Government who is firmly resolved to carry out our important demands here.'[16]

Antonescu preferred Fabricius's solution to the parliamentary government he knew Maniu and Brătianu would insist on. He told the King that he would accept his offer only if he became head of state and if certain of the royal prerogatives were transferred to him. By his own account, he ran the risk of being arrested and executed because Carol, knowing that he had virtually no support in the country, had still not altogether given up the idea of appointing his chief of staff as premier and battling on. According to Antonescu, only when Fabricius told the King – whether in person or by telephone is not clear – that the Reich attached no importance to his remaining in the country and was 'looking up time-tables for him' did he finally accept defeat.[17]

Many of us were at the Athenée Palace bar on the night of 5 September. One experienced journalist – I think it was Walter Duranty – went to bed leaving instructions to be called at four o'clock. He knew that abdications always take place in the early hours. King Carol's was announced at 5.30 a.m. Prince Michael, a shy young man of eighteen, musical, strong-willed and said to be more interested in aero-engines than politics, took the oath a few hours later.

Chapter 7

The Iron Guard Revolt

Little was known of the Iron Guard members of Antonescu's government. Their somewhat insipid leader, Horia Sima, who had returned from Germany with ideological but no administrative training, became Antonescu's deputy. Of the non-Legionaries, Antonescu's friend, Professor Mihai Antonescu, became Minister of Justice and later combined the duties of Premier and Foreign Minister. Meanwhile, Manoilescu retained the Ministry of Foreign Affairs. Maniu and Brătianu had refused to serve in the new administration. Other public figures with known Allied sympathies – even the dubious Tătărescu – had vanished from the scene.

One thing soon became clear: with Antonescu in charge, the Reich would have a freer hand in Romania. What we did not know was that on 20 September 1940 the German Supreme Command had already decided to move in a whole division, ostensibly to train the Romanian army but with a secret brief to protect the oil installations and to prepare for Romanian and German forces to advance eastwards in case of war with Russia. The key sentence in a guidance telegram from the German Foreign Office is 'Every suggestion that it is an anti-Russian move must be energetically denied.'[1]

Antonescu was faced with the choice that Ada's father had warned me about. Russia had taken Bessarabia and North Bukovina. Germany had given the more precious North Transylvania to Hungary. Yet Antonescu had no hesitation. On 23 November he went to Berlin to sign the Tripartite Pact with the Axis and announced that 'Romania on her own initiative has entered the political sphere of Germany and Italy.'[2] At the signing ceremony Hitler spoke to Antonescu about the recent 'unfortunate' Italian invasion of Greece; if the British moved in to help the Greeks and established air-bases in Greece, Ploeşti would be threatened. He asked for permission to move German troops southwards through Romania if necessary, and Antonescu agreed subject to provisioning arrangements.[3]

In October the Joint Intelligence Committee (JIC) in London had given as one of five possible courses of action open to Germany – not at this stage including the invasion of Russia – 'an advance south east through Bulgaria' into Greece, the object being to prevent the use of Greek harbours by the British fleet.[4] No mention was made of RAF raids on Ploeşti.

The German troops behaved well in Romania and their discipline and good manners impressed us all. Yet Romanians resented them. They could send home a five-kilogram parcel each week, which later amounted to a considerable food export. They turned Romanian soldiers out of their barracks. They were paid about three times as much as Romanian troops and appeared in fashionable tea shops on the Calea Victoriei which a Romanian peasant-soldier would never dream of entering. To make matters worse, although they were there for everyone to see, the German authorities felt that to confirm their presence would give the British a pretext to sabotage the Ploeşti installations. This evasiveness irritated the average citizen, and when the authorities finally announced that German troops were in Romania on a training mission Romanians saw more in it than training. When, later on, transit troops on their way to Greece disrupted the railway system for over a week and no official explanation was given, Romanians jumped to the conclusion that Antonescu and Hitler were preparing to recover Bessarabia.

Following the Vienna Diktat, the Soviet Government had told Berlin in a memorandum of 21 September that while they recognised the Reich's special economic requirements in Romania, the German Government should not assume that, after the solution of the Bessarabian question, only they had interests in Romania and the Danube Basin.[5] On 12 November Molotov had an angry meeting with Hitler in Berlin. 'No foreign visitor had ever spoken to him in this way in my presence,' wrote Paul Schmidt, Hitler's interpreter.[6] While the Führer waffled on about the New Order in Europe and the plunder that would be available when the British Empire collapsed, Molotov pressed home his precise, blunt questions. Would Hitler revoke the guarantee of Romania's frontiers? Hitler refused. Then Russia would consider giving a similar guarantee to Bulgaria, so putting Hitler's Greek campaign at risk. That evening a banquet at the Soviet Embassy – which Hitler did not attend – was disrupted by a British air raid planned for the occasion. In the shelter Ribbentrop still foolishly insisted that the war with Britain was virtually over, to which Molotov replied, 'Then whose are these bombs which are falling?'[7] Later Hitler told Antonescu of his strong impression that Russia's ambitions were not yet satisfied.[8] No doubt Molotov left Berlin with the same impression about Germany's.

The British in Bucharest could not have known that Molotov's visit to Berlin marked a watershed in Russo-German relations. In any case the local situation was giving us plenty to think about.

Antonescu, like the Iron Guard, had a flamboyant, mystical side to him and on 8 September, the Sunday following the King's abdication, he called on everyone, wherever they were, to kneel at eleven in the morning and pray for their country. I stayed indoors. On 6 October, there was a great

Legionary rally: the streets were full of marching, bare-headed, long-haired youths wearing their green shirts openly for the first time and demonstrating against the Vienna Diktat. Unlike the Communists who supported Russia's claim to Bessarabia, the Iron Guard were essentially a nationalist and populist movement with strong fascist overtones. They gave Antonescu the fascist salute to which he replied, 'Long live the Legion and the Captain.'[9]

Having tasted power, the Iron Guard wanted immediate revolution. Under a Legionary Minister of the Interior and a Legionary Prefect of Police they formed their own police force, which acted as police, judge and executioner. And since these thugs were out of Antonescu's control the Legation had no effective official channel to go to when British subjects were attacked.

Legionary intimidation was worst at Ploeşti, where there was no British consul. At about nine in the morning on 25 September two young guardists flashing police identity cards took an English chemist from his laboratory. Other oil people, including one wife, were rounded up and accused of tampering with oil tankers en route for Germany. By the time the military attaché and the Bucharest consul had located them, none of the prisoners could stand. The men had been bastinadoed, kicked and hit with revolvers, and one had lost his teeth.

Clare Hollingworth had been the *Daily Express* correspondent in Poland at the time of the German invasion, and had crossed the frontier into Romania at the very last minute. On 1 October, the Iron Guard came to arrest her in her bedroom but she had the presence of mind to strip and dare the youthful Legionaries to escort her out as she was. She then managed to get to the telephone in the next room and contact the Legation. It was typical of Clare, but she had been lucky.

Alexander Miller, a leading official of the Shell affiliate Astra Română, lived at my digs in Strada Spătarului. On the evening of the day Clare Hollingworth saved herself, he was abducted from the company's sports club at Sinaia and taken to a house three hours' drive away. According to Eric Berthoud's minute to the Minister of 5 November,[10] his ill-treatment was progressive, starting with a few blows on the first night, worse on the second, and a severe beating with heavy sticks on the third.

Finally he 'confessed' that he had passed to one of the engineers four boxes, each containing thirty ampoules of a substance which, when dissolved in a tank car of petroleum, would cause the petrol to explode in an aero-engine. He was then driven down to Legionary headquarters in Ploeşti and next morning handed over to the Bucharest Security Service. As he entered the Siguranţa building, he was recognised by an employee of Astra Română who informed the Legation. Now that he was in official hands, Ian Le Rougetel* – the newly arrived counsellor – and Eric Berthoud could intervene with the administration.

The Siguranţa agent who questioned him found the confession ludicrous; his problem was how to get rid of the case without incurring the revenge of the Legionaries who, as he said, had 'worked so hard on it'. In Miller's office the Siguranţa man turned a blind eye to the fact that the door had been forced and incriminating documents removed, and accepted some quite innocuous papers as examples of Miller's London reports. Together they then wrote a new confession based on these. On Saturday 12 October Miller was taken before a judge who released him.[11] We saw him briefly at Madame Arditti's and David Walker examined his bruises. He left the country on the Monday afternoon.

On 8 October 1940, Sir Reginald Hoare received authority to withdraw the British Legation at his discretion as soon as British interests had been quietly liquidated. Some officials and their wives left for Istanbul immediately but two interesting experiences awaited those of us who remained – a large-scale earthquake, and an armed insurrection.

There were two tremors on 22 October, but the big 'quake took place at 3.50 a.m. on 10 November. Anne Windham, Bobsie Samuelli and I were spending the weekend in a *pension* in the mountains. We had to share the dining room with a German officer, and after dinner, the girls and I went for a walk and then to bed. They and the German were on the ground floor, and I was upstairs. I took the first tremor to be a repeat of the October one, and turned over to go back to sleep. Next moment I found myself on the floor. The lights had failed. We must have been in the habit of locking our doors, and in the dark and the shambles the room was now in, I could find neither my key nor my trousers.

The others had gathered in the garden, and when they realised that I was missing the German got hold of a spare key and let me out. We all stayed up talking, waiting for the next big tremor, too excited to go back to bed. The officer was keen to get through to Bucharest, and when the telephones were working again he told us about the destruction there. Travelling back through the Prahova valley next day, Anne, Bobsie and I looked in vain for damage to the oil installations.

There was one major tragedy. A twelve-storey block of flats over the Carlton cinema had collapsed. A night watchman on the roof simply stepped off on to the rubble under which were some five hundred people; the Green Shirts, soldiers and police worked themselves to exhaustion to rescue them.

* Later Sir John Le Rougetel, High Commissioner in South Africa.

The Iron Guard were treating the British badly but the Romanians far worse. I noted, 'It is difficult to believe that Antonescu sanctioned the murders that took place this autumn.'[12] One night in November, they entered Jilava prison and shot sixty-five politicians awaiting trial for alleged implication in Codreanu's death and this piece of rough justice reflected badly on the strong-man image of Antonescu who had just been to Berlin to sign the Tripartite Pact. Shortly afterwards Romanians were deeply shocked by the brutal murder of the aged historian Iorga. Madgearu, Secretary General of the National Peasant Party and a close friend of Maniu, was killed in a typical Legionary way; the murderer called on him at two o'clock one afternoon to discuss an agricultural scheme, took him away in his car, shot him in the woods near Bucharest and was back in his office by four. Three months later, Maniu wrote to Antonescu, the assassins though well known had still not been arrested.[13]

A week after Madgearu's death a group of us were in a restaurant where Maniu happened to be dining. Although the place was crowded with Germans, he sent us a message to say how glad he was to see us so cheerful; we must not imagine that the present government represented the country. When the restaurant was almost empty we stood up and toasted him and he and his companions, clearly moved by our gesture of solidarity, raised their glasses to us.[14] We had nothing to lose but, only a week after one of his closest friends had been murdered by the Iron Guard, Maniu had identified himself publicly with us. In such ways he was fearless. In others, as we shall see, he was irritatingly hesitant.

From their *pension* on the Calea Victoriei Denis and Iona Wright watched the reburial of Codreanu and the other thirteen 'heroes', which lasted for three hours with 'row upon row of frozen Green Shirts'. Shops and restaurants were shut for the occasion and street lamps were draped in black. The funeral march, headed by Antonescu and the moon-faced Fabricius, was immediately followed by an impressive display of German military power, for which they were joined on the reviewing stand by King Michael. A large crowd turned out, but there was no cheering.[15] Four days later Horia Sima, under pressure from Antonescu, issued an order dissolving the dreaded Legionary police and, except on official occasions, forbidding the wearing of the green shirt, which had become a kind of terrorist *passe-partout*. The Legionary Prefect of Police, however, remained in office.

Bucharest seemed calmer after the dissolution of the Legionary police. The news from the BBC was better; we were winning the air battle over London, and the threat of invasion had receded. The first offensive in the desert was going well. Christmas was coming. Children were singing carols from door to door, sometimes carrying a huge star made of coloured paper and furiously ringing a bell. Shopkeepers, though particularly busy just then, always stopped serving for a moment to give them something. Sometimes two or three peasants would go round, one with horns on his head and wearing a brightly coloured cloak. His friends played their flutes while the 'goat' danced, and once again a hat was passed round.

Over Christmas and New Year there were parties; at a particularly splendid one given by a member of the passport office and his beautiful Polish wife we had caviar, vodka, pheasants, champagne, gypsy musicians, dancing and Russian songs. When most of us left at about 4 a.m. Ian Le Rougetel was still dancing; he could dance all of us younger ones into the floor.

The cheerful interlude did not last. On 11 January Antonescu in a friendly and frank interview with Sir Reginald Hoare confirmed that he had tried unsuccessfully to get rid of the Legionary Prefect of Police. He referred to a 'sleepless spirit of revenge' but, having no assurance that the Germans would not use a disturbance as a pretext to establish complete control, he had to tread carefully.[16]

Maniu had written to Antonescu pointing out that 'illegal acts of revenge merely prolong a condition from which it is only a step to the collapse of the state.'[17] Incompetent Iron Guard commissars were already bringing about that collapse; the National Cooperative Institute, of which Madgearu's assassin was commissar, had lost over 25 million *lei* in a matter of weeks; Hitler was beginning to see that the Iron Guard might well have outlived its usefulness.

When Antonescu went to Berlin in the middle of January to seek the assurance he had mentioned to Hoare, Hitler, with ironic clairvoyance, remarked that any movement which relied on force and had not the backing of the people would not outlive its founder. Relations between the German National Socialist Party and the Iron Guard could be severed immediately if the general so wished. Antonescu diffidently declined the offer, only asking that his own authority should not be put in doubt. Horia Sima, who had also been invited to Berlin by some visiting Nazi VIPs, had decided not to go at the last minute and when Antonescu returned he was told that Sima had stayed behind to prepare an armed revolt. Nevertheless, he was fairly confident. Had not the Führer made it clear in Berlin that he valued Antonescu more highly than his fifth column?

Things moved quickly. One night while some of us were dancing at the Melody Bar, a German major was shot on the pavement outside, and the Legionaries blamed the British. Antonescu fired General Petrovicescu, the Legionary Minister of the Interior, for incompetence but the Prefect of Police again refused to go and even rearmed Legionary police and installed them at his headquarters. On 21 January, we heard sporadic shooting in town and several Green Shirts were reported killed. Restaurants closed at 9.30 that night and people were warned to be home by ten o'clock. The

Associated Press correspondent discovered that no one could buy petrol – the Iron Guard were intimidating garage owners. On Wednesday 22 January only two newspapers appeared, both Legionary, and one, *Cuvântul*, published a letter from the president of the National Union of Romanian Christian students, which gives an idea of the anti-British atmosphere.

> Romanians,
> A German major has been killed in the streets of the capital – murdered in a cowardly way by an agent of the Intelligence Service under orders from England . . . the heroic soldier and man of character, General Petrovicescu, has been forced, because the British Legation and Masonry required it, to leave the government.
> We call on General Antonescu to do justice to Romanians.
> We desire the removal from the government of all stuffed Masons.
> We desire a Legionary government.
> We desire the punishment of those guilty for the assassination of the German major.
> Romanian students will not allow German soldiers to be slaughtered by British agents on the streets of the capital.
> Romanian students want a Legionary government.[18]

By then Green Shirts had occupied the Prefecture, the broadcasting station and the telephone building and had barricaded themselves into their headquarters known as the Casa Verde which was next to Antonescu's office. They were well armed, with plenty of ammunition and food. Tram drivers came out in sympathy and their trams were used as barricades. Posters declared the Legionaries to be the enemies of 'British Masonic Judaism'.

Fabricius telephoned Hitler to suggest that Antonescu be given a free hand to suppress the insurrection. The Führer said, 'Good, good, but what is left of Codreanu's ideology?' Fabricius told him that nothing was left of the movement's idealism – everything now was 'dishonest and anarchic'. After a little hesitation but no real resistance, Hitler agreed that the revolt should be suppressed[19].

The Romanian soldiers, whose discipline was excellent, at first shot over the heads of the Legionaries whilst themselves under fire. Later they were ordered to shoot to kill, but the Legionaries still held out.

Romanians went about their business as usual. A British governess walked through the cross-fire; when we remonstrated she replied that, being English, she had nothing to do with their stupid war. Denis and I dropped in on Clare Hollingworth, back after her clash with the Legionary police. We remained there until the curfew and amused ourselves dodging patrols on our way back to the Legation. That evening Antonescu assured Romanians that he would never allow interference in Romanian affairs by 'judaeo-masonic conspirators' – a reference to the Legionaries' description of the British. If attacked, Romanians should 'call in the authority of the state' and until its arrival 'protect your home without hesitation.'[20] That was easier said than done with a group of trigger-happy Legionaries threatening you and the telephone not working.

At one moment, King Michael set off from Sinaia to drive to Bucharest, but General Antonescu, fearing that he might be held hostage by the Legionaries, peremptorily ordered him back. In the circumstances the King deferred to him though the Marshal's dictatorial behaviour did nothing to improve relations between them.

There was a terrible pogrom on the night of 22 January. According to one level-headed Jewish journalist whose report we sent to London, Jews were taken in numbers to the Jilava and Baneasă woods and machine-gunned. Some were murdered at the abattoir with the machines normally used on animals. A large number were tortured and mutilated. Next morning hardly a shop in the Jewish quarter of Strada Lipscani was undamaged and there were long queues outside the morgues. The Iron Guard riff-raff planned to deal with their other enemies the following night.

At 5 a.m. on the 23rd, a proclamation – supposedly from Horia Sima, who was in hiding – ordered Legionaries to leave public buildings and 'return to normal life.'[21] Many assumed this to be a trap laid by Antonescu, and fighting soon became general again. It was then that Antonescu turned to the German military mission for help. We watched German troops parade that afternoon before opening fire on the Legionary-held police headquarters. They also prevented Legionary reinforcements from entering the town. The Iron Guards, who had naturally counted on support from a country in which many of them had been trained, were so shocked by this betrayal that they collapsed. By evening the trams were running again and telephones working for local calls. Antonescu proclaimed that every Legionary would be brought to justice 'from Horia Sima down to the lowest cut-throat',[22] but Romanians had noted that he had had to call in German troops to suppress the uprising. Constantin Brătianu in a letter of 21 February warned Antonescu that over-commitment to any one power would always jeopardise Romania's existence.[23]

We were horrified to hear the BBC describe the Legionaries as 'patriots', on the assumption that anyone who opposed the quisling Antonescu must be pro-Allies. The night-duty officer had misread the FO guidance;[24] it was one of the BBC's rare wartime gaffes.

No protection had been given to the Jews during the revolt. At least 800 died – tradesmen, lawyers, doctors, their wives and children – but the number has been put as high as 1,800. During that one night in Bucharest one of the worst brief pogroms of the war had taken place, yet when the official casualty figures for the Iron Guard revolt were published this Jewish massacre was not included. If he were to have the good relations with Hitler on which his whole foreign policy now depended, Antonescu, who was certainly not behind the pogrom, dared not run the risk of being thought soft on the Jews. Churchill minuted the Foreign Secretary that it might be as well to let General Antonescu know that if such a vile act occurred again the Allies would hold him and his immediate circle personally responsible 'in life and limb.'[25]

By now von Killinger was about to take over from Fabricius as the German Minister at Bucharest. In his late forties and already too heavy for his height, von Killinger in Slovakia had already gained a reputation for brutality and had been given the name of 'butcher'. This, of course, was known in Bucharest. A member of the Italian Legation was walking with him one Sunday morning in Floreasca, a fashionable quarter of Bucharest, when they passed the back door of a villa where the cook was sitting with a knife and a chicken in her lap. It is considered bad luck in Romania for a woman to kill a chicken, but instead of addressing the younger man, she asked von Killinger, '*Tai găina?*' – 'Will you kill the chicken for me?' The Italian was quite embarrassed.[26]

On 25 January von Killinger, who had been made personally responsible for the problem of the Iron Guard, received a telegram from Ribbentrop which, taken with his own reply, gives a clear insight into the deep mistrust that existed between Himmler's people and the Foreign Ministry. Could it be, asked Ribbentrop, that in spite of the Führer's express instructions, some German agency had encouraged the Iron Guard? He asked for independent reports from Fabricius and Neubacher,* 'unadorned and without any consideration for persons', and covered by von Killinger's confidential comments. Ribbentrop added that they could not judge in Berlin what part, if any, the British had played in the revolt.[27]

A month later,[28] von Killinger replied that although no German had been directly involved in the revolt itself, the Iron Guard had strong sympathisers among the German Security Service (SD), certain members

---

* Neubacher, leader of the underground National Socialist organisation in Austria, 1933–8, had been appointed Ribbentrop's special envoy in Bucharest for petroleum negotiations. At the time of the Iron Guard revolt he was in charge of all economic questions at the Legation and was considered by us to be one of the best informed and most dangerous Germans in Bucharest.

of the Legation close to the SD, some journalists and the Overseas
National Socialist Party Association; and that by their attitudes these
people had contributed to bringing the revolution about.

The SD representative had been hiding nine Iron Guard leaders in a
Legation building, and to von Killinger's embarrassment Antonescu
himself had been the first to tell him of this. The head of the SD also knew
Horia Sima's hiding place but refused to disclose it because he had given
his word not to. A German police officer liaising with the Iron Guard
police had publicly described the murder of the Jilava prisoners as no more
than 'popular justice', and when challenged by von Killinger had argued
that this was the Führer's own opinion. (Hitler had, in fact, spoken on
these lines in one of his interviews with Antonescu.) 'I advised him,' wrote
von Killinger to Ribbentrop, 'to keep quiet about it if that was actually the
case.' The Russians and SIS, he added, had played no part in the revolt.

In a personal telegram of 6 March von Killinger reported that a month
before, Horia Sima had sent Himmler a long report such as 'is not sent to
someone not familiar with one's plans'.[29] Two days later Antonescu asked
for eleven named German officials to be recalled and, in the event,
Himmler withdrew, if only temporarily, all SS and police deputies from
Romania. By then we British had also left the country.

Since Iona had already gone to Istanbul, Denis and I gave a joint party at
Clare's flat on 8 February. In spite of an outgoing bag and a cypher crisis,
almost everyone came including Ian Le Rougetel, Robin Hankey, Clare
herself, Anne Windham, Frances Flanagan, May Hartley, Gertie Gellender, Desmond Doran, Annie and Bobsie Samuelli, Olympia Zamfirescu
and her brother, David Walker and his nice red-haired girl friend Greta
Novak, Eric Berthoud and Bill Burland. Those who were kept back at the
Legation joined us later for dancing at Le Rougetel's house.

It was, I think, our last Legation party. Two days later, on 10 February
1941, the Minister informed Antonescu by note that since Romania was
being used by Germany as a military base 'without one word of dissent
from you', he and his staff would be withdrawing on 15 February or as soon
after as a ship was available.[30] In fact, we left for Istanbul on the 12th and
while most of us thought we would never see Romania again, I was not so
sure.

Colonel Bill Bailey, SOE representative in Istanbul, had visited
Bucharest over Christmas, and he and Sir Reginald Hoare had agreed on
SOE's programme in Romania. He had also persuaded the Minister to
allow de Chastelain, who was now his Number Two, to return as a
diplomatic courier. De Chastelain brought in the diplomatic bag on 15
January 1941 and again after the Iron Guard revolt. He contacted all the
key people SOE intended to work with after the Legation had left,

including Maniu, Georgescu and Popovici who had been de Chastelain's assistant at Unirea. During the next two months Popovici was to recruit a network of agents among whom were a wireless engineer and a radio operator. At some point de Chastelain also had a talk with Prince Matei Ghica. Matei Ghica owned a plane with a range of 1,200 miles, and in September 1939 had offered to fly to British territory and join the RAF. Although the Legation's reply was, he says, 'équivoque', clearly he had not been forgotten. De Chastelain now asked him whether he would be ready to fly Maniu out of the country, and Matei agreed so long as his only contact was through his old friend, Rica Georgescu.

Bailey and de Chastelain had also talked to me about SOE. It was, they said, a kind of club: you were invited to join. There were academics like Hugh Seton-Watson, oil men, bankers and regimental soldiers; all had to be ready to collaborate with civilians, opposition leaders, monarchists, anarchists, Communists, anyone who could harass the Germans, and be ready by any means to blow up bridges, derail trains and help create civil disobedience. If I joined I would have a chance to return, possibly with de Chastelain, to liaise with Maniu.

I had not quite committed myself when we left, but the informality and independence of SOE certainly had a strong appeal.

PART TWO

February 1941–December 1943

Chapter 8

Collapse of the Romanian Network

I was to wait almost three years to return to Romania.

During my first stay in Istanbul I spent many hours wandering among the old, wooden houses of Stamboul, often with the Wrights who were waiting to be transferred to the Consulate at Trebizond. We visited St Sofia – birds flying wild in that magnificent dome while Western scholars uncovered the mosaics. In the windows of shops near the University were huge bowls of yoghurt covered with a thick, creamy, yellow crust such as one never finds on the sanitised stuff we keep in our fridges today.

The grandeur of the former embassy, where SOE was housed, was a reminder of the one-time importance of the Porte. The intelligence group was inclined to stick together. There was a popular restaurant on the Bosphorus with a tree growing through the roof. There were the night clubs for Europeans and the Turkish *jeunesse dorée* where you ordered your whisky by the bottle, the seal unbroken, and as an added precaution felt the base for the tell-tale glass blob which would indicate where a substitution had been made. During the dimly lit dancing one of our party would always remain at the table to protect the glasses from German skulduggery.

Georgescu had learnt how to make invisible ink and was already sending us messages. On 13 February, the SOE Office had assured London that Maniu could be expected to leave Romania 'any day now', though Robin Hankey who had had a talk with him shortly before we left Bucharest had concluded that the old man would never abandon his people to physical risks which he himself would not be facing if he were abroad.[1] In any case Maniu was never one to make up his mind in a hurry. The Zamfirescus, whose father made those delicious chocolates, told a story about him. When Prime Minister he came to their shop one morning to buy a small present for Queen Marie. Since he was lunching with her in Sinaia a carriage for him had been attached to the regular train. He took so long choosing his chocolates that their father had had to telephone the station master to explain that, 'for reasons of state', Mr Maniu would be delayed and would he kindly hold up the train.

When I left Istanbul for Greece, the Germans were already moving south. I had a reserved compartment but was soon helping Greek refugees and their belongings in through the window. For most of the journey I sat on half a large peasant basket, back to back with the owner. From Athens I flew to Cairo. It was my first-ever flight, and I still remember the clouds below changing from blue to yellow as we crossed the African coast, and a glimpse of the Pyramids as we circled to land.

Cairo was full of British uniforms; for the duration it seemed to have slipped back into protectorate status. The Commander-in-Chief, Middle East, had an extensive theatre covering the desert war, the war in Greece and, later, the Italian campaigns, and including Romania. In July 1941, a Resident Minister of State was sent out to take up some of the load, and one of his tasks was to keep the peace between the intelligence departments – SOE, SIS, PWE – which were all quarrelling among themselves, with the service departments and with the Foreign Office. Cairo – particularly in the hot, humid summer – seemed to act as a catalyst to inter-departmental jealousies.

On 1 March I joined SOE as a civilian. My symbol was DH88 and I was employed in the Romanian section with offices in Rustem Buildings. At the time we went under the name of GSI(J), but the Egyptian taxi drivers always referred to Rustem Buildings as 'Secret Service Headquarters'. On 4 April Istanbul announced their first radio contact with Maniu. One of his nephews, Balan, was head of the repair shop at AEG, the German electrical manufacturers which had a branch at Bucharest. He normally had on his bench a whole raft of components; for his transmitter he used sixteen of these, wired up but not assembled into any kind of cabinet. After each transmission he disconnected and scattered them, so that the security people never noticed anything out of the ordinary. Popovici, Chas's assistant at Unirea, had recruited Jean Beza, a wireless operator with the Romanian airline. (His brother, George Beza, was already in the Middle East.) Jean came to AEG to meet his schedules, while another of Maniu's collaborators, Augustin Vişa, brought Balan the messages to be transmitted. The fact that the Germans unwittingly provided the transmitter and paid the electricity bills for this contact with the Allies was always good for a laugh.[2]

In Cairo I set up a card index on which we noted information from Romania – local regulations etc – which might help a British agent keep out of the outer police net. Though London thought the project valuable, Cairo abandoned it as soon as I left.

In the Continental Hotel I had a large, airy room cooled by a slow ceiling fan. On the hotel roof garden, a happy hunting ground for Italian agents, we younger ones were entertained by a glorious belly dancer and the loose security talk of the senior officers around us. Hugh Seton-Watson, when duty officer for the week, once found in an unlocked drawer in Rustem Buildings a book listing all our Balkan agents, together with their symbols.

In the desert, the Tommy's favourite song was 'Lili Marlene', his favourite general, Rommel. When we ran out of gin we had to put up with rum daiquiris. Life in Cairo was little more than a sequence to the phoney war we had known in Romania.

Pussy Nasta, daughter of the journalist Liviu Nasta, used to leave in the middle of dinner to broadcast back to her country, always afraid that her voice might be recognised and harm come to her family. There was Madou Faucigny-Lucinge who later married Lord Forbes, and Hermione Ranfurly,* personal assistant to General Wavell, whose husband was a prisoner of war. The favourite dance tune at the time was 'Begin the Beguine' which the orchestra could never play enough of. Julian Amery† was there working on Yugoslavia and Albania, and we sometimes ate pigeon in a restaurant beside the Nile and discussed the kind of Europe that might emerge from the war. I must have been an odd mix of uninformed intelligence, conformity and liberal instincts with a zest for adventure – intellectual and physical – rather than for the intrigue which seemed to occupy the more senior people.

I spent some time with two Poles with the code-names of Christine Granville and Andrew Kennedy. Andrew may well have been the only one-legged parachutist in the war. Christine was preparing to go into France but could not take him with her because, as she said, his French was not good enough – he would insist on saying: *couché dans le soleil*. During the German occupation of Poland the Countess Gizycka, *née* Krystyna Skarbek – otherwise known as Christine Granville – had established a ski escape rout through the Carpathians. She told me how once, when the Germans were after her, she had met a wood-cutter who, with great presence of mind, had taken her in as his daughter, sick in bed – authentic, fairy-tale material. She was a slim, fair girl, very fit, beautiful and optimistic about the outcome of the war. She was later awarded the George Cross for her outstanding bravery and initiative in France but was never able to return to Poland. There was a high proportion of women in SOE – about a third of the total strength by the middle of 1944 – many of them foreigners, many in the field and in situations of great danger.

In early February, before we left Romania, Hitler had already approved the Barbarossa plan for the German invasion of Russia, timed for mid-May. It was delayed five weeks owing largely to the stubborn Greek resistance he met on his flank, which possibly cost him Moscow. Meanwhile, Count von Schulenberg, the German Ambassador in Moscow, tried personally to convince the Führer that, as was the case, the Russians had no intention of attacking the Reich. Von Schulenberg's arguments

* Lady Ranfurly, wife of the Earl of Ranfurly
† Now the Right Hon. Julian Amery, PC.

were brushed aside with 'You can't trust them.' In a brief memo intended for Hitler's eyes, the wise Weizsäcker pointed out that the sole consideration should be whether the invasion of Russia would bring closer the collapse of England. He concluded that it would not. Nor would taking Moscow defeat Stalin, who would withdraw eastwards. The passive resistance techniques of the Slav were well known.[3]

Unlike the German Foreign Office Antonescu, for whom Hitler had a high regard, was spurring him on. The day before von Schulenberg's interview, the General had assured him that the Germans would break through before the Russians could bring up their reserves. Most of us in Cairo would have been more inclined to agree with Antonescu's estimate than Weizsäcker's; on 22 June, when Germany and Romania invaded Russia, friends in GHQ were unofficially giving the Red Army six weeks. Yet everyone hoped for a miracle. If the Russians could hold the Germans until the winter, Britain might no longer have to carry the whole burden of the war. At this stage we saw Romania as no more than a nominal ally of Germany, going along for the ride, as it were, in order to recover the eastern territories Russia had taken from her twelve months before. We knew that the great majority of Romanians were with the Allies, and we did not foresee the extent to which the country would become enmeshed with Germany or its consequences for our relations with the Romanian opposition.

In June, when he promoted himself Marshal, Antonescu was confidently looking to the Führer for recovery of the eastern provinces and, to this extent, Maniu went along with him, only urging that once they were Romanian again they should enjoy a more enlightened administration than in the past. However, both he and Brătianu called for Romanian withdrawal from the war as soon as Bessarabia and North Bukovina had been recovered. 'It is inadmissible that we present ourselves as aggressors against Russia – today the ally of England, the probable winner – for any other objective except Bessarabia and Bukovina.'[4] Romanian troops, they contended, had no right to be on Soviet territory proper.

In the heat of war Antonescu found the proposal impracticable, and as the military situation worsened Maniu and Brătianu held him solely responsible. In the memoranda they sent him regularly they argued that if the Marshal pursued his policy Romania would find herself on the losing side, an enemy of her traditional allies, and defenceless against Soviet reprisals. They proved right. For three years the Romanian soldier fought on in the most terrible conditions. He was tough, stubborn and could survive on less than the German. He was always kept short of equipment – especially tanks and anti-tank guns – and was given the more unpleasant jobs like path-finding through mine-fields. By the end of the war with Russia, when Bessarabia and northern Bukovina had been reoccupied by the Red Army, Romanian casualties would amount to 620,000 dead, wounded and missing.

In August, two months after the invasion of Russia began, we heard that Rica Georgescu, code-named 'Jockey', had been arrested along with the whole of the Popovici network. This was a major disaster. Maniu had no flair for the nuts and bolts of resistance – the wireless telegraphy (W/T), cyphers, couriers, security etc on which his communications with the Allies depended. Without Georgescu's drive and administrative ability our chances of doing anything worthwhile in Romania would, we feared, be greatly diminished. De Chastelain, backed by Cairo and London, searched desperately for ways of saving Jockey's life. But this was to be done on the spot by his wife Lygia, by Maniu and by Antonescu himself.

The network of fifteen which Popovici had set up in Bucharest included a certain Constantin (Dinu) Mircea. Mircea married the divorced Australian wife of our Legation's legal adviser, and they moved to Istanbul to apply for his Australian visa. Since the application had to be referred to Canberra and was delayed, his wife went on ahead. This was a disastrous decision. Mircea promptly fell for a Romanian night-club dancer called Stella who was also the steady mistress of the Gestapo representative. Mircea at the very least gave Stella a hint of what was going on in Popovici's group, which she passed to her German lover.

For a time SOE kept Mircea busy as a cutout between them and Romanians arriving in Istanbul from Bucharest. After the invasion of Russia, when there were fewer Romanian visitors, they packed him off to Palestine. Weeks later, he was back. When his Turkish residence permit finally expired, de Chastelain, who must have known how dangerous he could be to the Romanian network, tried again to get rid of him. But Mircea refused to return to the Middle East 'unless accompanied by a woman against whom our security authorities had objections'. Prompted by her Gestapo lover, Stella now persuaded him to return with her to Romania. De Chastelain records that efforts were made to prevent this 'but the Turks let us down – more likely by design than by accident.'[5] Turkish Intelligence almost certainly apportioned their favours fairly evenly between the British and Germans.

So far, this story has been pieced together from the official records and from what Georgescu has told me. The rest is entirely Georgescu's. Dinu Mircea and Stella travelled to Romania with the German and were arrested on arrival. Captain Barbulescu, the examining magistrate, told Mircea that the girl would be released if he provided a list of the Romanians he had known at school in England who were now either friends of his or employed by British firms. Engineer Popovici was mentioned.

In fact Mircea named only Popovici, but that was enough. Popovici had had news that morning of his brother's death at the front, and was in no state to stand up to interrogation. He gave away the names of the whole group. All of them, including Balan and Beza, were picked up immediately and, in the hope of saving themselves, declared that they were working for Maniu.

Only Rica Georgescu was not arrested on 15 August. He was having lunch at Predeal with Maniu and the US Minister, and that weekend knew nothing about the collapse of the network in Bucharest. But when he returned to his office at Romano Americana on Monday, he found Barbulescu and a German waiting for him. He was arrested at about 1 p.m.

After the German had left them, Barbulescu took Rica to see his chief, Colonel Velciu. Velciu's first question concerned Maniu: had Georgescu any contact with the leader of the National Peasant Party? Georgescu replied that of course he had, since Maniu was his godfather*. But he was no politician; the work of managing Romano Americana gave him quite enough to do. He was not even a member of Maniu's party.

Colonel Velciu then asked for Popovici to be brought in. When he saw Rica Popovici broke down and admitted that he had told Barbulescu the whole story; everyone, including Georgescu, had been blown. Of course this was a great shock for Georgescu but he decided that everything was not lost if Maniu's name could be protected. He asked the colonel as a good Romanian to tell him the truth: had Maniu been mentioned in the declarations? Yes, Velciu said, he had. And had the Germans seen these declarations yet? No, the colonel replied. Rica pointed out that if the Allies won the war . . . but the colonel said he believed in a German victory. Yes, Rica persisted, but if against all the odds the Allies did in fact win, it would not go well with Velciu or his service if they had been responsible for incriminating the leader of Romania's anti-German opposition. If he could keep Maniu out of this business he, Georgescu, would accept full responsibility for the network. In the end the magistrate was persuaded to have the declarations retyped, substituting Georgescu's name for Maniu's as the head of the conspiracy. But in that case, the colonel pointed out, there must be some monetary evidence that part of the British funds had stopped with Georgescu; a million *lei* must be found in his house next day.

Rica was allowed to telephone his wife who came to the prison in tears. He asked her to raise a million *lei* and plant it in their house where agents of the Military Judiciary† could discover it next day. Lygia was always

---

* Godfather in the Orthodox Church is a sponsor of the bride and bridegroom at a wedding.

† The Romanian Military Judiciary were responsible to Eugen Cristescu, head of the Secret Service, for investigating and court-martialling in the capital military and civilian personnel accused of treason or of crimes against the state.

ready to try the impossible. She first saw Maniu, but he had nothing like that amount. He referred her to the party treasurer, who said there was not a million *lei* in the coffers. She then turned to her uncle, General Ion Manolescu, the head of one of the royal domains: realising how serious Rica's and Maniu's situation was, he promised to raise the money somehow by morning.

The Georgescus had two houses – their own and the one provided by the oil company. At eight next morning, Rica realised that the police were going to search the wrong one. He telephoned his wife, and she managed to switch the money in time. It was duly discovered, the Military Judiciary received their legal twenty per cent of booty found, and next day the National Peasant Party returned the million *lei* to General Manolescu.

Lygia knew that the death sentence would be almost mandatory – there is documentary evidence in Bucharest that Georgescu's execution was, in fact, intended – and she set about trying to save him. Through one of Antonescu's aides, she managed to arrange an interview with the Marshal, and she persuaded Antonescu to receive Maniu. But when she told Maniu what she had done he was not pleased. Perhaps he felt that she should have consulted him first; perhaps he had other plans, and did not wish to be under an obligation to the Marshal.

Lygia lost her temper with Maniu. Yes, she said, Rica had confessed to giving the Allies information about oil production and oil exports to Germany but did Maniu really think the story would stand up in court? Couldn't he see that unless the trial was stopped his own name would be dragged in by the prosecution or by one of the other defendants? The authorities would then have a pretext for restricting his pro-Allied activities. Was he prepared for that?

His response was typical; he was unwilling to commit himself at short notice, but became very positive once he had had time to think it through. He finally went to the Marshal and told him that if Rica Georgescu was tried, he, Maniu, would be the first witness for the defence. This shook Antonescu, who had never lost sight of Maniu's popularity in the country. It was too late to prevent the trial altogether; the prisoners had already been marched through the streets to the Military Court and indicted of treason. But Antonescu was able to suspend the sentence *sine die*. We do not know what explanation he gave the Germans, who were furious; as I was to discover later, the Marshal could be very obstinate on such matters.

In solitary confinement, Rica was very badly treated for six months. One night in the spring of 1942 he developed kidney trouble and was in great pain but was refused even a cup of water. Next day Colonel Velciu, who was governor of the prison, came to his cell for the first time. He was shocked by Rica's condition, allowed his wife and personal doctor to see him and, according to Rica, gave the warder hell. From then on Lygia and

Alecu Ionescu, Rica's assistant at Romano Americana, visited him regularly and his health slowly improved. On 1 May, Velciu came to a small celebration in Rica's cell for Lygia's birthday, and Lygia began to invite him to some of the parties given by her friends and relations. Eventually Rica was moved from cell Number 12 to cell Number 2 where he had a refrigerator and use of the adjoining cell as a sitting room.

As Lygia's car had been requisitioned, her long trips to the prison carrying food were made by tram and on foot; she was always followed by a Siguranţa car. On one occasion she tried a ploy which I was to use with the Siguranţa some years later; she waited in the snow for it to draw level and asked whether, since they were going in the same direction, they could give her a lift. They refused politely. The only diplomat friends who dared to see her were the delightful Bova Scopas – the Italian Minister and his wife – and the Argentinians. The latter would even meet her at the prison gates, flag flying on their car, and drive her home so that she had time to change before going to a party at their house.

Meanwhile, Rica was building up goodwill in prison. To begin with he persuaded warders and duty officers to break the rules in small ways – not to padlock his door, for instance, unless there were Germans about. Later, provided there was no chance of a German visit, they let him walk in the garden and feed the colonel's goose. In the end the officers and warders began to work for him. Although Rica's strong, likeable personality was partly responsible, these security men were risking their careers, families and lives to help the British cause. Even senior people in the Antonescu régime sympathised with us. As in every society, the extent to which any of them were prepared to put his or her convictions on the line varied considerably, but Colonel Velciu, his successor, Colonel Radu Ionescu, Captain Barbulescu and a certain Major Oatu decided, as we shall see, to take very considerable risks.

Chapter 9

Radio Communication Re-established

Soon after Jockey's arrest I was sent to Teheran to escort a group of pro-Allied Germans to the SOE training camp at Haifa. In Teheran, Sir Reader Bullard was Minister. Robin Hankey was Head of Chancery. Francis Buckley and his delightful wife Audrey were there. Christopher Sykes* introduced me to polyglot rug dealers. Nancy Lambton rode a bicycle, entertained Persian writers and teachers rather than diplomats and was probably already more familiar with Persian literature than most of her Iranian guests.†

I greatly preferred Teheran to Cairo but eventually had to take my Germans away. I must have dumped them – they were a decent lot – at a transit camp near Baghdad for I spent an evening with a friend drinking black velvet on a verandah standing over the Tigris and next day had tea with Freya Stark who wore a large hat against the sun and seemed a very practical person. Then I took the Germans via the Nairn brothers' bus to Haifa and after handing them over to the camp authorities, fell sick.

I had either diphtheria or polio and since military drugs were not available to civilian personnel, I was to be left in poor health for the rest of my life. I owe my survival to a Viennese doctor – one of a group of refugees who had blown up their boat in Haifa harbour rather than run the risk of not being allowed to land – a Russian throat specialist, and the daughters of the hotel where I stayed on Mount Carmel. Three pictures stay with me from the *khamsin* of that summer, while I lay in bed, with a twisted face and a throat that had almost closed. One was a delirious dream that I was drinking iced fruit juice. Another was of my highly-strung Viennese doctor plunging his arms into cold water before giving me a heart injection. And, when I was a little better, I remember Patrick Leigh Fermor standing at the foot of the bed swapping Romanian words with me. The Moldavian word for 'sheet'

* Author of *Four Studies in Loyalty, Orde Wingate, Troubled Loyalty: A Biography of Adam von Trott*, etc.
† Ann K.S. Lambton, Emeritus Professor of Persian, University of London. A most distinguished Persian scholar.

was the Slav *prostire* from *prost* meaning 'simple' and *a prosti* to 'stupefy' or 'bemuse'. But the Wallachian equivalent, *cearceafuri*, was of Turkish origin, pronounced 'chiarchiafuri' and drawn out long with just a hint of the 'i' at the end to obtain the full onomatopaeic effect of silken Ottoman sheets.

When I found my feet I was in no state for either a military operation or the training that would precede it. I was in Jerusalem during the emergency evacuation of Cairo, and took a light ten-day course at the SOE Middle East training camp learning morse and how to operate the SOE suitcase transmitters which, like Enigma, had originated in Poland.

In Cairo, I shared a flat with David Russell* who, wearing German uniform, had just rescued two officers and eight other ranks from Tobruk. The flat was over an open-air cinema and if we were foolish enough to go to bed early we lay awake until one in the morning listening to incomprehensible Arabic drama. David had a Sudanese servant who would sometimes wrestle with him after dinner.

After the arrest of the Romanian network in August 1941 de Chastelain, who was now head of the Istanbul office, had no radio link with Bucharest and had to make do with the occasional courier. Since these were slow and unreliable SOE's first priority was to restore wireless communication. When in April we heard that a Romanian W/T operator from one of the Goeland Company ships had been interned in Palestine, Colonel Ted Masterson, head of the Romanian Section in Cairo, went to interview him. Nicolae Turcanu, the operator, was given paramilitary and parachute training while I looked into possible routes for him into Romania. One, via Mihailovic territory, was eventually used for the Ranji operation, led by David Russell with Nicolae Turcanu as his W/T operator.

In January 1943 I was packed off back to Istanbul to recuperate, living in an SOE house by the Sea of Marmora and being fed *kaimak* by a motherly Turkish housekeeper. I learned enough Russian to make tea-time conversation with a lady in Istanbul, and practised my morse in the evenings with one of our stations in Palestine. Later, I was joined by a cheerful Romanian Navy type called Alexandru (Sandy) Stiubey, who was also waiting to go on an SOE operation, and we would row across the bay for a beer or a *zabib* at the café. I still found swallowing difficult.

From my house I travelled to Istanbul by tram and steamer. There was a plague-scare, and I used to scratch in the tram for imaginary lice, remembering the health hazards our ambassadors had run when Constantinople was at the height of its glory. The solid steamers, built by Brown

---

* Commissioned in the Scots Guards, April 1940. Posted to SOE, April 1942. Awarded the MC, January 1943. In June 1943 he led the 'Ranji' operation into Romania where he was murdered.

Brothers of Glasgow in the 1880s, were bounced against the landing stages until the gap became narrow enough for people to jump off and on. Turkish traitors were said to be dropped down the funnels of these steamers.

De Chastelain told me of his attempts to keep in touch with Maniu after Jockey's arrest. In March he had sent in a W/T set to replace Balan's, but Maniu had failed to come on the air. I met Tozan, the man who had smuggled it in, a glamorous character who, when Ataturk had forced all Turkish citizens to take a surname, had called himself after the smallest thing he could think of – a speck of dust. Lufti Bey, as he was known in Istanbul, had a way with him not only in the Balkan countries but as far away as Budapest. When arrested there he had developed a pain and been taken to hospital, where he knew there were SOE agents. His gall bladder, which was perfectly healthy, was removed and during his convalescence the surgeon and nurses helped him escape.

In January de Chastelain, desperate for links with Romania, had thought that he might replace the Georgescu-Popovici network with a businessman called Bursan, a Tătărescu Liberal who regularly brought him political and economic reports. In June, with Turcanu in mind, he had asked Bursan to find a suitable reception area and by August had high hopes of an estate near Craiova. Turcanu was ready to go in at the end of September. However, this arrangement fell through and in November Bursan, on his last visit to Istanbul, told Chas that the Craiova estate had been sold. That same month a Romanian called Gheorghiu, whom Chas knew for certain to be a genuine courier, passed him a warning about Bursan from Jockey and the contact was broken.[1]

Georgescu (Jockey) and his wife had arranged the Gheorghiu visit. Growing anxious about the long breakdown of communication with the Allies, and with time on his hands, Rica had had the idea. Lygia had then put it into practice. She convinced her friend Florica Stoicescu, wife of the Chairman of Creditul Minier, Romania's only purely Romanian oil company, that Rica had a proposition to put to her husband of such interest that it would be well worth his while to visit him in prison. An admirer of Antonescu, Stoicescu was at first horrified at the idea of visiting a political prisoner, but Lygia and Florica finally prevailed on him to pocket his somewhat exaggerated sense of propriety and announce himself at the prison gate as Georgescu's uncle.

Rica proposed to Stoicescu that Romania should buy rather than appropriate Allied property. Creditul Minier could probably obtain the British company Unirea's two refineries and marketing network for a song. One of Romania's biggest oil conglomerates would then become Romanian and not German. Stoicescu was impressed. He consulted the Marshal, who was anxious to limit German exploitation of Romanian oil; and two weeks later 'Operation Lygia' had been approved.

Gheorghiu, the managing director of Creditul Minier, then came to see Rica to discuss the details. Rica suggested that he should contact de Chastelain in Istanbul for de Chastelain, an ex-employee of Unirea, could put the proposal to the British parent company. When it became clear during their conversation that Gheorghiu was one of Maniu's many admirers, Rica decided to take him into his confidence at that first meeting. He asked him whether he would be prepared to act as Maniu's courier. Gheorghiu agreed. If he had panicked and informed the authorities that could well have been the end of Rica Georgescu.

Since the Germans must be given no hint of what was going on, Antonescu asked Cristescu, his head of security, to vet Gheorgiu. Cristescu warned Gheorghiu that while in Istanbul where the Gestapo were active he should meet Unirea people only in the house of Economu, the Security Service representative. Though greatly shaken by the interview with the dreaded Cristescu, Gheorghiu was still game when he next saw Rica, and Rica gave him the password 'nightingale' which would let de Chastelain know that he was a reliable courier from Maniu and himself.

In Istanbul, Gheorghiu, as directed, met de Chastelain at Economu's house, and while their host was opening a bottle of *ţuica* he wrote the word 'nightingale' on a piece of paper and passed it to de Chastelain. Chas, who was an inveterate doodler, doodled a rendezvous among the data he was noting down, and slipped it into Gheorghiu's overcoat pocket as they were leaving. De Chastelain later picked him up near his hotel and drove him to a safe house.

There was another courier in Istanbul – Christu, who was heading a Romanian economic delegation to Turkey. Through Christu and Gheorghiu, Maniu gave de Chastelain an idea of his plans.[2] Since Romania was allied to Germany rather than occupied, he still had some room for manoeuvre. He stressed that sabotage would simply cause the Germans to tighten security, whereas a carefully planned *volte face* with the army behind it could do real harm to the Reich. Timing would be important; the *coup* must take place when German troops in the country were at their minimum. It must be prepared meticulously; he had already begun to place his men in key posts in the army and government ministries. If it failed or if the new government were unable to hold the Wehrmacht until the Allies arrived, Romania would then be occupied by Germany, and would have no second chance.

Maniu, Gheorghiu said, had been unable to find an operator for the W/T set Tozan had taken in and Chas, with Turcanu in mind, told him he would try to help. Meanwhile cypher messages would be sent to Jockey at the end of the BBC Austrian service. Gheorghiu took back a simple post code for his own use, but the BBC cypher for Jockey went in with the Swiss diplomatic courier a few weeks later.

Georgescu's assistant in Romano Americana was the quiet, conscientious Alecu Ionescu; married to an American, he had studied geology in the States and spoke English perfectly with an American accent. He visited Rica regularly in prison. Alecu and his wife deciphered the messages now being sent via the BBC. As a partial check, since the Ionescus' flat was close to tramlines which could interfere with radio reception, Rica would also listen on the prison wireless and note down what groups he could. By this means Rica – and through him Maniu – learned of the proposed Ranji operation, to be led by David Russell.

During a subsequent visit to Istanbul Gheorghiu was given an introduction to Captain Radu Protopopescu, who was a friend of Turcanu – the wireless operator we had found in Palestine. Turcanu thought that Protopopescu might know of a reliable radio operator inside the country. It was now all-important to find someone to work one of Maniu's two transmitting sets for apart from the one Tozan had taken in, Balan's original set had been copied and it too was lying idle.

In March 1943 Gheorghiu, then back in Istanbul, was urged by de Chastelain to take possession of one of these sets, and to ask SOE to send in Turcanu to operate it. At the same time, he should look for a reception area where Turcanu could land. We heard nothing more from Gheorghiu until May, and then his message in the post code he had been given was indecipherable. De Chastelain felt that 'it was useless to hope for quick action from Maniu . . . the only solution would be the despatch of a party under a British officer to provide a reliable means of communication and the necessary incentive to act.'[3]

On the night of 15 June, David Russell and Nicolae Turcanu dropped into a reception area at Homolje in Yugoslavia with a brief to penetrate Romania for the purpose of 'opening up W/T communications, effecting contact with Maniu's organisation and organising a reception area in the Romanian Carpathians'.

I returned to Cairo and spent most of the summer training. I was commissioned on 27 August and driven straight from Acre to the SOE camp at Haifa where I had deposited my Germans the year before. I had trained to be an officer in an abandoned POW camp; and now, in a disused monastery, a mixture of British and Balkan students were learning ancient and modern tricks of subversion.

We were taught to handle a steam engine, to drive an explosion deep – the bee-hive effect – so as to cut through a steel girder with no more 'chocolate' than we could carry in our pockets. The plastic gave one a bad headache. Our detonators – 'pencils' we called them – were timed by a simple device; when you pinched them, an acid started to eat through a metal wall which varied in thickness according to the delay required.

Stas Lazarowicz, a one-eyed Pole, taught us to shoot from the navel. We used to clatter down some steps into a dark room and blast away at wooden figures using one stiff arm, not two as they do on the box today. I still remember his great good humour, his only complaint being that we had not enough ammunition to become familiar with our weapons.

From Mount Carmel I went straight to the parachute course at Kabrit. Since I suffer from vertigo, the worst part of the ten-day course was jumping harnessed from a tower; once off the ground everything seemed easier. After our first jump in a stick of five through the door I was still rolling up my parachute when the next man landed close to me, delighted because he had just completed a sonnet which had been giving him trouble for days. Once the parachute had opened (we had no auxiliary in those days), the descent was pleasant enough until the ground suddenly rushed up and you had to decide how to land.

We also jumped through the floor of an old Wellington. My brother had been flying them in 1939, and by 1943 this one was hardly airworthy. One night I somersaulted, tangled my legs in the rigging lines, and was coming down fast and upside down; with someone hollering at me from the ground, I spent some of the coolest five seconds of my life disentangling myself in time so as not to break my neck.

We made six practice jumps, the lowest from about five hundred feet. We learned to drop free from our harness, which was useful in a wind though the timing had to be just right; and we practised rolling off the back of a truck at 40 mph.

On my free Sunday afternoon, I walked to a kibbutz, drank a glass of milk, and saw a film. Years later, when I was Ambassador in Senegal, my Israeli colleague, who was of Romanian origin, told me he had been working at that kibbutz at the time, and reminded me of my visit. He said he was unlikely to have forgotten the only Romanian-speaking British soldier he had ever met.

Back in Cairo I found Captain Charles Maydwell,* who had joined SOE while I was away in Turkey. I heard that Russell and Turcanu had crossed the Danube on 2 August with a Serb chetnik guide, and towards the middle of the month had made contact at Varciorova with Maniu's representative. They camped outside the town and sent their first radio messages to Cairo on 12 and 13 August. On 4 September Russell had been killed: he is generally thought to have been murdered by the Serb guide for the gold sovereigns we always carried on these operations.

---

* Charles St George Maydwell was with Standard Oil (NJ) before the war. In March 1941 he was commissioned in the Rifle Brigade, served in the western desert and joined SOE in February 1942. After working with the Kurds in Northern Kurdistan he came to the Romanian section in April, 1943.

After Russell's death Georgescu's assistant, Alecu Ionescu, took charge of Nicolae Turcanu. He brought him to Bucharest, rented a flat from Protopopescu and installed him there with his wireless transmitter. There were two particular advantages to this arrangement: Protopopescu was a friend of Turcanu; and the flat was only a hundred metres from the main post-office transmitter which broadcast a news bulletin at seven every morning on a frequency adjacent to Turcanu's, and this served to blanket Turcanu's own transmission locally.

A cyphered radio message from Cairo would be passed by Turcanu to Ionescu, who decyphered it. Ionescu would then take the open message to Georgescu in prison. Often it was intended for Jockey himself, but if not, Lygia would carry it in the lining of her cigarette packet to Maniu. She enjoyed offering the governor of the prison a cigarette with a message only a millimetre from his finger tips.

The success of the operation depended on their appearing to do nothing out of the ordinary. It was quite normal for Alecu Ionescu to visit Georgescu in prison with news of Romano Americana, and for Lygia to visit her husband daily, and her godfather Juliu Maniu from time to time. With Maniu surrounded by his supporters, what could be more natural than for her to take her old friend aside for a moment?

With his powerful political following, Maniu had succeeded as promised in appointing some of his supporters to key administrative posts. Since they were among the most talented people available, and since no purges were practised under Antonescu, it would have been difficult to ignore them even if the Marshal had wanted to. But Antonescu recognised the value of Maniu and his followers. So when in September Alexander Cretzianu, one of Maniu's supporters, was appointed by Antonescu to be the Romanian Minister to Turkey, he found himself liaising with the Allies on behalf of two masters. One of Maniu's men was now deputy chief of staff and several generals had discreetly made known their support for a break with the Axis. As head of the Foreign Ministry's Communications Department, Niculescu-Buzeşti used his own cypher to keep in touch, via official channels, with Maniu's people in missions abroad. By the time Alexander Cretzianu was installed as Minister in Ankara, George Duca, son of the murdered prime minister, had taken up his post as Counsellor in Stockholm with a brief from Maniu.[4] Duca was soon to discover that his Minister, Frederick Nanu, had also been briefed – by Mihai Antonescu, the Foreign Minister, and by the Marshal – to put out feelers to the Allies.[5] On 24 September the British Minister reported that Nanu's first words to the Secretary General of the Swedish MFA had been that 'opinion in Romania is wholly on the side of the Allies.'[6]

The situation was becoming increasingly complex. As early as March 1943 the Romanian Foreign Minister had put out tentative peace feelers, and in July he had told the Turkish Minister in Bucharest that as soon as a practical understanding could be reached with 'the Anglo-Saxons' the government would hand over to someone like Maniu who had popular support.[7] On 2 October the Romanian military attaché in Ankara handed his British colleague a memorandum from the Marshal himself listing the troops and supplies that would be available to any Anglo-American force entering the Balkans ahead of the Russians.[8] Yet to all these approaches the British Government seemed to be reacting negatively.

By October Chas, Charles Maydwell and I were ready to go in on an operation which had been given the code-name 'Autonomous'. With the collapse of Ranji we had technical problems – particularly in finding a secure jumping area – but these, we thought, could be overcome. We would carry out straightforward sabotage operations on German communications. The only really unpalatable aspect of the operation – particularly for Chas – was the knowledge that Maniu would be expected to surrender his country unconditionally to the Russians without any kind of guarantee regarding her future independence or restoration of democratic government. The meaning of 'our cause', a phrase used often by Churchill in the early days of the war, seemed to have changed perceptibly over the years and this would not be easy to explain to Maniu.

Chapter 10

Maniu and the Allied Powers

In the summer of 1940, when the British Government had reached their understanding with Maniu, Britain and the Empire had been fighting alone against the Axis. By the end of 1943, when the Autonomous operation went in, she had two allies each more powerful than herself, each with a different historical background and outlook and, in many ways, different war objectives.

Although in June 1941, she suddenly found herself allied to the Soviet Union, Britain's policy towards the small east European states did not change overnight. On 12 August Churchill issued a joint declaration with Roosevelt – the Atlantic Charter – identifying certain common principles of national policy to be applied to the post-war world. The two leaders wanted no territorial changes except in accord with the freely expressed will of the people concerned. They respected the right of all peoples to choose the form of government under which they would live. They wished to see sovereign rights and self-government restored to those who had been deprived of them. Churchill still hoped eventually to rally the East European countries against Germany. The Atlantic Charter would then apply to them all, including those which had been forced against their will into the German orbit. A few months later he gave way to Stalin's insistence that he declare war on Hungary, Finland and Romania, but he continued to oppose Stalin's ambitions in Eastern Europe and the Baltic.

When, in December, Eden went to the Soviet Union to negotiate an Anglo-Russian treaty, the battle for Moscow was at its height. The determination of the Russian people and of their leader – who, unlike the rest of his government, remained in the Kremlin throughout the war – was impressive. The Foreign Office hoped Eden could sell Stalin the idea of a post-war Balkan confederation backed by the Great Powers, ostensibly as a bulwark against Germany. But Stalin was not so easily taken in. He was quite frank about his East European objectives. He would recover the territory he had acquired after his pact with Hitler and before the German invasion – known loosely as the 1941 frontiers. By now the Romanians had retaken Bessarabia and North Bukovina but, he told Eden, he would want them back at the end of the war plus naval bases on the Romanian Black

Sea. Hungary should return northern Transylvania to Romania. Britain, he suggested, should herself establish bases in a now weakened France. Although taken aback by this attempt to commit him to cut and dried post-war plans for Eastern Europe, Eden undertook to consider Stalin's proposals with the Dominion and US governments on his return to London.

The telegrams he exchanged with Churchill in Washington about this underline their different reactions to Russia's war aims, just six months after she had become their ally. Himself an idealist, Eden felt the need to inject into Churchill's strong idealistic strain his own concept of Realpolitik. After the war, he argued, the void left by Germany would be filled by the USSR. American troops would withdraw from Europe and Britain, the only European country left standing, would not be able to resist Soviet pressure. We should, therefore, establish a good working relationship with the USSR during our common war against Hitler and Stalin considered our agreement to his ambitions in Eastern Europe to be the 'acid test' of our friendship. As for any 'apparent conflict with the Atlantic Charter' – to which Stalin had subscribed – the frontier proposals could be made subject to a plebiscite, since the Russians 'would foresee no obstacle, when the time came, in arranging for the necessary vote in their favour'.[1]

Churchill's reply opened with the ominous words 'Your telegram surprised me.' We have never, he said, recognised the 1941 frontiers. 'They were acquired by acts of aggression in shameful collusion with Hitler. The transfer of the peoples of the Baltic States to Soviet Russia against their will would be contrary to all the principles for which we are fighting this war and would dishonour our cause. This also applies to Bessarabia and Northern Bukovina . . .' Apart from certain cases where strategical security could be invoked, 'transference of territory must be regulated after the war is over by freely and fairly conducted plebiscites very different from what is suggested in your para. three.' In any case, there could be no question of settling frontiers before the Peace Conference:

> When you say in paragraph two that nothing we and the US can do or say will affect the situation at the end of the war, you are making a very large assumption . . . It seems probable . . . that the US and the British Empire, far from being exhausted, will be the most powerful armed and economic block the world has ever seen, and that the Soviet Union will need our aid for reconstruction more than we shall need theirs.

Churchill admits that he must honour Eden's undertaking to examine Russia's claims, 'but there must be no mistake about the opinion of any British Government of which I am the head.'[2] The two members of the Cabinet who gave Churchill whole-hearted support on this issue were Attlee and Bevin.

When Churchill visited Stalin for the first time in 1942 with the unenviable task of telling him that in spite of their promises the Western Powers could not mount a Second Front that year, Stalingrad was under siege, and the Wehrmacht were sacrificing as many men to take one street as they had to take a whole West European country in 1940. British and American troops were involved in Africa and the Far East but in Europe, where Hitler had eventually to be defeated, the Red Army was carrying almost the whole burden of the war.

After Stalingrad, Russia's image changed. There was an upsurge of patriotism for the fatherland rather than the party. The heroes of Tsarist times were recalled. The Holy Synod of the Greek Orthodox Church was restored. Political commissars were made subordinate to military commanders. Épaulettes were reintroduced, guards regiments revived and Stalin himself put on a marshal's uniform. In May 1943 the Cominform was dissolved.

According to Isaac Deutscher, by the summer of 1943 in Russia 'two parties, a party of revolution and a party of tradition, only half conscious of themselves, led a silent existence in the thoughts and feelings of the people and in the mind of Stalin himself.'[3] Churchill and Roosevelt were aware of this. Their mistake was perhaps in hoping that the party of tradition would be less suspicious, less evangelical and expansionist than the party of revolution. Had not Count Kisseleff written, in February 1832, that 'Russia has not marched for more than a century from the banks of the Dnieper, merely to stop upon the banks of the Pruth'?[4] Just as the Romanian socialists were sure in 1917 that the revolution must have purified Russia of chauvinism so, apart from the Foreign Office, most of the senior advisers around Churchill were muddled in a different way by their woolly ideas on bolshevism. They were far from being kremlinologists as we understand the word today. When Churchill sent Cripps as our ambassador to Moscow he recommended him to Stalin for his socialist background, though Cripps's kind of socialism, particularly in a vegetarian who did not drink, must have been anathema to the Kremlin. Roosevelt, with nothing like Churchill's broad sense of history and international affairs, had cut himself off from his State Department where any US expertise lay and Harry Hopkins who seemed to compound the President's prejudices, but not Secretary of State Hull, attended the critical summit meetings of 1943. Hopkins looked forward to a post-war world without the 'colonialist' Churchill but seemed quite unable to assess Stalin's imperialism. The Western leaders may have felt a twinge of guilt for having ostracised a country which was now proving such a gallant ally, but they went on to hope that once they had made Stalin a member of their club he would behave like a club member. When he spoke of 'democracy', many of them thought that he meant what they meant.

Among the annexes to the Foreign Office record of confidential agreements reached at the Foreign Ministers' Conference at Moscow in October 1943, Annex 7 deals with the British proposal for a confederation of Balkan States. 'Soviet Government considers liberation of small countries and the restoration of their independence and sovereignty as one of the most important tasks of the post-war arrangement of Europe and in the creation of lasting peace.' Moscow is, therefore, opposed to pressing confederation on East European states. 'Such an important step as federation with other states and possible renunciation of part of their sovereignty is admissible only as a result of a free, peaceful and well-considered expression of the will of the people.'[5] Western leaders may not have been particularly well versed in Marxist dialectics, but Molotov had certainly mastered the jargon of Western democracy.

The British delegation returned from Moscow in a state of near ecstasy. Three months later the head of Northern Department was writing a personal and secret letter to Jock Balfour in Moscow about the need to get the 'great ones here' out of the habit of extremism – either throwing their hat high in the air because Molotov or Uncle Joe have turned on their kindly and responsive mood, or 'in a flap' when the Soviet press is a bit naughty. All this, he says, is most prejudicial to a sound conduct of policy: 'We have suffered much from the suppression of all public criticism of the Russians, and if it went on it would lead easily straight to disaster. For it would mislead the Russians . . . and will lead straight to a policy of appeasement . . . I am afraid I think that the Teheran and Moscow conferences were dangerously wrong in this respect . . .'[6]

Underlying the different ideologies and social backgrounds, the bonhomie, the drinking bouts and the respect for each other – Churchill left a deep impression on the Soviet leaders as 'a farsighted and dangerous "bourgeois statesman"'[7] – was a deep mutual suspicion. When the Western Allies twice broke their promise of a Second Front on grounds of shortage of landing craft, this must have seemed to Stalin a poor excuse from the two most highly developed industrial countries in the world. For some time he believed that the Western Allies would not intervene until Russia and Germany had exhausted themselves. On the other hand, Churchill and Roosevelt were afraid that once Stalin had recovered his 1941 frontiers he would do a deal with Hitler. According to Liddell Hart Ribbentrop met Molotov in Russia in May 1943[8] and six months later we know from a minute Churchill sent to Attlee that the Prime Minister was still worried by the possibility of a separate peace – which would have meant the subjugation of the whole of Europe to the two great tyrannies. It is not surprising that by then the government's primary concern was to keep Russia in play until Britain could make a proper contribution to the war in Europe. Britain would do nothing, therefore, which might help to drive

Russia into the arms of Germany, and would certainly not oppose Russian ambitions in Romania. Romania's troops had been fighting in the Soviet Union for two years; we considered her to be a Soviet affair, and made this clear to Stalin and Molotov at every opportunity. We had moved a long way from the sentiments expressed in Churchill's telegram to Eden of January 1942.

By the end of 1943 when de Chastelain and I went into Romania, Stalin had no intention of giving up any territory the Red Army might occupy after so much devastation in Russia and such an enormous loss of life. Whether he had already decided that the *cordon sanitaire* on his western frontier – of which London approved – must necessarily consist of Communist governments with absolute allegiance to Moscow, it is difficult to say. He did tell Tito that 'This war is not as in the past; whoever occupies a territory also imposes on it his own social system.'[9] But that was in 1945.

How does Maniu fit into this picture? In the summer of 1940, he had told Chas that he would leave the country to set up a government-in-exile and, what was more important, had undertaken to bring about a Transylvanian uprising when finally the Germans were forced to leave the country. His plans a year later were far more ambitious – a full-scale *volte face* against the Germans involving the whole country and the national army. To achieve this he felt that he should stay in the country, and by the end of 1941 London were agreeing that he would be more use to the cause in Romania than setting up a government-in-exile. In a well-reasoned report made orally in Lisbon at the end of 1941 by one of Maniu's collaborators, Vasile Serdici, Maniu explained that instead of fomenting revolution or sabotage he preferred 'a well-prepared *coup* so that the entire force of the Rumanian army could be turned against the Axis'. Although Maniu was no Tito, and had an instinctive dislike of violence, Pierson Dixon of the Foreign Office commented to SOE in January 1942, 'We entirely share the view that Maniu is our best hope of starting an anti-Axis movement in Rumania'.[10]

But there was an impractical side to Maniu. In 1942 he had planned to take Georgescu with him out of the country, and Matei Ghica – who was to fly them out – refers drily to the feasibility of transferring a fugitive from prison to a spot a hundred miles away at the precise date and time of a planned escape. Ghica also remembers a conversation with Maniu the night before he was ready to fly him out, on Good Friday, 1943:

Maniu: Why will two mechanics have to be there?
Ghica: Because the engines, propellers and wheels are hooded, and these have to be taken off. Also the nights are cold and we need the field battery to start up.

Maniu:	Why does the sentry have to be at the gate?
Ghica:	Because that's his duty point.
Maniu:	Can't you send him somewhere else?
Ghica:	Not without making myself most suspicious.
Maniu:	Why not do away with that point tomorrow night?
Ghica:	Same answer.
Maniu:	What if he tries to stop us or shoot us?
Ghica:	He won't; he's under my orders.
Maniu:	But then anyone could get in and get a plane.
Ghica:	I'm not anybody. I'm the Duty Officer and he knows me. I am his master after God so long as I don't interfere with his standing orders.

Maniu dropped the matter and after fussing about the clothes he should take agreed to have no further contact with Ghica until eleven the following night, when they would meet at the main gate of the base. However at 7.30 next morning Maniu's chief of staff telephoned to say that Maniu did not consider an escape safe with a sentry there. The operation was called off, and two weeks later Ghica's squadron was transferred to the Black Sea.

This was the nit-picking side of Maniu. Yet he was in so many ways far-sighted, and his integrity always difficult to ignore. He embarrassed London by his failure to extend to Stalin the trust he had put in us. Had he been less principled, he would have been easier to deal with in the cirumstances of war. Sir Reginald Hoare once said of him that he 'preserved a rugged and obstinate adherence to principle in this land where expediency rules supreme'.[11] By the end of 1943 expediency may not have ruled supreme in the councils of the three Allied Powers, but it certainly played an important part. To stand any chance of defeating Hitler the three had to stick together, which meant that, even if they refused to admit it, the Western Allies had to forfeit the principles of the Atlantic Charter to Stalin's ambitions in Eastern Europe.

On 16 January 1944, three weeks after Autonomous went into Romania, Churchill minuted to Eden about the position of Russia's western frontiers. After referring to the strong line he had taken in January 1942, after Eden's trip to Moscow, he said:

> Undoubtedly my own feelings have changed in the two years that have passed . . . The tremendous victories of the Russian armies, the deep-seated changes which have taken place in the character of the Russian State and Government, the new confidence which has grown in our hearts towards Stalin – these have all had their effect. Most of all is the fact that the Russians may very soon be in physical possession of these territories, and it is absolutely certain that we should never attempt to turn them out.[12]

Maniu never seemed to grasp this fact. He knew the long history of British opposition to Russian expansion. He overestimated Britain's military power and Churchill's influence with his two partners. He assumed that Britain was preparing either diplomatic, economic or even military moves to prevent Eastern Europe from becoming a ring of Soviet satellites. When London urged him to trust the USSR he seemed to be asking them 'to come clean', 'to come off it' – as if incapable of believing that their protestations of faith in Stalin were genuine.

When he sent us a message via his close friend Cornel Bianu in October 1942 he still felt that he could be entirely frank with the British Government. He could not come out against the Axis, he said, unless he knew positively that the Allies would exclude a Russian invasion of Romania once the eastern front had collapsed. Britain, of course, could give no such guarantee; it would have been as meaningless as the Anglo-French guarantee of 1939, and the USSR would have seen it as an unfriendly act. Eden hoped that the Soviet Government would stand by the principles of the Atlantic Charter, but since only they could give the Romanian opposition the assurance they wanted, the most useful thing he could do, he felt, would be to put the Russians in direct contact with Maniu. He proposed this repeatedly to the Soviet Government, who invariably replied that they were not interested. Then in March 1943, when Eden was again in Moscow, Molotov sent him a personal letter suggesting that since Maniu's was the only effective opposition in Romania a basis might eventually be found for collaboration between him and the British and Soviet governments. Eden saw this as the green light from Moscow. SOE proceeded with Ranji and our own operation, Autonomous.

London's reaction to the flurry of Romanian peace feelers in the summer and autumn of 1943 was similar to their reaction to Maniu's request for a guarantee. By March the Foreign Office had already decided that, since only Russia was in a position to help Romania, any peace feelers from that country should be referred to Moscow, and the Romanians should be told that no future approach could be considered unless addressed to all three Allied Powers. This procedure would apply to government and opposition alike. London then proposed that the tripartite conference of Foreign Ministers, which was to meet in Moscow in October 1943, should formally adopt their *ad hoc* formula.

This would have been bad enough for non-Communist Resistance groups in satellite countries, but – thinking aloud to the press at the Casablanca Conference in January – Roosevelt, without consulting Churchill, had announced that unconditional surrender would be enforced on 'all our enemies'. The Russians followed this up at the Moscow conference by insisting that unconditional surrender be applied to German

satellites. Taken together the British and Russian proposals meant that in
practice only unconditional surrender to the Soviet Union would now be
considered by any of the Allies, even if an opposition leader like Maniu
were to overthrow the pro-German régime in a satellite, break with the
Axis, and bring their country to the side of the Allied Powers. The effect
on the friends of the Western Allies in Eastern Europe was devastating.
Yet Churchill continued to make statements in the House of Commons
exhorting satellite countries to 'work their passage home' – in other words,
to earn their post-war independence by shortening the war. This
contradiction between, on the one hand, a suggestion that in certain
circumstances the principles of the Atlantic Charter would apply to
German satellites and, on the other, our determination to treat them as a
purely Soviet affair, was to befuddle our satellite policy to the end. When,
in September 1943, Colonel Pearson of SOE suggested to the head of
Southern Department that an encouraging message should be sent to
Maniu based on Churchill's public undertaking of a week before that
satellite states 'suborned and overawed' could if they helped to shorten the
war be allowed to work their passage home, he must surely have known
that the Foreign Office could do no such thing.[13]

In effect, we now had no Romanian policy. We had a Russian policy,
which incorporated Romania. We rightly argued that the defeat of Hitler
must take precedence over the fate of East European countries. Yet we
were urging Maniu to surrender unconditionally, even if this led to
German occupation and so ruled out a *coup* which could bring victory
appreciably nearer. Our chiefs of staff recognised that while there was
much Romanians could do 'to work their passage home' we should not
insist on unconditional surrender[14] since, in the unlikely event of their
agreeing to such surrender without our military support, we could not take
advantage of it. Commenting on the conclusions of the chiefs of staff, a
realist in the Foreign Office remarked that although our policy was dictated
by the wishes of the Soviet Government, 'we should . . . recognise that
this uncompromising line is not likely to lead to any practical results.
Unconditional surrender . . . offers no inducement whatever to Roumania
to come out of the war so long as she can possibly avoid it.' The 'work their
passage home' formula advocated by the chiefs of staff was sensible and
would appeal to Romanians, but would not be accepted by the Soviet
Government. 'In spite of the fact that Roumania's war effort is directed
entirely against them they have always shown a surprising lack of
enthusiasm for any scheme calculated to lessen that war effort.'[15]

Moscow's attitude was understandable. They had little faith in Maniu's
ability to bring off a *coup* and, in any case, preferred to overrun the
country without incurring obligations towards a devotee of the Western
Powers. They suspected him as they suspected the British. For a long time

they did not believe British protestations that, in spite of our considerable pre-war investment in Romania, and the fact that we had the only effective intelligence network in the country, and the great majority of Romanians behind us, we were, nevertheless, ready to go along with them on every aspect of our dealings with Romania.

At the Moscow Conference of Foreign Ministers in October 1943 Britain lost all room for political manoeuvre on Romania and at the Teheran Summit Conference a month later any prospect of an Allied landing in the Balkans – however slight it might have been before – was finally shelved.

In the early days of the war Churchill had seen the East European countries, including the satellites, as potential military assets. British troops would return to Greece. Guerrilla operations should logically lead to a landing of regular troops. British officers, trained in the Balkan languages for liaison with the regular army, were being held in readiness in Turkey. In spite of his later denials, for some time Churchill continued to hanker after an Allied landing and an attack northwards through the 'soft underbelly' of Europe. His main object may have been to take pressure off the Red Army, though at no time could he have overlooked the longer-term political implications. Orme Sargent minuted bluntly on 11 January 1942 that one way of countering Russian penetration into the Balkans was an expeditionary force at the end of the war.[16]

Americans, for whom the Pacific was far more important than the Mediterranean, were inclined to attribute Churchill's continual harping on that part of the world to his imperial heritage. Roosevelt saw no political advantage in involving American boys in Eastern Europe though naturally he did not want to appear to be 'selling the Balts down the river' – his way of expressing Eden's view that Stalin's claim to the Baltic States should be met only at the peace settlement, 'otherwise we should certainly have a clamour here and abroad about violating the Atlantic Charter.'[17]

Churchill's interest in the eastern Mediterranean unfortunately fed a misunderstanding held by the US chiefs of staff that he was not whole-heartedly in favour of Overlord. The soldiers had to keep one overriding consideration in mind. The defeat of Germany could only take place in Central Europe. All other theatres – Africa, Italy, the eastern Mediterranean, the Balkans – must be made subsidiary to the Soviet drive from the east and the Overlord drive from the west. Guerrilla activity and a deception strategy for Eastern Europe were acceptable if they tied down sufficient German divisions. But the success of a landing, even on the Greek islands, would be largely dependent on the doubtful proposition that Turkey would enter the war on our side. Any such operation could well snowball and become an unjustified drain on men and material to the detriment of the main operation. Moreover, another postponement of

Overlord would revive the threat of a separate peace. The US chiefs of staff felt, therefore, that they had sound reasons for opposing Churchill's 'exotic' schemes and for pulling Roosevelt up short whenever he seemed to be showing any real sympathy for them.

When the three leaders came together for the first time at Teheran in November 1943, Roosevelt and Hopkins were determined to get on with Stalin even if this meant that there would be no agreed Western position; Roosevelt had tried to meet him for several years but Stalin had always played hard to get. 'Sure,' Hopkins told the British just before the conference, 'we are prepared for a battle at Teheran. You will find us lining up with the Russians.'[18]

On the grounds that they had intelligence of a plot on the life of one of the heads of state, the Russians offered Roosevelt the secure hospitality of the Soviet Embassy, and Roosevelt jumped at it. The British were appalled. Apart from any bugging of the President's apartments, Roosevelt and Stalin would be physically closer. Roosevelt had already side-stepped the Prime Minister's attempts to go to Teheran with an agreed Western strategy. He now invited Stalin to a *tête-à-tête* to sound him out on the possibility of Russia declaring war on Japan as soon as the war in Europe was over, and he dropped a hint, as one anti-colonialist to another, about Churchill's sensitivity over the Mediterranean.

Chairing the first plenary meeting, the President emphasised that operations in the Far East together with a shortage of landing craft had delayed the opening of a Second Front intended for 1943. Unless there was a major operation in the Mediterranean, Overlord would now take place in 1944; a minor Mediterranean operation would delay it by up to three months. He invited Stalin's views.

Stalin undertook to enter the war against Japan when the European war was over. Since the way to Germany was through France, he wanted Overlord to start as quickly as possible. He showed no enthusiasm for an attack in the Balkans.

Churchill argued in vain that Mediterranean forces should not lie fallow for six months. They could be used either for a landing in the South of France or an attack from a bridgehead high up in the Adriatic, with greater activity in the Balkans, more support for Tito, the enlistment of Turkey in the war and a direct supply route into the Black Sea ports, all of which would cause a political landslide among Germany's allies. Overlord, to which there was a firm commitment for the spring or summer, would not suffer.

Stalin opted for an attack in the South of France in support of Overlord. Undoubtedly he preferred to keep Anglo-American troops as far westward as possible. But he also had good military reasons for supporting the Americans against Churchill. The Russian campaign was going well but was by no means won, and Overlord was the only West European military operation which, once a bridgehead had been secured, could be certain of relieving the enormous burden on the Red Army. If, as the US chiefs of staff contended, Churchill's schemes for the eastern Mediterranean would delay or even weaken Overlord, then Stalin could be expected to oppose them.

Churchill was so upset by this outcome that, in a private talk with Stalin before lunch on 30 November,[19] he accused Roosevelt of wishing to divert the landing craft required for his Mediterranean operation to an operation in the Bay of Bengal. The choice, then, lay not between the Mediterranean and Overlord but between the Bay of Bengal and Overlord. Thus Stalin had confirmation, if he needed it, that his Western allies were at odds over the best use of their military resources, and the Prime Minister had made things worse by explaining at the beginning of the conversation that since he was himself half-American, nothing he was going to say should be taken as disparaging of the Americans.

Though Churchill never quite seemed to abandon his hopes of action in the eastern Mediterranean if Turkey entered the war, the possibility of Anglo-American troops coming anywhere near the Romanian frontier, however remote it might have been before, was now ruled out.

Since Hitler was still afraid of an Allied landing in Eastern Europe, the three heads of state agreed that a Balkan landing should be included in their cover plan to 'mystify and mislead the enemy . . . to be concerted between the staffs concerned'. The British controlling officer advised that in their negotiations with the Romanians the British should speak from the false assumption that 'during April, Anglo-American and Polish forces will be established in Greece and Albania'. Romanians should therefore 'be ready from end of March onwards to declare for the Allies immediately a landing in Greece was announced'[20]. The object of the deceit was to persuade the German High Command to keep forces in reserve to deal with an Ango-American landing in the Balkans. As many as nineteen divisions are said to have been immobilised in this way. Though I have seen no evidence that the British ever hinted to the Romanians that such a landing would take place, they were always very careful not to rule out the possibility.

Yet it would be a great distortion to suggest that Churchill's 'soft underbelly' policy had been conceived as a deception strategy from the start. When his two more powerful allies and most of his own military advisers persuaded him that such a policy would not be militarily feasible, he made the best of a bad job by adopting the deception strategy – though not without some residuary grumbling through most of 1944

I was in Cairo in December when Churchill passed through on his way back from Teheran. Bill Deakin,* who had married Pussy Nasta earlier

---

* Later Sir William Deakin, Warden of St Antony's College, Oxford.

that year and had led the first British mission to Tito in May, was in Cairo. An historian and Fellow of Wadham College who had helped the Prime Minister with his literary work before the war, he told us how the PM would talk over brandy until three in the morning and knock at his door by 7.30 next morning, asking why he wasn't yet up.

When SOE learned after the Foreign Ministers' Conference of October 1943 that unconditional surrender to the Red Army was the only way open to Romania, de Chastelain questioned the point of continuing with his mission to Maniu. As for the Teheran Conference of November, for obvious security reasons we went to Romania without knowing what had been agreed there. According to Victor Rădulescu-Pogoneanu, a reliable member of the Romanian Foreign Ministry, the US military attaché in Ankara asked his Romanian colleague shortly after Teheran what would be his government's reaction to an Allied landing in the Balkans advancing towards Sofia. When Cretzianu, the Romanian Minister, was sent posthaste back to Ankara with a positive response, he was told by the Americans that the question was no longer current.[21] Romanians could quite reasonably have seen our mission, which was headed by a more senior officer than would usually go into the field, as the advance party to a landing in the Balkans. Certainly all Maniu's plans were based on the assumption that, just as General Berthelot had arrived on the Danube during the First World War, British or American troops would appear at the right moment to support his *coup* against the Germans.

Chapter 11

Autonomous Goes In [1]

Some misunderstanding almost always creeps into communication between an intelligence headquarters and its agents in the field. In the case of SOE Cairo and the Romanian Resistance it was made worse by a two-year break in their radio link. At the end of 1943, during the run-up to the Autonomous operation, Cairo had little idea of the operational set-up in Romania. The travellers – Bianu, Serdici, Gheorghiu, Christu, Bursan and others – had brought back reports on Maniu's plans and on general political and economic developments. They knew that Jockey's trial had been postponed probably *sine die* but were not familiar with the day-by-day working of the network he had built up from prison.

On 20 September, after weeks of silence, Turcanu (now code-named Reginald) sent Cairo a radio message reporting Russell's death and his own arrival at the Protopopescus' flat.

The loss of David Russell, an outstanding and popular officer, was a hard blow for the Romanian Section. After establishing radio contact between Maniu and Cairo he was to have found a secure reception area, or DZ as we called them. The RAF were familiar with parachute drops into Yugoslav or Greek guerrilla-held territory, where DZs could be marked out with flares. But no such extensive area of friendly territory was available in Romania. Flares might well be spotted by the authorities, and flash-lamp signalling was difficult to see from the air. Even for a specially trained officer like Russell, establishing a workable DZ in Romania would have been difficult enough. Without him, and with jumping weather only likely to last another couple of months, the situation had become critical.

But once Cairo had recovered from the shock of losing Russell they began to see possibilities in the Turcanu-Protopopescu network. By now they were sure that Reginald was not working under hostile control. Protopopescu had obtained false papers for Turcanu, and was employing him as a clerk. He had friends ready to help – a man called Brener, for instance. Also Virgil Tabacu, Chief Inspector of Number 2 Police District in Bucharest and Sandu Ioan, an air force captain, and the air commander at Ploeşti. Turcanu asked Ted Masterson, Head of the Romanian Section, to trust him. Get supplies to his group, he said, and someone to train them, and they would form sabotage teams. His comment that Maniu's people 'were afraid of their own shadows' reminded one that Turcanu himself was inclined to be impulsive. However, one of SOE's principal objectives was to harass the enemy by the kind of paramilitary operations British liaison officers were reporting from Greece and Yugoslavia and which were acclaimed in London. Maniu's inactivity in this respect had been an embarrassment to the Romanian Section. Not surprisingly Cairo seized on Turcanu's offer and, knowing Maniu's objections to sabotage, decided to keep the Turcanu-Protopopescu and the Maniu-Georgescu operations in separate, watertight compartments. They warned Turcanu not to discuss his plans with Maniu's people.

Protopopescu suggested a drop on to the estate of an anglophile general who was also a close friend of Marshal Antonescu's. Although in Romanian terms the idea was not altogether absurd, Cairo thought it unwise and asked him to try again. Meanwhile they prepared to send in a British officer of Romanian origin as an instructor in the use of explosives. Silviu Meţianu was in his fifties – to me, in my twenties, he seemed an old man. A Transylvanian, he had fought in the First World War and then emigrated to England. He looked like the god Pan; smallish, square, with a large tapering head and a weathered face, he was extraordinarily fit and tough and an excellent shot.

On 16 October Cairo received Jockey's first message via the Turcanu (Reginald) radio. After answering Chas's queries about Romanian friends and twitting him for some previous indiscretion, Jockey got down to business. Since Maniu's *coup* had to be coordinated with the Allies, he asked whether Anglo-American operations in the Balkans or the Black Sea could be expected soon.

In mid-October Maniu had been dissuaded from leaving Romania; had he popped up 'like a rabbit out of a hat' in the middle of the Foreign Ministers' conference, Russian suspicions, the Foreign Office felt, would have been aroused. Now, on 30 October he returned to the charge. He and three collaborators wished to leave the country in order, with British help, to contact the Russians. At the same time Jockey repeated his military query. We referred Maniu's request to SOE London, who obtained a reply from the Foreign Office which was word for word the formula agreed in Moscow. Maniu had no need to leave the country in order to overthrow Antonescu and then surrender unconditionally to the Russians. From prison Jockey commented that 'The cold shower we have received does not alleviate our suffering for the common cause'; and four days later he asked 'In the event of the Romanian Government offering unconditional surrender what will you, the British, do? Can we count on your immediate help?'

De Chastelain knew, of course, that such questions would be more difficult to duck once he was face to face with Maniu. Perhaps he could convince him that, after two and a half years of fighting on Russian soil, Romania was now dependent on Soviet goodwill; but that if she broke immediately with the Axis and surrendered unconditionally to the USSR she might still win favour with all three Allied Powers. Though we respected Maniu for putting his country's future independence before everything else, we would do our best to persuade him to take the leap in the dark. Because we considered Maniu to be loyal to the democratic cause and a friend, ours would be a difficult and not altogether honourable mission, but one that had to be attempted.

Maniu showed characteristic resilience in the face of London's rebuff, and on 9 November announced his intention of sending out a special delegate. Where, he asked, should he land? Again, we passed this message on to London, expecting another brush-off.

So long as he expected to leave Romania, Maniu had pressed de Chastelain to wait for him in the Middle East. After the 'cold shower' he agreed that his friend had better come in. The other two officers Cairo were pressing him to accept – Charles Maydwell and myself – should, Jockey suggested, delay their journey until Chas had had an opportunity to assess with Maniu's people the technical difficulties on the spot.

Meanwhile Reginald had sent Cairo the coordinates for a new DZ which he had checked personally. The recognition signals would consist of nine flash lamps in a cross, with one indicating wind direction. So far so good. Cairo asked him whether Maniu knew of the DZ or his plans. Turcanu replied that Maniu's people knew of the DZ – they had found it together – but not the sabotage plans. This, from Cairo's point of view, was bad enough. But when Chas agreed, under pressure from Jockey, to go in alone, adding that he would use Maniu's, not Reginald's radio, he was told that they were one and the same. (We should, surely, have realised this in Cairo.) The final blow came on 17 November, when Jockey sent his coordinates and recognition signals which proved to be identical with those Cairo had received from Reginald four days earlier. So much for their efforts to operate two watertight networks – one for sabotage, one for liaison with Maniu. Cairo immediately told Reginald that the Meţianu operation was 'stood down', that one officer would go in on 21 November without sabotage equipment and, if unsuccessful, would try again on the following nights. On Jockey, Chas urged the utmost discretion – not only did both networks know of the DZ, but there had been mention in his signals of such an unlikely person as a military magistrate. The military magistrate was, in fact, Major Oatu from Rica's prison, who had undertaken at great personal risk to accompany de Chastelain in uniform when he was driven to Bucharest.

On 20 November the Foreign Office received the following unexpected telegram from Moscow:

The Soviet Government agrees that Maniu be informed that he can send his emissary, but only on the understanding that latter's sole function is to discuss operational details for the overthrow of the present régime in Romania and its replacement by a Government prepared to surrender unconditionally to the three principal Allies.

The Soviet Government added that since Romania was the country concerned, it was absolutely necessary for a Soviet representative to take part in the negotiations. Stalin was taking no chances; three months before, the British and Americans had concluded an armistice with Badoglio's Italian government without allowing the Russians any part in the negotiations.

London were, of course, delighted with this apparent Soviet change of heart. They suggested that de Chastelain should take the message personally to Maniu, with BBC confirmation following in twenty-four hours. De Chastelain – who was already at Tocra, near Benghazi, from where the RAF operated their SOE flights into the Balkans – also felt that the message would get Autonomous off to a good start; he should, however, be allowed forty-eight rather than twenty-four hours to reach Maniu before confirmation was sent.

It was at this point that Autonomous changed from a predominantly military to a predominantly political operation. Earlier it had been planned as a classical SOE operation – to disrupt German communications – though the Foreign Office had had no objection to our also working for the overthrow of the Antonescu régime. But now de Chastelain's primary task was to brief Maniu and his emissary about Romania's position and the overriding necessity for her to accept unconditional surrender to the Russians.

It was hoped that cover for de Chastelain's flight would – at Jockey's suggestion – be provided by the bombing of the Giurgiu oil depot. This proved impossible though mines were dropped in the Danube and leaflets over several towns. The flight was put off for twenty-four hours until 22 November, and that night some of us sat up waiting for news. The weather was good and at first we were optimistic, though annoyed that there had been no radio contact with Reginald during the critical twenty-four hours before take-off. But when the plane failed to return to Tocra we knew that things had gone badly wrong. Next day – a bleak day – the news came through in driblets. The Liberator had stooged too long over the target looking for signals; their radio had broken down; they had misnavigated over Albania, run short of fuel and had all bailed out off the Italian coast near Brindisi, not knowing whether they were in friendly or enemy territory. Chas and the crew had survived; the aircraft had been lost.

Ştorobăneasa, the estate chosen for our landing, was to the south-east of Alexandria, a town roughly twenty miles north of the Danube. The estate belonged to the Racotta family. It had been Sandu Racotta, one of three sons, who with Rica Georgescu had had that extraordinary interview with Antonescu when they were students in England. Sandu visited Rica in prison and on one occasion Rica asked him if he could help with Autonomous. The Racotta family had agreed and Sandu, who had taken charge, had been code-named Ştefan – indeed at the time I only knew him as Ştefan.

Jockey reported that Reginald and Ştefan had waited at the DZ in good weather until three in the morning of 22 November, which explained why there had been no contact with Reginald's radio in Bucharest on the 21st. However, bad weather and the fact that their car had broken down meant that there had been no one at the DZ the following night. Not unnaturally, Chas sent off a blistering telegram. Tension grew when Jockey referred to Alecu Ionescu – of whom Cairo had never heard – as one of few reliable people. 'Then who can we trust?' de Chastelain asked. Jockey asked him to be patient, explained who Ionescu and his wife were and, in an effort to defuse the situation, said he was sorry for what had happened on the night of the 22nd – though being in prison a hundred miles from the DZ he could hardly be held responsible.

Meanwhile, Maniu had received the Soviet message together with a reduced background briefing via the BBC and had been told that his representative was awaited in Nicosia. Only twenty-four hours' notice was required. A note of 28 November from Lord Moyne, Minister Resident in Cairo, to McVeagh, the US Ambassador in Cairo with responsibility for Balkan questions, reflects the excitement and sense of urgency felt by the British. A senior Romanian officer was expected within the week and negotoiations with him, Moyne said, should be completed as quickly as possible 'in order that the *coup d'état* against the existing régime in Romania, followed by unconditional surrender, may be achieved before the enemy can take adequate counter-measures'.[2] However, arrangements inside Romania were not that simple; Maniu's representative was not to leave for another three months.

Reginald was still pressing for Meţianu and explosives, and had to be told that this would not now be possible for the time being. Ted Masterson urged him to procure his explosives inside the country and 'get down to work'. Fortunately Turcanu did not act on this. He would almost certainly have been caught before he had achieved anything worthwhile and SOE would have lost one of their best wireless operators and their only radio link with Romania.

Jockey had now agreed to take two bodies and Chas and I were in Tocra, expecting to jump on the night of 5 December or on one of the following two nights. Ted Masterson in Cairo was exhorting Reginald to stay with his W/T in Bucharest and make contact twice a day.

On the 5th we flew in a Halifax. On the journey out we had perfect weather. We saw the Danube clearly and the gleam of smaller rivers north of it. We even saw lights in the cottage windows. Yet over the target there were no lights. Perhaps Ştefan and his people had not judged our direction in time to point their torches at the nose of the aircraft while we were still far enough away to see them; perhaps they were waving them about when the aircraft was already too close or overhead. Whatever the reason, the pilot made several runs across the target without seeing the all-clear signal to let us jump.

Before returning to Africa, the despatcher heaved up the heavy lid of the hatch and hurled the lightly strung packets against its edge so that they burst and our propaganda roared through the slip-stream and floated down to the woods below. Sometimes a packet went through intact, hitting the ground with enough force to kill rather than persuade. Only days later, this same despatcher lost his balance and went through with one of his packets.

On our journey home through deteriorating weather we were disheartened and disgruntled with our Romanian friends. This crew had put in many operational flying hours; the pilot was a quiet, impressive character in whom we had complete confidence; the weather had been better than one would expect for the time of year. A chance like this was unlikely to occur again.

There were strong cross-winds at Tocra and we were diverted to an abandoned airstrip where we spent the night in the plane – cold, hungry and angry. A few days later, the same aircraft turned over and caught fire; it staggered home, but on landing destroyed itself and a Spitfire. After the loss of the Halifax and de Chastelain's Liberator, the despatcher's death, and the evil eye on Ştefan's signals, Chas and I began to joke about Operation Autonomous; it seemed the only thing to do.

Jockey then reported that Ştefan (Racotta), Reginald (Turcanu), Sorin (Ioan) and the military magistrate had all been at the DZ with transport. The lights had been lit as agreed. We had circled over them, and they could not understand why we had not jumped.

On 12 December Reginald told us that as Sandu Ioan had now been appointed commander of the area to the south-east of Bucharest with his headquarters at Roşiori de Vede, a town not far from Alexandria, Reginald would install himself there with his W/T. Four days later he notified his arrival. Since the police were now looking for him under his original cover-name, he had new papers in the name of Popa, describing him as a civil servant. Cairo informed him that we would come 'as urgently as possible' once the DZ and recognition signals had been arranged. Reginald told us that, on this occasion, the DZ would be four kilometres south-east of Roşiori de Vede between the road and railway. Cairo then modified the signalling: they now wanted five lamps twenty-five metres apart, four forming a square and the fifth in the centre, and a sixth a hundred metres from the centre to show the wind direction – all pointing at the plane, which would approach from the south-east.

The mission – which would consist of de Chastelain, Charles Maydwell and myself – would be attempted on Monday 20 December or the following nights between 11 p.m. and 2 a.m. On the 18th, Cairo told Reginald and Ioan that if the aircraft failed to pick up their signals on its first run over the DZ it would continue on the same course for about seventy kilometres and, returning, drop us blind at a point six kilometres from Roşiori de Vede 'where the railway bends and is nearest to the road'. Some of the reception party should therefore wait at this point. Reginald confirmed this, and urged us to come in under a thousand metres. By now, of course, Rica Georgescu (Jockey), being locked up in Bucharest, had no access to Reginald in Roşiori de Vede; his last message, until after the operation, had reached Cairo on the 9th.

On Monday the 20th we had to postpone the operation due to bad weather. On the 21st Reginald signalled 'Today, Tuesday morning, weather very fine and calm. Please come today. We can't wait much longer because of W/T security . . .The officers will also hear from the road horn of *Sorin*'s car, two short blasts at small intervals . . . Good luck.' Cairo replied on our behalf, 'Wait for us without fail tonight, Tuesday 21st December . . .'

The nine o'clock met. report on the morning of the 21st was discouraging: there was mist over northern Greece, and night mist was expected over the Danube, including the target area. In the middle of the morning, Chas, Charles Maydwell and I met the Wing Commander and the pilot in an old Turkish castle, part of which Wing used for offices. It had been agreed that if we did not see lights on the outward flight we would fly on to Piteşti, a town on the river Argeş, and after dropping our diversionary leaflets, jump blind at a point south of Roşiori de Vede where the road and railway came closest. It was as near to the target as we could hope to get with reasonable visibility but no ground signals.

We could see the road, railway and river on Wing's wall map, and the pilot kept on saying 'piece of cake'. 'See that river, sir, I'll follow that. Piece of cake, sir.' Wing had cancelled the operation the night before, when the mist had been no worse than was forecast for tonight. But now he said nothing. No one did. The pressure was on us all to put Autonomous in that night. This, we felt, would be our last chance; it was important for Chas to talk to Maniu and his emissary before the latter left Romania which he was expected to do at any time. We were therefore ready to take great risks though not impossible ones; if de Chastelain was lost then the whole operation was lost.

I raised a question of security. As a diversionary tactic SOE proposed to leak to the Germans that we had jumped into the Piteşti area. I argued that to admit that we had dropped anywhere would lead to an immediate general tightening up of security and that it would be better to revert to a straightforward leaflet cover. This was agreed.

Before lunch we were fitted with parachutes and packed our kit. The precious W/T set was in a rhomboid-shaped container made of a new, strong, light material – presumably an early plastic – and wrapped in our civilian clothes for further protection.

During the afternoon de Chastelain had instructions from London to take Silviu Meţianu, the sabotage expert, instead of Charles Maydwell; Maydwell would follow once we were established. It seemed a strange decision and hard on both Maydwell and Meţianu. While paramilitary operations might come later, our immediate objective was to ensure that Maniu's emissary was given a realistic brief for his talks with the representatives of the Three Powers. Maniu would not understand why we had brought a sabotage expert on what had become primarily a political mission.

The met. report at one o'clock was a little better but still, I felt, not good enough. However Reginald gave us the go-ahead at four o'clock and that settled the matter. We discussed whether we should be armed: I had a Colt 38, but since Chas was keen that, as Maniu's friends, we should go in unarmed, I asked Charles Maydwell to keep it for me. Meţianu, we discovered later, held on to his weapon.

At about five o'clock we were given the customary bacon and eggs. An hour later, standing in the cool Turkish courtyard, we again went over the plan, and again the pilot said that it would be a 'piece of cake'; he virtually guaranteed to drop us that night. Then we drove inland from the sea to the airfield – take-off had been fixed for half past six.

The Wing Commander, Chas, Charles, Silviu and I stood at smoking distance from the Liberator, waiting for it to warm up, cubist faces appearing from time to time in the flame of someone's Zippo lighter. Chas and Wing ran through their stock of last-minute problems. I wandered off, stopping to watch the exhaust fires, the shaded green light in the pilot's cabin, the red identification light on the line of hills overlooking this part of the coast, the mild, moonless, North African sky, telling myself that even if Wing or Chas had put into words what was on everyone's mind, they could still have done nothing about it. The pilot's 'piece of cake' was so much blarney, but no one was going to say so.

When the aircraft was finally ready, at about half past seven, we said goodbye to Wing and au revoir to Charles, and climbed up through the hatch into what seemed the enormous belly of the plane.

For take-off we crowded forward into the radio operator's den, four of us crammed into his narrow vibrating bulkhead, but once airborne we took the cat walk over the bomb racks back to the big compartment where the leaflets and jumping hatch were located. As Chas and I stacked the packets for something to sit on, someone remarked that each one carried a ten-pound charge of Allied subversion. Silviu was sorting through private papers, deciding which to destroy. The despatcher put his hands in his pockets, chatted with us for a while and then went forward. Chas extracted a leaflet, read it, grinned, screwed it up and threw it at me. It was addressed to the citizens of Bucharest but would be dropped a hundred miles from the capital, not far from Curtea de Argeş, itself the old capital of Wallachia after the barbarian invasions, before Wallachians had decided to trust themselves again to the plain. I grinned back and shook my head, agreeing with him. The noise was deafening.

We climbed slowly away from the North African coast. We would cross the Mediterranean, Greece and Bulgaria and, once north of the Danube, head for the DZ. Last time, in good weather, we had failed to see Ştefan's signals; why should we do any better on a misty night with a cock-a-hoop pilot? Why not, I asked myself. A break in the cloud, a chance glimpse of those electric lamps, and out we would go. That's the way the cat jumps, sometimes.

I pushed through the leaflets to the large rhomboid which held our transmitter and the carefully vetted civilian clothing we would wear until we could find local things. Each garment, the eagle-eyed women in Cairo had told us, could be had in Romania; we could even say where we had bought it. I touched the new-fangled material of the rhomboid and glanced at my fingers. It felt strange, like a new era. I tugged at the small canvas bag tied to it; it contained our binoculars and the hard rations we would need if anything went wrong. Then I stumped back to my parachute, sat down with my back to it, and slid slowly on to the hard, ribbed floor, using my pack as a pillow.

The jump was winding up inside me, though that was no reason for feeling so sick. Perhaps I had drunk too much sherry before lunch. My face felt pale. My fair hair was cut short. My hands were deep in my pockets for warmth and my thin though rather stocky body was curled up. I tried to shut out the cold and nausea, to let myself go with the noise and vibration of the aircraft. But for a long time I was aware of the army fat stuck to the roof of my mouth, and the ball of propaganda moving uncertainly this way and that at my feet. Then I slept.

When I woke, I looked at my watch and came up on one elbow. It had stopped. SOE had given me a special watch which had packed in in less than ten hours. We had spent a hundred thousand pounds on the operation yet had skimped on this vital piece of equipment.

I stood up, heavy with cold, and stumped across to Chas. He nodded. By his watch – he had wisely turned down the army issue – it was already twenty past twelve. 'We're losing height,' he shouted. We were, and the height, of course, had accounted for our sickness; that was why the despatcher had disappeared forward, looking for oxygen.

The despatcher came back with a thermos of thick, sweet tea. We had our ration of rum, then a sandwich and more tea, and felt a great deal better. The despatcher told us we had flown most of the way at 17,000 feet, between two banks of cloud. At one moment they had had difficulty finding the Danube, but now had a pinpoint and were navigating straight to target.

Chas talked to the pilot by intercom, reminding him that on the way out we dropped only on lights. Then we put on our harnesses and tied up to the wire that ran down the middle of the compartment. Each one of us made sure he was firmly attached for unless the line tore off the parachute cover once you were clear of the aircraft your parachute would not open. Back on the intercom, the despatcher told us we had about six minutes to go. Chas was sitting on the edge of the hole looking through. I was behind, the spring very tight now. Silviu Meţianu was third. The despatcher kicked some packets aside, dragged the rhomboid into place behind Silviu and tied that up as well. He went back to the intercom and almost immediately turned and shouted something. I felt sure that the six minutes were not yet up, but the red light came on, and then the green, and we were out.

I pushed myself too violently forward: my helmet struck the front edge of the hole and my pack the back edge, correcting me as I dropped through the roar of the slip-stream, and those two long, silent seconds of freefall. When the line snapped tight and released the parachute, I was aware only of thick mist. I breathed it in, and it blinded and befuddled me. Perhaps, I thought, it was only scattered cloud. Perhaps the pilot really had spotted Ştefan's signals through a break in it. I made a turn but could see no lights. I listened, but could not hear the motor horn that should have been hooting at regular intervals. I took out my red torch and when a black mass rushed up at me, put it quickly away again. But it was not the ground, only a thicker bank of mist. Then I was sure: as I went through it I knew that we were lost. Ştefan would not be waiting for us down there.

A few hundred feet from the ground I started to oscillate but was too angry to bother to turn and face the impact; the skyline sprang up at me, and I landed in a backward roll on a ploughed field.

PART THREE

December 1943–March 1944

Chapter 12

Capture

After two and a half years in the Middle East, the warm, damp earth of Europe smelled good. For a moment I lay there feeling a great affection for my continent. To be spreadeagled in a ploughed field at one in the morning, three days before Christmas, and hundreds of miles inside enemy territory, was the kind of contradiction I would always enjoy.

Then I scrambled to my feet, unharnessed and folded the parachute and felt in my pockets to make sure I had dropped nothing. I blew my whistle softly and Chas replied. I found him quite quickly, but spent twice as long looking for my parachute, cursing myself for leaving it behind. Chas dropped his own beside it, sat down and said, 'Our pieceofcake couldn't have seen a damn thing through this.'

We smoked a cigarette. If we were within walking distance of the target, we might still find Ştefan. He and his people would have green lamps; we had red. Our password would be 'Caut pe Ştefan' – 'I'm looking for Stephan' – and theirs, 'Ştefan e acasa' – 'Stephan's at home'. Ştefan had a hole dug for our gear. He had guns and game which would make sense of the shooting jackets we were wearing over our uniform. He would get us safely to Bucharest, with a military magistrate in uniform sitting next to the driver: a member of the Romanian Judiciary Police would help us to make contact with the leader of the Romanian Resistance. Everything now depended on Ştefan. We had no escape route. We had only a few sandwiches and the hard rations in the bag tied to the rhomboid. We had plenty of money, but were unarmed except for coshes. And if we had landed south, instead of north, of the Danube, the Bulgarian women, according to RAF myth, might well lynch us. I listened, already feeling myself a wilder, more sensitive animal than the one who had jumped out of the plane. Yet I heard nothing but the chatter of my own thoughts; the mist remained as thick, ubiquitous and silent as ever.

It was now about one o'clock in the morning of the 22nd. First we must find Silviu Meţianu. He had either dropped late, or hurt himself when landing or he had had a 'Roman candle' and been killed. I decided to reconnoitre while Chas stayed with the equipment. I pulled the compass out of my fob pocket, a little unsure of myself; our training in night navigation had been rather different in Palestine in that we had worked in pairs or threes, there had been no mist, and we could rely on a good breakfast at the end of the exercise.

South-eastwards brought me to the edge of the ploughed field. There was no answer to my whistle, so I returned to Chas and then tried to the west. This time I came to a wood but, again, there was no answer. To the north-west lay the same wood, and I followed it to its edge. On my fourth recce, this time to the south, I walked for some distance parallel to the wood and finally heard Silviu's whistle. I moved back slowly towards Chas, keeping in touch with Silviu, and soon afterwards he joined us. He had landed in a tree and had had to cut himself free.

By now, it was well after two o' clock. Chas had heard cars and trains some distance to the north-west and thought that perhaps we had dropped to the south-east of both the road and the railway, instead of between them. We also heard dogs barking to the north, only much nearer – the sign of a village.

According to Silviu, the wood was fairly deep. We squeezed the red celluloid out of our torches to see better, scuffled the earth, and made for the corner I had reached on my third recce, where we spent the rest of the night in a hollow. After a walk to get warm at about six o'clock, Chas and Silviu reported what seemed to be a disused airfield with mounds like machine-gun posts, but as soon as it was light enough we saw that these were humps of earth and the 'airfield' a large meadow. We camouflaged our kit as best we could with the little foliage available at that time of year and then turned to the meadow, squaring it methodically, taking twenty minutes to find the rhomboid and dump it with its parachute in the wood. But the small sack was no longer tied to it, and hard rations were now more important to us than the transmitter. We knew it must have dropped between Silviu and the rhomboid. We searched for almost an hour, hiding whenever a *caruţă* – a village cart – came down the path, and eventually trudged back to the edge of the wood without it. We each ate a sandwich and one of the ~~hard~~-boiled sweets Pussy Deakin had given us – they were good for thirst.

I glanced at my watch, remembered that it was broken and swore softly. We had asked for an accommodation address in Roşiori de Vede but had not been given one. After Reginald's morning schedule, Ştefan would know that we had jumped and, if possible, would wait at the target. We must expect our equipment to be found within forty-eight hours or so. We had finished our boiled sweets and without rations we would soon be driven into the open. We had maps on silk but they were small-scale and of no help in our present situation. First, we had to orientate ourselves, then, if we were right in thinking that the target was within walking distance to the north, we had to contact Ştefan that night.

By ten o'clock visibility had improved to about one hundred yards. Some women arrived to collect firewood, and as soon as we heard them talking we at least knew that we were in Romania. Chas asked Silviu to get into conversation with them but when he returned an hour later he had not been able to do so. Having been out of the country for twenty years and being, in any case, a stranger to the district, it would have been difficult without arousing their suspicions.

By now the mist had lifted enough for us to see a line of trees to the north running east-west – almost certainly alongside a macadamised road. We left our hiding place and set out for the village. We passed several peasants, remembering not to greet them with an Arabic 'saida'. The village was about three kilometres away; it lay in a hollow and, according to a board on the hill, was called 'Plosca'. Although in the mist it had looked bigger than it was, it was too small to appear on any of the maps we had seen.

A woman was pottering in her garden on the edge of the village and Chas suggested that Silviu, since he was the only one of us who looked Romanian, should ask her how far we were from Roşiori de Vede. Silviu thought it too risky. Perhaps he was right; perhaps it was the need for human contact that drove Chas and me towards the village – that and the fact that Chas, in particular, considered these people to be his friends. Two things, had we known them, might have dissuaded us. The leaflets had been dropped on Roşiori de Vede, not Piteşti; instead of acting as a diversion, they had concentrated security in this very district. Secondly, since my card index of Information Useful to a Traveller in Romania had been discontinued, we were not aware that peasants had been offered a reward of 20,000 *lei* for reporting to the authorities any strangers seen in or around their village who might turn out to be parachutists.

Despite Silviu's reservations, Chas approached the woman, who at first said we were thirty kilometres from the town, and then fifteen – but, as Chas pointed out, country people were always vague about distances. Fifteen kilometres seemed about right – roughly eighteen kilometres from the wood. Judging from the sounds of trains and cars we had heard when we landed our target area – where the road and railway lines came closest – must be only about ten kilometres from the wood.

Chas proposed that we stay in the wood until nightfall, whereas I felt that having been seen we should now leave the district and be within easy reach of the target before the mist thickened again. We all agreed that if we missed Ştefan again that night, our chances of survival were slim. So we decided to set out immediately.

During the walk back to the wood one peasant took a particular interest in us – later he claimed the reward, though it was the woman in her garden who got it. We reached the wood just before one o'clock, put more camouflage over our kit, and were about to leave our shelter when we saw a group of men – civilians and gendarmes with rifles – approaching from the direction of Plosca. We worked our way through the wood to the western edge and then walked away as casually as we could, still hoping against hope that they were not, in fact, looking for us. But they were, of course. At first they shouted, and then fired over our heads. The wood was not large enough for cover, and we would have been shot down in the open before we had run fifty feet. We were also very hungry and thirsty, and that must also have influenced our reactions.

To improve our chances if caught before meeting Ştefan, we had decided to wear uniform under our civilian clothing. All we had to do now was to remove our jackets before the gendarmes reached us, and this we did.

Chapter 13

We Return to Bucharest

Once de Chastelain had explained to the NCO in fluent Romanian that we were unarmed and we had shown him our identity cards which were stamped over in Romanian to say that we belonged to the British Army, an enemy soldier was immediately transformed into a friendly Romanian peasant. We were, he said, in the commune of Plosca. He apologised for having to arrest us, and as we tramped cross country to the road and down the road to the gendarmerie, he shouted 'sunt prieteni' – 'they're friends' – to anyone we passed. It was a heartening reception for three captives who were feeling more than a little nervous about the future.

On our way to the village, we managed to have a few words together in English – virtually our last before the interrogation. To keep out of German hands, we agreed to say that we had come with messages for the Romanian Government and must, therefore, be taken as quickly and as discreetly as possible to Bucharest. Our object was to keep out of the hands of the Gestapo for as long as possible; we had no idea that this, our first cover story, was to light a fuse which, five months later, would lead to an almighty explosion.

A group of villagers had gathered outside the gendarmerie, but they were curious rather than hostile, talking amongst themselves as they made way for us. We tramped through the guard room and up four steps to a dormitory, separated from the guard room by a glass partition through which people could stare at us.

To the left as we entered was a large window giving on to the street, and by standing on their toes people could see us through this as well. Near the door were a table and two chairs, and down the room were three iron beds made up with clean, off-white sheets, brown blankets folded to make a strip down the middle, and, at the foot of each bed, a pair of the wooden clogs Romanian soldiers wore off duty. But for us prisoners, suffering as we were from cold, hunger and shock, and carrying false civilian papers, only one thing in the room mattered: the unlit stove at the far end, the large, wood-burning, porcelain *soba*.

Being a local boy, the sergeant in charge could not keep the villagers out. The mayor arrived with his secretary, then the deputy prefect, followed by the vet, the village doctor, local teachers and the chief tax collector and his clerks. Towards the end of the afternoon, all the peasants returning from the fields came along to see what it was all about. They tended to come in small groups, rather nervously, listening while one of them made conversation, then all shaking hands and filing out again. The priest asked us a few questions about the sensation of jumping and, on leaving, remarked, 'May we have peace among us soon.'

I remember in particular one old woman who came in alone. She perched herself on a chair and made little gestures of encouragement with her head and hands while she talked. Silviu, she said, must be Romanian, and she stroked his head. About Chas, she was not sure, but thought he was probably English. As for me, I was certainly German. Since we were none of us Russian, we must all be Romania's friends, and she asked whether we had come across her grandson on the eastern front. We were cold, she said, and told the sergeant to light the stove. Half an hour later, when she returned with tea and bread, the damp smell had gone out of our clothes, and our false papers and radio schedules had been dropped into the *soba*.

Altogether two to three hundred people must have dropped in to see us but only one, a teacher, was unfriendly; he was a small, intense man who insisted on speaking florid Balkan French and setting himself up as a German propagandist. We gathered that he was a Legionary, a member of the Iron Guard, and unpopular in the village. Since Chas was the senior officer and fluent in the language, he bore the brunt of these encounters. Several times I asked whether we could have some food, at which people would nod and smile and do nothing about it. But eventually a burly sergeant-major arrived, turned almost everyone out, took a dig at 'these intellectuals' – he was referring to the school master – 'who pester everyone with their views', and ordered a hot meal.

Three Germans from the local direction-finding station, who must have plotted our Liberator's course during the night, watched from the street but were not allowed in. When they finally gave up and left, presumably to report our arrival, it became all the more urgent for us to leave the district; the sergeant-major seemed a tough and independent type, but I would not have backed him against a senior German officer.

De Chastelain told him that we must see the colonel in charge of the Turnu Măgurele gendarmerie headquarters as soon as possible. The sergeant-major telephoned and did his best, but the colonel – who, he said, was a good man – had gone to Bucharest for the day, and the captain in charge was already on his way over with a truck. He sounded far less enthusiastic about the captain.

Chas then asked to speak privately to the sub-prefect. With him he followed up the cover story we had agreed when we were arrested, telling

him that we were on a mission to the Romanian Government. Could he
help us to contact a senior official quickly, with as little publicity as
possible? He promised to do what he could and left.

The sergeant-major sat by the door, making a short report of our
landing and capture. He added an inventory of our belongings, but
agreed that the rhomboid Silviu and a corporal had brought in from the
wood should be opened only in front of the colonel. Eventually, the meal
arrived – *ţuica*, meat, potatoes and wine – and the sergeant-major and
Chas got going in Romanian. The atmosphere was, in fact, so warm that,
as Chas remarked to Silviu and me in an aside, we could not have had a
much friendlier reception if we had been Romanian POWs returning
home from the front.

It was not to last, however; when the officious captain arrived from
Turnu Măgurele the temperature dropped to zero. He grudgingly
accepted a glass of wine from Chas but without the usual '*Sănătate*' or
'Good health'. He approved the sergeant-major's report but complained
– quite rightly, I thought – that too many people had been allowed to talk
to us. This remark was directed in particular at the sub-prefect whom he
accused of holding an unofficial interrogation; the gendarmerie, he said,
would stand for no interference from the prefecture.

After this short, heated argument he told us to get into the truck. He
put Chas into the warm driver's cabin, and joined him there. He ordered
a chair to be placed at the disposal of Silviu and me, which, of course, we
ignored, pulling ourselves up by the tailboard along with the sergeant, the
guards and our kit.

I sat with my back to the cab, rubbed the grit out of my palms and put
my hands into my pockets. A group of villagers watched us leave and, as
the truck jumped and then started down the road, someone shouted '*La
revedere, Englezi*' – 'Goodbye, English' – and Silviu and I called back.

It was another raw, misty night and the going was slow. As I dozed, I
wondered whether Ştefan had heard of our capture. He could be in any
of the cars which were passing us on their way to Bucharest.

When I woke the truck had stopped. The prefect of the county of
Teleorman and the regional inspector of gendarmerie – the colonel – had
met us with a car. Chas got in with them and they drove on ahead.

The truck reached Turnu Măgurele at about eleven o'clock, and Silviu
and I were examined in turn by the colonel, a large, decent-looking man
with a brusque manner. I gave him a brief account of our landing and
capture, and told him that we had been sent in to contact the Romanian
Government. De Chastelain's cyphers were on the table and since mine,
too, would be discovered as soon as my clothes were examined, I told
him where they were hidden. At no time did Chas or I disclose the key to
the cyphers, which we had memorised.

The transmitter, civilian clothes and compasses (except for Chas's, which had mysteriously disappeared during the trip from Plosca) were laid out on the floor. When the colonel had made a report and inventory of what had been found in the rhomboid and on our persons, his wife gave us a light meal. It was our second supper, but we were glad of it. The colonel told us we would leave with him for Bucharest at six in the morning. It was then 1.30 in the morning on 23 December 1943.

After dossing down on the guards' beds for a few hours, we were taken out to a small Ford car in the courtyard. The colonel's programme had unfortunately changed, and the captain would now escort us to the capital. After the colonel had gently ticked him off for fussing, we eventually started – Chas, Silviu and the captain behind, while I was sandwiched between the driver and the burly sergeant, greatly preferring this arrangement to having to make conversation with our officious escort.

On the outskirts of Turnu Măgurele, the captain left us for a quarter of an hour while he went into a house with coloured glass and an electric bell on the front door and the noise of disturbed pigs and hens behind – as if it were unable to make up its mind between an urban and a rural existence. While we waited, I thought of a woman in bed, still warm with sleep.

In Alexandria we stopped for tea and rum, which the captain let Chas pay for out of the small change the sergeant-major had returned to him. There were German posters on the café walls, and the little girl who served us stared at us suspiciously through tired eyes. When we were ready to leave, the captain put on his hat and told her and the few men around at that time of the morning that we were his prisoners. They all came out to see us off, giving us just the kind of publicity we wished to avoid.

Then on to Bucharest, stopping only to buy some Plugar cigarettes, the strong, cheap kind that the peasants and King Michael smoked. Once again a group gathered round our car, as if our fame had gone on ahead of us. We passed several patrols which did not stop us, and I realised how easily we could have travelled with Ştefan at the wheel and a member of the Judiciary Police in uniform beside him. In Bucharest we avoided the Boulevard Brătianu, Calea Victoriei and all the familiar streets, skidding several times on the winter mud of the side streets before stopping at the gates of the gendarmerie headquarters at 51 Şoseaua Ştefan cel Mare, without having seen much of the city. During the whole journey I had noticed only two Germans in uniform.

Chapter 14

Antonescu Protects Autonomous

We drove into gendarmerie headquarters, passed the main entrance and stopped unexpectedly at a side door. There was a casual, off-duty air about the place which was deceptive; as I climbed out of the car, glancing up at the walls, the heavy gate and the faces of the guard at attention by the door, I could see no point of escape.

The captain returned the guard's salute absentmindedly, as befitted an officer carrying heavy responsibilities. I was glad when we were turned left off the stone-flagged corridor into a waiting room, while he walked straight on and out of our lives. The sergeant-major smiled and nodded before following him, just as keen no doubt to arrange transport back home for Christmas.

We passed the morning on a bench, crossing and recrossing our legs, staring at the yellow, distempered walls, at tiles washed cold until the dirt had become part of their design. The aroma of spices sweetened the smell of coarse uniforms. Romanian newspapers which a courier had carried every week to Cairo were lying on the table but when I touched one the guard shifted and said 'Nu'.

A captain entered and we stood up, hoping for action or at least companionship. But the smile on his face was merely a permanent fold of flesh. When de Chastelain asked to see the general urgently, he looked at him with expressionless eyes and did not reply. He told the guard that the prisoners were to speak only Romanian and left.

Later, a thin-faced, sharp-nosed captain with inquisitive eyes took us to the colonel. Colonel Teodorescu, a large man, was in charge of gendarmerie security. He sent out for cigarettes, chatted about our adventures, and discounted the idea that we had come in to contact the Romanian Government – sabotage more likely, he said. We couldn't have arrived at a worse moment. This he thought funny, for quite a number of good holiday plans, including his own, had been upset. He had nowhere suitable to house us, but since the cadets had left for Christmas, we could use their infirmary.

The captains who had come to the waiting room were called Ionescu and Ungur. Whenever the colonel was called away a Captain Duţa or a Captain

Dobrojan came in to talk to us. By the end of the morning, when Dobrojan escorted us two floors up to the Sala de Bolnavi, the sick room, we had met most of the gendarmerie's security section.

We were to spend Christmas and the New Year in the sick room, with its three beds, kitchen table and large cupboard. Judging by the noise of the traffic, the window overlooked Ştefan cel Mare, a broad street named after a fifteenth-century ruler of Moldavia, who subdued a Polish king, entered Wallachia to defeat the Ottoman armies and had been patron of some of Moldavia's most beautiful architecture.

We were given bean soup, white cheese and black bread; when I heard someone say that it was quite good enough for English spies, the seriousness of our position struck me for the first time. Our shoelaces had been removed, and a notice pinned up instructing the guard to observe us at all time and to stop us approaching the unbarred window in case we tried to jump out. This unexpected preoccupation with suicide shocked me. In Plosca I had handed over my red cyanide pill to the kindly sergeant-major without any sense of loss.

Eight soldiers had been detailed to guard us. Two were on duty day and night at the door. To the right, beyond a small lobby giving on to the staircase, there was the guard room, normally the pharmacy. To the left were the bathroom and w.c. Standing orders did not apparently forbid the use of the razor I had in my pocket, and we all felt fresher after a cold shave. A few days later we found the right stop-cock and had hot water.

Since the guard had been ordered to prevent us speaking any language but Romanian we decided what not to disclose at the interrogation by using a kind of anglicised Romanian which sounded like the language but could not have meant much to our guards. We slept for an hour, and just before three o'clock we were wakened and handed our shoelaces. My head felt as though it had been stuffed with cotton wool and my mouth was bitter with lack of sleep. More than anything, I wanted a cup of tea. We were first taken to the colonel, who was as friendly as ever and told us we would probably have a hard time of it for a few days. Chas was called in first; at about 4.30 it was my turn.

The interrogation room was smaller than I had expected; I had to edge my way round a trestle table on which were laid out pens, ink-wells and squared paper. There was no sign of the electric lamp which figured in every Hollywood interrogation scene. In fact the window was behind me, with the tram cars noisy and reassuring at my back.

I was glad to see Teodorescu there. Two duty officers muttered and fiddled with their papers, but when the general, accompanied by a civilian, came in we all stood up. They took their chairs and the general asked me if I preferred to speak French rather than Romanian.

General Tobescu, the head of the gendarmerie, was in his fifties. He was heavily bemedalled and stout, with a benevolent face and a weakish chin; his overall roundness was offset by a long nose, long fingers and a sky-blue stripe down his trousers. The civilian on his right must, I felt sure, be Eugen Cristescu, head of the Romanian secret and counter-espionage services. He was the fattest man I had ever seen, pale with his large eyelids drooping over a heavy face. His voice had the roughness of too much drink. His enormous presence gave him an otherworld – though somewhat flabby – unscrupulous charm. He would, I thought, make the perfect criminal mastermind in an Edgar Wallace film. Cristescu probably had more dirt on members of the present and past régimes than anyone living. We prisoners were to nickname him Willy, and it was he who usually interrogated us on behalf of the Romanians.

First, the general took me step by step through the landing, up to the time of our arrest. As agreed with Chas and Silviu, I was frank about this and am sure that we corroborated each other. It was when the general moved on to the purpose of our mission that Cristescu began to intervene. When I explained that we had come in to persuade the Romanian Government to break with the Axis, he said it was far more likely that we were here to contact the opposition. I assured him that Cairo had lost faith in Maniu's so-called *coup*; only the Marshal, with the army behind him, could hope to reorientate Romanian policy. Though what I said was partly true Cristescu was not convinced.

He tried several familiar techniques. Since we had landed in civilian clothes we should be treated as spies. I had told him far less than de Chastelain, though I must be almost as well informed. He hoped to treat me in a civilised way and not to have to turn me over to the Gestapo. I had been warned of such interrogation tactics so they did not upset me as much as he probably expected, and when he asked me who were my Ploeşti friends I knew he was completely off beam. Chas had been in oil, so he had jumped to the conclusion that we had been sent in to sabotage the oil installations. The US Air Force, I pointed out, had already done this. He replied that he had a higher regard for the British secret service than I seemed to think; they knew as well as he did that the American raid had been a complete fiasco and the damage minimal. (Unfortunately, he was right). No, he said, he was convinced that we had been sent in to do from the ground what the Americans had failed to do from the air. Hadn't I attended a sabotage course? Yes, I replied, such courses were routine – anyone going into the field learnt sabotage techniques, parachuting and something about wireless telegraphy. Nevertheless, we had not been sent in to sabotage oil. This time I was speaking the whole truth, and it is extraordinary how much assurance telling the truth can give one. I refused to show him how to use the cyphers, and he said that next time we met he would force me to talk. That cliché was his parting shot, and since he had chain-smoked throughout the interrogation perhaps he was not such a formidable adversary as I had at first thought.

I was then taken to a small room where I remained, cold and hungry, until well after midnight. Captain Dobrojan dropped in for twenty minutes and talked about people he knew in Ploeşti, trying, presumably, to extract from me what I had not told Cristescu. Since I knew no Romanians in Ploeşti he did not get far. But for some weeks I wrongly suspected him of being, like Cristescu, a German agent.

At about one o'clock in the morning, I was finally taken back upstairs and, in spite of my sixty-five sleepless hours, Chas's news kept me awake a little longer. His first interview had been similar to mine. But while I was being prodded by Dobrojan he had been called in a second time and had met General Piki Vasiliu, the Under-Secretary of State at the Ministry of the Interior with overall responsibility for the gendarmerie and a good friend of the Marshal. To him Chas had admitted that our mission had been to Maniu and had gone badly wrong.

At first I was furious. We had agreed to protect Maniu and in that respect I thought I had done quite well. Later I saw Chas's point. Although our cover story had helped us keep out of German hands in Plosca, it was unlikely to stand up to serious interrogation in Bucharest. Better, therefore, to abandon it voluntarily in the hope of winning the Marshal's goodwill.

Antonescu had sent word to Chas that although we had come in as his enemies, he would protect us from the Germans. The Germans must be given no legal pretext for taking charge of us and to this end Professor Mihai Antonescu – the Premier and Foreign Minister, who had a knowledge of international law – would help us draft our statements. On no account must we admit to being sent in to sabotage oil because, oil being a strategic commodity, the Germans would then have a valid reason for taking us over. Vasiliu and Cristescu, Chas told me, had added that they were sorry we had been arrested; any good we might have done would now be greatly diminished. I had not met Vasiliu, but if Cristescu had said this, I felt sure, from what I had seen of him, that it must have been with his large tongue lodged firmly in that enormous cheek. When I dropped off to sleep, I was still annoyed with Chas but excited by the new possibilities the Marshal's attitude had opened up. Here was one of Hitler's closest allies – a quisling – arresting three British parachutists; but then offering them his protection, and having his Foreign Minister brief them for their interrogation by the Germans. How many people at home – taught to see the war in only the most general and unequivocal terms – could believe such a thing possible?

Next day, Christmas Eve, we spent writing our declarations and these were to be changed twice before Mihai Antonescu – who was nicknamed Ica by Romanians – finally approved them. In their final form they stated that we had come in to prepare an up-to-date report on the economic situation, with particular reference to crops and oil, to ascertain the likelihood of Romania remaining in the war and to obtain an overall picture of the political situation. We planned to stay in the country for three or four weeks and then to cross the Danube into Tito's territory. Our declarations were not, of course, identical. In mine, I said that our report would be used partly as material for propaganda back to Romania, partly for training civil affairs officers. Though I did not know it, the British were, in fact, training civil affairs officers for Greece and Yugoslavia, though not Romania. So, hopefully, I might have misled the Germans about our plans for Romania.

On Christmas Day we were given extra food but saw no one. On Boxing Day we again saw no one, but next day we saw Teodorescu. On the 28th de Chastelain saw Tobescu, Vasiliu and Cristescu, after which we added to our declarations, though I do not now remember what.

On New Year's Eve we were given our first exercise in the courtyard and that evening a special supper was sent up at midnight. Next day, New Year's Day, Vasiliu sent us a bottle of champagne and a delicious cake baked by the wife of one of the colonels. In the evening Chas saw the three of them again and handed them notes on our cover story.

One evening two little girls who had seen us in the yard came upstairs. The older one told us proudly that, since their parents were giving a party, they had been able to slip out without anyone noticing. The guards were their friends and had let them in. We cut them some of the cake and while they were eating it the conversation between the elder one and Chas went something like this:

'*Ce faceţi aici?*' – 'What are you doing here?'
'*Stăm*' – 'Hanging around.'
'*Dece staţi?*' – 'Why?'
'*Suntem prizonieri*' – 'We're prisoners.'
'*O, ce păcat*' – 'Oh, what a pity.'

And, their curiosity satisfied, they ran downstairs.

That little scene is now far more vivid to me than any part of the official interrogations which were to continue, off and on, for the next four months.

Chapter 15

German Interrogation

On the top floor, meanwhile, a permanent prison was made ready for us. It had been a general's flat and was far less cramped than the sick room. There was a lobby for the guards, a large room in which we ate, received visitors and played cards, an interrogation room which had a telephone and was kept locked, a bedroom for Chas, and a larger bedroom for Silviu and me, off which was the bathroom. Hot water, though rationed, was usually enough for ourselves and our laundry, and a sheet served as an ineffectual bath-towel.

We moved in on Tuesday, 4 January. Our greatest immediate luxury was to have windows fitted with bars, so that we could stand for hours on end looking down into the street. On one corner was a milk shop and opposite a newspaper and cigarette kiosk. The centre of activity was the tram stop. Tram Number 26 headed towards Piaţa Victoriei and the University, while Number 9 turned right to the fashionable suburb of Floreasca. Women with heavy shopping baskets let themselves down from the platform and hurried across the street, never looking to see whether traffic was coming in the other direction. 'In the winter,' I noted in my diary, 'people stamp their feet at the tram stop and hunch their shoulders and keep to themselves. In the spring, they are cheerful, walk lightly, become more communicative. We see only a few Germans in uniform, usually taking tram Number 9.'

Our food came from Cioc, a nearby restaurant, and was paid for out of the currency we had brought with us. We had no meatless days. The markets were full of unrationed food. We were each allowed a bottle of wine a day with ţuica or şpriţ (white wine with soda) as an apéritif, and fruit and white cheese on squares of bread. Wartime Romanians had far better food than most of their neighbours. 'The peasant,' I noted, 'can live. Civil servants have a harder time.'

On 11 January, Captain Ungur came up with some of our personal things – socks, handkerchiefs, playing cards and my dice. The general had refused to return my Romanian dictionary or to allow me an exercise book. Ungur was friendly. He rolled the dice on the table, smiling when three kings and two tens came up. He smoked from a long cigarette holder which he held between two fingers, tapping it gently over the ash tray when there was no more ash to fall, finally ejecting the stub with a little push device and putting the holder back into his breast pocket.

Next Monday I noted that 'I have my dictionary now and work on Romanian much of the day. Do a daily translation for Chas to correct.' Cristescu's people had examined my dictionary for marks; as they suspected, it held the key to my personal cypher – but no marks.

Cristescu and the gendarmerie officers lent us a mixed bag of books in English, Romanian, French and German, including Jean Stratton Porter, Upton Sinclair, John Ruskin, P.G. Wodehouse and Bernard Shaw. We also had Romanian newspapers.

Physically, we passed through several stages. To begin with, in the sick room we simply slept. There followed a period in which we needed all the exercise we could get, and would walk our duty officers off their feet in the freezing courtyard, discussing the international situation and breathing in great lungfuls of strong January air. After moving into the flat we felt less constricted, and during the political activity of March and April we sometimes declined any exercise at all. Our routine was described in my diary a few weeks later:

> Besides reading, we have passed our time in various ways. Only Silviu has never found anything definite to do. He usually sits in Chas' room reading the papers or looking out of the window or talking.
>
> Chas took to needlework and produced three parachute badges which we are wearing. Since then, he has been improving his Rumanian and now has a notebook of very choice words, with some Turkish. I began to do something about my Rumanian almost as soon as we arrived. I was refused a note book until very recently and wrote my words on the back of Plugar cigarette packets. In this way I collected some three thousand and have now transcribed them into my exercise book. I thought it would be too much to ask for a Russian grammar though this language interests me most and now would have been a good opportunity to improve it. I have also amused myself writing bits of verse and keeping this diary. This has been done on the greased inside papers of my Regale cigarettes. They pack easily and burn quickly though, in fact, there is nothing here that needs to be burned.
>
> And so our day goes something like this. We get up later now and have our herb tea and roll. Chas and I put our second roll on the radiator to get crisp for lunch. Then we shave if there is hot water. About once every five days either the boiler or the piping breaks down and we are sometimes without any water for several hours. Not

much of a hardship in the circumstances. While we are in the bathroom the boys clean our rooms and make the beds. I then read German until after noon, learning words or grammar and thus the time passes until the gong sounds at 12.30 in the nursing home opposite where Marion de Chastelain had their first child. Sometime between 12.30 and one o'clock we begin to play bridge and continue until lunch arrives at two o'clock. The best part of lunch is the *ţuica* and cheese we have before it. After lunch, we finish our rubber and then I read the papers or write some verse while Silviu sleeps. And later in the afternoon, usually read some Rumanian or write this diary until seven o'clock and at seven we play bridge or talk to the officer on duty who very often comes up. So usually late to bed, I reading and Silviu talking to Chas until the early hours and then coming into our room and usually waking me.

And every Sunday morning there came along Ştefan cel Mare the same old man who had played his barrel organ under Madame Arditti's flat.

There were occasional red-letter days. Once, we saw some Russian prisoners moving logs in the nursing home garden, wearing *căciule* (fur hats) and short jackets with K.G. – *Kriegs Gefangene* – on their backs, guarded by two German soldiers with old-fashioned carbines. On 25 February, there was a slight earthquake, a mere echo of the 1940 disaster.

Next day Silviu went downstairs to see his family for the first time since 1917. He was not allowed to talk to his brother, only to shake hands. Afterwards, his sister returned to her home near the new Hungarian frontier but his mother stayed on in Bucharest in the hope of seeing him again. Next day, she sent us a parcel of ham, bacon, sausages, cakes and jam which for a few weeks made our breakfasts far more appetising.

For a German satellite press, Romanian newspapers were surprisingly informative. The outcome of the war was widely discussed. Large chunks of British official and press comment were quoted verbatim.

The New Year press was pessimistic. Allied handling of the Polish problem, said Şeicaru, the influential proprietor of *Curentul*, should dispel any illusions Romanians might have about the help they could expect from Great Britain and America. 'Will Europe in 1944,' he asked, ' preserve its noble traditions or will it be Russified?' When I remarked to Chas and Silviu that if Europe were Nazified it would hardly be better off, I had missed the point. Şeicaru like most Romanians had already discounted a German victory. If part of Europe came under Soviet influence 'even Britain,' he wrote, 'would become subordinated to a Russian and American-dominated Europe.'

According to the papers of 20 January, *Pravda* had accused Britain of trying to negotoiate a separate peace; two English politicians were alleged to have met Ribbentrop. My diary noted that the Russians had not published the British denial in full. I did not know that Churchill, haunted by fear that the *Pravda* article might herald another attempt at a separate peace, had sent Sir Archibald Clark-Kerr, our Ambassador, posthaste back to Moscow and had written to Stalin urging him to do business through the proper channels rather than the press, adding, 'I try night and day to make things go the way you wish and the way our triple interests require.'[1]

Clark-Kerr concluded that the *Pravda* article was a direct consequence of the publicity surrounding Autonomous. In effect we had invented three cover stories in ten days. The first – that we carried messages to the Romanian Government – had been in line with our fallback plan agreed before we left. Its purpose had been to keep us out of German hands until we could contact someone close to the Romanian Government. The second – Chas's admission that we had come in to contact the opposition – did not disclose our brief to Maniu or the names of any of the people involved except Maniu himself. The third – that we had come in on a short fact-finding mission – was worked out with the Romanians and during the German interrogation, we had to be careful not to confuse it with the other two.

The first of these stories was to cause trouble both for the British and Romanian governments. On 18 January 1944, the Turkish press started a rumour that we had brought in for Antonescu a copy of peace terms proposed by Germany to Russia at Romania's expense. The Romanians were embarrassed. The Russians suspected complicity between the British and Romanians. On 21 January the British Communist Party newspaper, the *Daily Worker*, accused us of negotiating with the 'quisling Antonescu' in order to 'upset the decisions of the Teheran Conference' – a line which was most probably inspired by Moscow. Chas was described as 'a gentleman holding a high post in a British Government office in Cairo', whereas either Silviu or I was 'a man who was at one time understood to be a large financial backer of the pro-Nazi Iron Guard'. Though a full account of our mission was given to the NKVD at the end of January[2] the Russians still suspected London of trickery. Incidentally, when my father was told by the War Office that I was a POW, he wrote to Denis Wright in Trebizond. Denis saw no reason why he should not know what had already been published in the Turkish newspapers and told him where we were.

The German interrogations began on 10 January, continuing through January and February and thereafter intermittently for several months. Captain Petermann, number two in the Bucharest branch of Germany's Military Intelligence, took the chair. He was the caricature of a regular German officer – tall, rigid, correct, even wearing a monocle. On 17 April he was joined by a smooth, quick-witted Austrian Gestapo man from Berlin whose name I do not remember.

Opening the first session Cristescu said that, though completely independent of Germany, Romania felt duty-bound to invite a German army representative to take part in the interrogation. Perhaps de Chastelain would first confirm that the rumours circulating about him were without foundation – that on landing we had not gone voluntarily to the gendarmerie, had not brought diplomatic papers for the Marshal and had not dined at the Military Club in Bucharest. As previously agreed with Tobescu, de Chastelain, in the words of a later German report, 'gave us to understand by his replies and his gestures that these rumours are completely erroneous'.[3]

We repeated to Petermann the details of our landing and capture, giving as the object of our mission the version agreed with the Romanians. The Gestapo man, when he arrived, could not believe that our escape route into Yugoslavia had not been worked out in detail. Their people, he said, were always given precise escape routes – 'it is only fair to an agent.' When, off the cuff, I replied that SOE relied far more than German intelligence on an officer's initiative, he was clearly not convinced.

The Germans were particularly interested in the intelligence set-up in Cairo and Istanbul and without Cristescu's list of the twenty-one questions they proposed to put to us, Chas and I could have been in difficulties. I could not claim to know much less than Chas. Silviu, who had not worked at headquarters, was in a stronger position. When asked whether we had proposed 'to contact any political group inside Romania and, if so, which', we said we had had specific instructions not to do so. When asked whom he knew in Romania, Chas gave the names of eight people of no importance. He gave away none of our contacts, and we denied any knowledge of W/T communication with Romania. The Germans knew that we were holding a lot back but, thanks to Romanian protection, never had an opportunity to work on us.

On 31 December 1943 the German Intelligence Service in Bucharest had given Berlin an accurate summary of our background including the fact that I had taught at Bucharest University. (The Foreign Office, in their reports on Autonomous, always described me as an oil man.) The Germans assumed that de Chastelain 'wished to re-establish his personal relationships with various Anglophile elements – the Romanian General Staff and Maniu, the most popular exponent of English-Romanian cooperation'. By these means he would aim to create in Romania a situation similar to that which existed between Badoglio and the Allies in Italy.[4]

On 6 January 1944 von Killinger reported a conversation he had had with Cristescu the day before. To the question why he had been removed and sent into the field after being chief of the Intelligence Service in Istanbul, and then head of the politico-military section for Romania at GHQ Cairo, de Chastelain, he said, had been evasive.[5]

Although there were certainly jealousies in Cairo, it was not intrigue that had forced de Chastelain into the field. He himself had planned and organised the Autonomous operation and had been desperately keen to lead it. He had, of course, never been in the SIS, let alone its head in Istanbul, and if the Romanians and Germans did not realise this he would not enlighten them. The telegram contained other inaccuracies, claiming that we had been interrogated at the British Legation, that I was a rocket technician, and that when we asked the peasant the way to Bucharest (*sic*) we had all been in uniform. Apparently Cristescu had not mentioned that we had arrived in civilian clothes, though at my first interrogation he had made a point of it.

In a long report, dated 20 January, the Head of the Bucharest Abwehr gave a detailed, accurate account of our arrival, based on the first four German interrogations of 10, 11, 13 and 18 January. Before the interrogation, he says, Captain Petermann was asked to behave 'in a friendly and comradely way' towards us (and, given his austere character, I think he did his best).

Among the report's conclusions were:

(a)   The fact that interrogation by a German began only two and a half weeks after our arrest, though admittedly it was the holiday period, shows that the Romanians wanted to hold on to us.

(b)   de Chastelain, personally, probably did not intend to organise sabotage, particularly of the oil fields.

(c)   Maniu had been too frightened to show himself in connection with our arrival.

(d)   The bureau admitted that its initial appreciation of this affair was not borne out by the present factual examination and should, therefore, be ignored.[6]

The 'initial appreciation' mentioned in (d) could well have concerned oil sabotage, from which Chas now seemed to have been completely exonerated. On 3 February, a brief telegram from the bureau partially corrected (c), reporting that Maniu had asked both Cristescu and the gendarmerie for permission to see de Chastelain and had been refused.[7]

On 30 December Maniu had, in fact, seen Mihai Antonescu for three hours and, according to Ica's private secretary, the Minister had emerged 'in high spirits'.[8] Maniu, of course, had assumed full responsibility for our arrival.

Chapter 16

Antonescu Says 'No' to the Gestapo

At the end of January Cretzianu handed the SOE representative in Istanbul an encyphered message in de Chastelain's handwriting. De Chastelain reported that we had not been dropped in accordance with instructions and, consequently, had been arrested within twelve hours. We were endeavouring to carry out our mission but required some indication of Romania's future without which it would be impossible to achieve any results.[1] I do not remember this message. It did not contain the conventional sign indicating that Chas was a free agent and for security reasons could not in any case have been answered. Yet it sounds authentic.

After the collapse of our mission to Maniu we had decided to work on Antonescu instead. We were in a privileged position since anything we told Vasiliu or Tobescu would be reported directly to the Marshal. We also felt fairly sure that so long as he saw in us a potential link with London Antonescu would keep us on ice and, if Maniu's assessment of him was right, could well eventually break with the Axis.

It was true, then, that we were still 'endeavouring to carry out our mission' which in its broadest terms was to bring Romania into the war on the side of the Three Powers by any means available to us. At every opportunity we urged Vasiliu and Tobescu to accept the reality of Romania's position: to see that no separate arrangement with the Western Allies was possible; that Romania's only way out was to abandon Germany, who did not deserve her loyalty, and to surrender unconditionally to the Russians; and that the sooner she contributed to the Allied war effort in this way, the better would be her prospects at the eventual peace settlement. They replied that Romanians would collaborate with Western troops – had been ready to do so since the war began – but could not be expected to put their country at the sole mercy of the Russians; if that was the only alternative to fighting the Red Army, the Marshal would fight on.

It was also true that we required 'some indication of Romania's future' in order to decide how far we could go with the Romanians. One reason for our failure to convince them that there was no point in their delaying a *coup* in the expectation of an Allied landing was the fact that we ourselves were not one hundred per cent sure that such a landing would never take place. Romanian wishful thinking continued to feed on the belief that, in spite of what we said, if they waited Allied support would eventually materialise, and that then they could work their passage home to the post-war independence promised in the Atlantic Charter and hinted at from time to time in Churchill's statements.

Meanwhile, we were gathering information; officers of all ranks confided in us with a clear conscience, knowing that we had virtually no chance of escape.

The guards were on duty three hours on, six hours off; Silviu lent them his watch. Two NCOs did twenty-four hours' duty alternately. Both soldiers and NCOs were, without exception, friendly and anti-German almost to a man. Nor did they all view the Russians with the antagonism common to officers. But they were changed every week – far too often for us to come to a working arrangement with any of them.

No one was allowed into our flat unless his voice was recognised by the soldiers on duty. When there was a crash of iron-shod heels, we knew that our visitor was an officer and, from the violence of the salute, whether a captain, the colonel or the general himself.

We had five duty officers, and one of them visited us once or twice every day. Most were friendly, a few suspicious and, during the Allied bombing of Bucharest, distinctly cool. No one was ever offensive. Two of the most sympathetic – one of whom was later on the point of passing messages to our friends in Bucharest – were sent to the front. Several were highly intelligent. Duţa, for instance, had in peacetime been assistant to the professor of law at Bucharest University and later *chef de cabinet* to Armand Călinescu, the Prime Minister who had been assassinated by the Iron Guard in 1939. Soon we were sitting on a mine of first-rate intelligence with no way of exploiting it. I did, in fact, encode data about Allied bombing and German positions on Red Cross post cards sent to friends in Cairo and Istanbul, but I managed my camouflage too well and no one thought of having the post cards tested for my personal code.

The newspapers reflected wartime Romanian society and carried much weighty editorial exhortation. According to *Universul* of 3 April a boy apprentice in a Ploeşti bakery had been condemned to five years' hard labour for trying to steal ten kilograms of barley during the blackout. That same day the editor of *Ecoul* berated two women overheard at the hairdressers. They had badgered the assistants because their masseuse was waiting for them at home, and complained about the shortages and hardships they had to endure; that afternoon, however, they had each bought twenty pairs of silk stockings, and could now face the future with greater courage.

A taxi driver told another newspaper about a newly-wed couple he had picked up at the Gara de Nord who had had nothing in their luggage but sugar. Her parents owned a grocery in Moldavia, and had decided to stay on in spite of the threat of Russian occupation. They had asked the newly-weds to take anything they wanted and they had chosen to bring only sugar.

The Jews were probably better treated in Romania than in most other parts of the German orbit. They did not have to wear the yellow arm band. They were not allowed to join the armed forces but Annie and Bobsie Samuelli, for instance, helped out in hospitals, folding blankets and doing similar jobs. As the raids grew worse, Jewish women in Bucharest took refuge in the country like everyone else. But in Bessarabia, Bukovina and Transnistria – the name given to territory beyond Bessarabia in Russia proper which, in spite of Maniu's warning, Romanians were now administering – the situation seems to have been very different. Jews were literally worked to death in Transnistrian labour camps, and the further they were from Bucharest the more Romanian officials vied with their Nazi counterparts in the maltreatment of the Jewish population.

A German occupation would, of course, have made the situation for Jews far worse in Romania itself. As it was, Queen Helen proved a good friend and Jews prayed for Antonescu, whom they saw as their protector. According to an unemotional, statistical assessment of the *Numerical Situation of the Jews in Romania* published in 1946, Dr Filderman, who had been their leader during the war and had himself spent some months in a labour camp, concluded that 'no other country that has at any time been under Nazi domination can show so large a proportion of survivors as does Romania.'

As for the gypsies, they were exported *en masse* to Transnistria. A friend who came across some of them in Romanian prisons told me that the persistence they showed when selling their flowers on the street stood them in good stead under duress. Unlike more intellectual prisoners, they were never provoked into any kind of discussion. They flatly and repeatedly denied whatever they were accused of without elaboration, and the police usually got nowhere with them.

Marshal Zhukov took command of the 1st Ukrainian Front on 1 March, and his major spring offensive began on the 4th. During the next two months the Red Army were to advance over 150 miles from east of the Bug to west of the Dniester. On the 21st they were across the Dniester and by the 26th had reached the Prut. In six weeks the Russians had recovered Transnistria. On 11 March I noted that the great German base at Uman had fallen; the way to Odessa was now open and German and Romanian troops in the Crimea in danger of being cut off.

Tobescu told us that the retreating Germans took with them 40,000 horses, 40,000 cattle and 30,000 sheep. In addition they withdrew 138,000 German minorities from Crimea and the Ukraine, all of whom were moving across the countryside. Since they could become a typhus hazard, every effort was being made to keep them away from towns and villages.

On 3 April I noted that

> Refugees are suffering greatly. Uncontrolled elements in the Soviet army are pillaging etc and most of the 'intellectuals' and some peasants are fleeing before them. But there is little organisation. Officials of one town evacuated fifty miles and when they discovered that the Russians were not, after all, going to occupy it, had to return.
>
> Ex-service men from the last war have offered to help in any way they can. The government has set up oxen stations on the route to help peasants up steep hills and over bad parts of road . . . The last few days have been hard for refugees: wet and snow yesterday and last night very cold.[2]

According to Vasiliu, Germans had looted the town of Cernăuţi, capital of Bukovina. Many had brought Russian women to Romania; they were no longer obeying their officers and were 'fit for nothing'. De Chastelain later informed SOE headquarters that 'the German High Command had to erect large road signs in German throughout Bessarabia and Moldavia reminding German soldiers that "The German soldier does not steal and if he does, he is shot."'[3]

Hitler had guaranteed Romania's frontiers – a promise that most Romanians no longer expected him to keep. Romanian casualties had already reached some 300,000 and Antonescu's obstinate loyalty to the Reich was becoming less and less popular. Several of our officers expected a change of policy during the Soviet spring offensive; they said that a *coup* by either Antonescu or Maniu would have overwhelming popular support. Tobescu even thought that, if we had not been caught, and had been able to work with Maniu, Romania could well have withdrawn from the war in April.

Although, as in the First World War, one could find pro-German Romanians among the middle and upper classes – Professor George Brătianu, for instance – relations between Germans and the civilian population as a whole had been cool since the beginning of the war. Women got up and left if a German in uniform sat down beside them in the cinema. German newsreels were often booed. Dragomir Niculescu's grocery shop on Calea Victoriei was like an informal club where men would meet at lunch time to discuss current affairs. A woman could join them if she did not mind being thought 'fast'. If a German entered the shop the conversation immediately dried up. Except at the very top, this attitude seemed to be true of the army as well. We saw an order informing gendarme officers that attendance at the third anniversary celebration of the declaration of war on Russia was obligatory; no excuse of any kind would be accepted. The ceremony was, in fact, a complete wash-out, since almost the entire Romanian section of the audience was there under orders.

On Tuesday 11 March I noted in my diary that we had had an eventful week. Spring had suddenly burst upon us. The heating was being gradually turned down. Just one week before, the corporal who came to collect our empty wine bottles had been stopped and the bottles examined. Returning with our meal from Cioc's restaurant, he had taken it into the guard room, where Duţa had checked it. The incident worried us at the time, but I now know that it was the result of a telegram from Berlin to the German Legation reporting 'as yet unconfirmed information' that an attempt would be made to rescue us.[4]

After the food incident our guards were as friendly as ever. When we received a parcel of coffee from Cairo they gave us a heater on which to boil water. Later Tobescu sent us a wireless. We reconnected the short-wave coil after which we had BBC news in English to pass on to our duty officers. I wrote a couple of stanzas about the jump:

> After the ride in the Wimpy's womb,
> Your despatcher feeding you rum,
> Senses walled in by the noise and vibration,
> Oxygen-starved and numb,
>
> Came the jump and the line was snapped
> And you hung in the night without plane or crew,
> The enemy ground swinging up,
> The briefing deep-frozen within you.

Otherwise, the routine continued as before – the inactivity, the deteriorating food, the herb tea (which I have never liked), the cards and the dice games, our fading hope of achieving something with the Romanian Government, the bugs (I killed forty-six in one night). And behind it all was the fear that in spite of Antonescu's assurance we would become part of the general withdrawal to Germany.

On 1 April, I wrote some of Silviu's vivid expressions in my diary – 'red-haired people are usually very highly sprung' – and then, 'Jerry has again made strong representations, this time for Chas alone.' According to Marion de Chastelain who was handling sensitive intelligence papers at the time, when the Prime Minister was told of the kind of material de Chastelain had had access to before his arrest, he sent a message to Antonescu holding him personally responsible for our safety. It is unlikely that this had already reached the Marshal by 23 December when he told us that we would not be handed over to the Germans.

As soon as they reported our arrival the German Legation had a telegram from Gestapo headquarters asking whether at least de Chastelain could be sent to Germany for a short time. 'De Chastelain offers us a unique possibility of clarifying questions of particular importance.'[5] On 24 January, von Killinger, transmitting a *procès verbal* of the interrogation to date, commented

> there is clearly no intention on the part of the Romanians to interrogate or treat de Chastelain or his companions roughly and this is yet another example, to which your attention has been drawn repeatedly, of their bland attitude towards the Americans and British. I have now made an official request for the transfer of de Chastelain to Germany although I do not believe – even if we bring up the big guns – that we will force them to allow de Chastelain to be interrogated in Germany.[6]

By 'big guns' von Killinger was presumably referring to Hitler who, we learned later, had intervened personally. In April German Security sent a representative to take part in our interrogation but were still not satisfied with the arrangement; they continued to press for de Chastelain to be sent to Germany and there were signs of friction between themselves and the Foreign Ministry over this.

On 28 April Killinger reported that the Marshal had once more refused, saying that he considered de Chastelain, a British colonel, to be a prisoner of war.[7] At the end of May, SOE reminded the Foreign Office that 'we have for some time past been extremely concerned about the safety of Colonel de Chastelain and his party in the event of a *coup d'état* taking place. Our fears are on security grounds as well as personal ones and from every point of view we are most anxious that these men should not fall into German hands.'[8] Early in June, Mihai Antonescu assured SOE that de Chastelain was safe.[9] On 15 June, we hear the last of this question; von Killinger has again approached the Marshal only to be told that his decision was final.[10] Apart from other considerations, Antonescu would have been seriously embarrassed if we had been forced to admit to the Germans that he had conspired with us to deceive them.

PART FOUR

March 1944—June 1944

Chapter 17

Negotiating for an Armistice

During January and February 1944, while we prisoners were being interrogated in Bucharest, London, unknown to us, was hard at work arranging a meeting between Maniu's emissary and representatives of the three Allied Powers. Overlord and a concurrent Russian offensive were timed for May, and a Romanian break with the Axis shortly beforehand would be a major set-back for the Reich.

Maniu had to find someone he could trust who had a legitimate reason for travelling abroad. He chose a close friend, Constantin Vişoianu, in whom the King also had full confidence. Vişoianu was a senior diplomat and a protégé of Titulescu but Mihai Antonescu who would have to issue his diplomatic passport considered him to be too left wing. According to Pogoneanu, who was working for the King and Maniu inside the Foreign Ministry, it was the Marshal himself who proposed Prince Ştirbey as an alternative. Ştirbey had business interests in Turkey and had negotiated with the Allies on behalf of King Ferdinand and Ionel Brătianu during the First World War. Vişoianu, it was agreed, could join him a few weeks later.

Ştirbey's instructions were to obtain military help against the Germans and the best possible terms regarding Romania's territorial settlement and independence, looking to the Western Allies for possible support against traditional Russian and Communist expansion in that part of the world.[1]

Alexander Cretzianu invited Prince Ştirbey and his daughter to stay at the Legation in Ankara, from where Ştirbey would be taken secretly to his rendezvous with the representatives of the Allied Powers. At first this was to be London, but Ştirbey had so many friends in England – including his son-in-law Colonel Eddie Boxshall, a senior member of SOE – that towards the end of February the meeting place was changed to Cairo. The Russians, it was feared, might otherwise suspect Anglo-Romanian collusion.

Colonel Ted Masterson met Cretzianu in Ankara and reminded him that the Prince must bring with him a declaration of unconditional surrender. Cretzianu retorted that Maniu and Brătianu would never undertake a *coup* with the sole object of surrendering unconditionally to the Russians. The matter was then dropped. Masterson did not refer to an Allied landing in the Balkans because none was planned, but Cretzianu put Masterson's silence down to the fact that he could not discuss military movements with an unauthorised person.[2] In fact Maniu told friends in Braşov to expect a landing 'very soon'. So the two major obstacles to an early armistice – unconditional surrender and Romanian belief in an eventual Anglo-American landing – were not properly addressed before Maniu's envoy met the Allied representatives.

Our first hint in prison that things were on the move came from Cristescu. Ted Masterson, he said, had been seen in Turkey 'looking as if he did not want to be recognised'. Sunday, 27 February, was a mild day and we strolled with Dobrojan in the courtyard for about twenty minutes. He was just back from Odessa. In our room I heard the barrel organ. On a Sunday morning it came by as regular as clockwork, whereas it had always worked its way past Madame Arditti's on a Saturday afternoon.

After lunch, Dobrojan, who was probably bored with his weekend duty, came up for a second talk. Hitler, he said, had invited Antonescu to his eastern headquarters, even sending his personal plane for him. It was high time too, Dobrojan said; Romanian troops in the Crimea were already as good as lost. Antonescu must either take the responsibility of fighting over Romanian territory and making a stand at the Carpathians, or he had better sue for peace.

The next day was Chas's birthday. We slept on until 10 o'clock – a record. We started playing cut-throat bridge earlier than usual and to celebrate opened a new pack, which was so glossy that we could hardly concentrate on the game. For our motto I suggested *paciencia y baraja* – patience and shuffle the cards.

My birthday present to Chas was a reserve of Player's cigarettes, though I have no idea how I had acquired them. Teodorescu came up in the morning with three bottles of a Transnistrian liqueur – filthy-tasting stuff but, as he said, the best to be had except for French liqueurs at impossible prices. In the afternoon Tobescu sat with us for an hour. He said that Antonescu had returned from Germany at 1.30 that afternoon and would see Vasiliu and himself on Friday. He did not mention our own future, though we knew that if Antonescu had decided to fight on we would probably end up in Germany.

Chas was asked to choose our dinner that night so we had *ciorba* (vegetable soup), lamb, cheese and a double portion of *ţuica*. Afterwards Ungur came up and we opened the bottle of champagne Vasiliu had given us for New Year. We talked with him until after two in the morning, mainly about Hungary.

1. Denis Wright, Anne Windham, Ivor Porter. Legation courtyard, 1940.

2. Boulevard Brătianu.

3. Corneliu Zelea Codreanu.

4. A road through the Carpathians.

5. Near Sinaia.

6. Ivor Porter in mountain woods above Timiş.

7. Christine Granville and Chas; and 8. Annie Samuelli and Ivor Porter on her terrace, 1944.

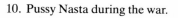

9. Lygia Georgescu before the war.

10. Pussy Nasta during the war.

11. Juliu Maniu.   12. Gardyne de Chastelain.

13. Dinu Brătianu; 14. Constantin Vişoianu; and 15. Prince Barbu Ştirbey.

16. King Michael; 17. Mircea Ionniţiu; 18. Baron Mocsoni-Styrcea. Taken in June 1944 during his last weekend off before the *coup*.

19. Strained relations between the two groups. Antonescu's chief spy in the Royal Military Household is saluting King Michael. The Queen Mother smiles ironically, Madame Antonescu (behind the Marshal) is amused and Mihai Antonescu (second from right) uneasy, while Ionel Styrcea (on right) is trying to spot the photographer, who is one of Cristescu's men.

20. Plevnei prison, morning of 24 August 1944. Rica Georgescu has an Allied agent on his right. Niculae Turcanu is on extreme right of group; 21. Also in Plevnei prison. On Georgescu's right is Alecu Ionescu, on his left Popovici.

22. The Royal Palace on 24 August 1944, after German bombing. Rubble of Casa Noua to right. 23. General Sănătescu.

24. The Georgescu family reunited in New York.

25. A demonstration, 1945, 26. 'Down with Maniu', 'Down with Brătianu'. 27. Anna Pauker with Petru Groza to her left, January 1945.

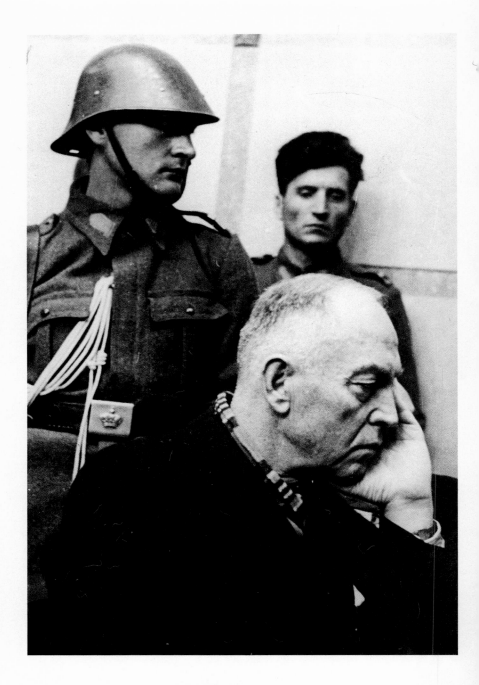

28. Marshal Antonescu at his trial.

Ştirbey was kept in Turkey for twelve days while the British Government made one last attempt to extract the text of an armistice from Moscow. Molotov refused, arguing that Ştirbey should be given no idea of the Allied position until the three Allies had heard his precise proposals.

As might be expected, Ştirbey's mission was leaked in Turkey – a hotbed of intrigue where the British Government had no powers of censorship. Either an American or the *Daily Mail* correspondent broke the story on 14 March. The BBC followed suit, announcing that Ştirbey had left with Antonescu's approval to negotiate Romania's exit from the war. I was unmoved when Tobescu described the leak as an outrageous breach of confidence, for I knew that the British Government would not puposely indulge in such a propaganda escapade. I was far more surprised at Maniu's delay. It was now three months since Chas and I had been taking unnecessary risks in terrible weather to reach him before his emissary left Romania. If we had known we could have waited for the spring.

When Ştirbey finally reached Cairo he was grateful to Ted Masterson for warning him that at the first plenary meeting held on 17 March he, and not the Allied representatives, would be expected to make the running.[3] The Allied delegates were Lord Moyne, Resident Minister in the Middle East, for the UK, Ambassador McVeagh for the USA and Ambassador Novikov for the USSR. Ştirbey, speaking in French, said that while he did not represent Antonescu, the Marshal was aware of his mission – otherwise he could not have obtained a passport. Antonescu was now 'under the pressure of events'. He had Germany's confidence and could prepare a *volte face* more easily than Maniu. A *coup* by Maniu would be premature and unlikely to succeed but if the Three Powers insisted on it he would require military assistance. Romania realised that she was defeated and hoped that her treatment by the Allies would be in accordance with the principles of the Atlantic Charter.

While Maniu could not formally renounce Romania's claim to Bessarabia, Ştirbey made the personal suggestion that were the Russians to hold a plebiscite while in occupation the result would then be 'a foregone conclusion'. Cornered by the Russian Ambassador on the question of 'Allied military cooperation', he said that he had had in mind Soviet landings at the port of Constanţa.[4] What he had really had in mind, of course, were Anglo-American troops at the Danube.

The Foreign Office were pleased with Maniu's 'unexpectedly realistic' proposals. Washington found them unobjectionable. Molotov, however, felt that since Ştirbey did not seem to be representing Maniu, and Maniu appeared to be a tool of Antonescu, there were 'no grounds for attaching importance to Ştirbey's statements'.[5] Possibly the Soviet delegation's inadequate grasp of French, together with Novikov's chronic fear of failing to anticipate his government's thinking, had something to do with Molotov's attitude. In any case, the events of the next few days were to put the Soviet Government into an unexpected U-turn.

On 19 March, while Horthy was at Berchtesgaden, German troops occupied Hungary. Antonescu was summoned to Germany and Romanians feared that, following the Ştirbey leak, their turn had now come. Mihai Antonescu sent a frantic message to Cretzianu in Istanbul who passed it to the SOE representative, asking what Allied help Romania could count on.[6] Since the Marshal was leaving for Germany the following day General Wilson, the Commander-in-Chief, Middle East, consulted neither the US nor Soviet Ambassador – his even-handed way of cutting out the cumbersome Soviet machine. He urged the Marshal on no account to visit Hitler and to order his troops to cease forthwith resisting the Red Army. Antonescu could count on air support.

Within twenty-four hours the C.-in C. had a message from Maniu also asking what military support he could expect from the Allies at the time of a *coup*. To him General Wilson promised that Romania's future was linked to her determination to overthrow the Antonescu régime. Maniu could never square this 'work your passage home' formula with London's insistence on unconditional surrender to the Russians; he told friends that he had trouble 'discovering Britain's intentions for Romania'.[7] Wilson assured Maniu of powerful air attacks on such targets as he indicated and would have added that 'no land assistance can be given from this theatre' so clearing up a vital misunderstanding between Maniu and the Allies, had not the Foreign Office for security reasons rightly removed this sentence from his draft.[8]

When Wilson's telegram to Antonescu reached Bucharest the Marshal had already left for Germany. Yet the general's gesture of independence, which was far more typical of the military than the politicians, and on this occasion annoyed Eden as much as it did Molotov, achieved the break-through with Moscow in days, which diplomacy had failed to achieve in months. Within seventy-two hours Molotov had told our Ambassador that the Soviet Government were now ready to deal with both Antonescu and Maniu. He suggested as a follow-up to Wilson's telegram one proposing that Antonescu should appoint a competent person to liaise between the Soviet and Romanian high commands. This message was transmitted to both Antonescu and Maniu via Reginald and when he received it Antonescu asked for an independent line of communication between himself and Cairo via the Autonomous transmitter held by the gendarmerie. In this way we prisoners were brought into the picture.

At the time we knew nothing of developments in Cairo and the duty officers seemed to be equally ignorant. They came up to see us with their usual snippets of news and much conversation but were clearly feeling the pressure of a deteriorating front. The Russians had bypassed Cernăuţi, and were threatening Iaşi, the ancient capital of Moldavia. They were about 250 miles from Bucharest. Waiting downstairs in the general's outer office one day, we had the impression of 'officers passing through all the time in a desperate hurry. The Adjutant having a hell of a time. The Colonel came in – he has been away for some time and very agitated about the situation.'

Captain Ionescu, the duty officer who had first visited us in that bleak waiting room on the morning of our arrival, paid us one of his rare visits. He had thick, wiry hair, seemed always untidy and was always smiling. Chas and I sat up with him and I noted that he saw the situation through pre-war eyes – 'every argument based on anti-Hungarian or anti-Bulgarian prejudice', as if nothing bigger was happening in the world at all.

On 26 March Vasiliu told de Chastelain that the meeting with Hitler had gone better than expected. The Führer had promised a spring offensive which would make the withdrawal of Romanian troops from the Crimea unnecessary, though I noted later that during the eventual retreat the Germans commandeered all available aircraft and that only 15,000 of the 40,000 Romanians in the Crimea escaped.

Vasiliu did not mention a remark Ribbentrop had made to Mihai Antonescu, to the effect that, in their relations with Russia, the British had now gone beyond the point of no return, and that nothing could come of the Ştirbey mission. Vasiliu did, however, say that on his return the Marshal had found General Wilson's telegram and now wished us to send a reply via our Autonomous cypher and radio. This was wonderful news. Perhaps our modest efforts with Vasiliu and Tobescu would, after all, help Antonescu to make the leap in the dark which Maniu had up to now refused. There were, I noted, three ways open to Romania. She could fight on until occupied, she could capitulate to the Russians and take the consequences, or she could turn against the Germans and reap the benefits at the peace conference. In just over three weeks I noted five rumours of an Allied landing in the Balkans, ranging from landings in Dubrovnik and Piraeus to speculation that the real purpose of the Italian campaign had been to clear the Adriatic for an expeditionary force. Two British airborne divisions were said to be standing by in southern Italy for use in Romania. That, of course, was why the RAF had not bombed Romanian airfields! We knew that much of this was Romanian wishful thinking. If some was also Allied deception, we were not aware of it. We were in an over-optimistic frame of mind; our mission, we felt, could still prove worthwhile.

The reply Antonescu wanted us to send to Wilson was disappointing. 'Do not ask an old man and honest soldier to end his days in humility,' he pleaded, addressing Wilson as 'a great and glorious soldier' who should not force him to throw his people 'into the bottomless pit of shame and destruction. We are your friends not enemies.' No country with its forces almost intact 'as are ours' could capitulate 'without some serious guarantee of her future'.[9] Chas had told Vasiliu that London were sick and tired of these requests for guarantees, and had suggested that the Marshal should redraft the message, offering instead some practical suggestion or other. But Vasiliu had insisted on its going unaltered. Perhaps he shirked from asking the Marshal to rewrite what was clearly a very personal draft. Perhaps, too, it sounded better to a Romanian than it did to us or would in Cairo, London, Washington or Moscow. The telegram was delayed owing to transmission problems and reached London almost a month later. Realising what a bad impression it would make on Molotov, and out of decency to Antonescu, Churchill and Eden decided to break their rule about copying all Romanian telegrams to Moscow, and on the grounds that it was now too out-of-date to be of any value, suppressed it.[10]

On 27 March when we were to send off Antonescu's maudlin message Captain Petermann called unexpectedly, his interrogation covering the transmission period. Nor were we available at the scheduled time on the following day.

It was not until noon on Wednesday 29 March that Chas and I went down to Tobescu's room where our W/T had been installed. I noticed that the aerial consisted of a very short length of wire and wondered whether the Romanians hoped that our signal would not be strong enough for their allies to pick up. I was tense, for this was really a job for a professional. But if we failed to get through, a wonderful opportunity would be lost.

These transmitters operated with crystals; the crystal set the transmitting frequency. One could double the frequency, but not tune through a range of frequencies. On this occasion the vital crystals for our particular set were missing. Tobescu told us that Captain Ungur who was responsible for radio must have put them away in a safe place. Unfortunately he had gone to the Dobrudgea.

But that evening Tobescu came upstairs greatly upset. The crystals, he said, had been stolen. He thought the Germans might have bribed Ungur. (We discovered later that Cristescu had given them to the Germans.) Tobescu was particularly nervous because the Marshal believed his message had been despatched two days before. That, we felt, was Tobescu's problem, but a rapidly deteriorating Russian front meant that if the Romanians were to contribute anything worthwhile to the war, they must act quickly. Chas confided to Tobescu that in the spring of 1942, SOE had sent Maniu a W/T set which had never been used; he suggested that Maniu should now be asked for the loan of this set and on Saturday, 1 April, the Marshal agreed. Chas was to see Maniu the following day.

That Sunday, 2 April, Silviu and I were taken for our first drive in town. Bucharest seemed little changed since 1941. There were, of course, more

German officers in the streets, mostly air force; one of them stared hard at me, surprised perhaps that someone looking like a German officer, and wearing such a scruffy uniform, should be in the hands of the Romanian gendarmerie.

Meanwhile General Tobescu drove Chas in his private car, fitted with false number plates, to a small wood a short distance from Bucharest where he met Maniu, who had been driven out by General Vasiliu. They had a private conversation. Chas argued that the military situation was now more favourable for a *coup d'état* than it was ever likely to be and Maniu, after referring to the promise of military help he had received from General Wilson, said he would now put his plan into action. His final words were 'the balloon is about to go up'; they would meet again very soon.[11]

But Chas felt that he had failed to tie Maniu down to anything specific. Maniu, I now think, was probably jollying Chas along. General Wilson had not promised him land assistance without which he did not consider a *coup* feasible. Chas, on the other hand, was trying desperately to get him in the short time they had together to promise immediate action and it would be like Maniu to put on a cheerful face for his young friend. Incidentally, he had told the authorities that in addition to the W/T set de Chastelain had mentioned to Tobescu, he had another which was already operating. As a result, Reginald was the transmitter used for Antonescu's messages, though why Maniu should have revealed its existence to the Romanian authorities, I could not think.

Persuasion from Wilson, de Chastelain and, indeed, Beneş – who had told Maniu that he was convinced the USSR intended to be a good neighbour after the war – had not changed Maniu's attitude to Russia one iota. On 2 April Molotov had assured Romanians in a broadcast message that his government did not intend to change the political or social order in their country. Maniu, when replying to Wilson's telegram urging him to carry out a *coup*, proposed that all three powers should jointly undertake to abstain from any interference of whatever nature in Romania and to recognise that all political and administrative powers would be vested in a government chosen by King Michael.[12] Such lack of faith in Russia's word exasperated London and Washington.

According to Rica Georgescu, Maniu at no time realised that the telegrams he addressed to SOE were seen also by the Russians. Yet the British told Ştirbey, during the week following the meeting of 17 March, that certain messages which Maniu had addressed to the Western Allies, instead of to all three powers, must have annoyed Stalin; and this clear indication that all Maniu's messages were going to Moscow must have brought home to Ştirbey the reality of Romania's position. Ştirbey found himself in a difficult position. To convince the obstinately anglophile

Maniu that he no longer had a special relationship with the British, using a laborious cypher in telegrams censored by Novikov would, he knew, be a difficult task. On 3 April after a long session with Novikov, he informed Maniu that if, in the light of the telegrams Maniu had received from Cairo and of Molotov's assurance of 2 April, he could still not take the action he had promised, 'then I must assume that you have grave and deep reasons for not doing so and conclude my mission here has no further point.'[13]

So the misunderstanding and disillusionment continued. Maniu did not believe that, in the absence of Anglo-American forces, Stalin would permit in Romania the free elections he had never permitted in the USSR. The Western Allies saw no democratic future for Romania unless Stalin for reasons of broader policy considered it to be in his interest to respect the principles of the Atlantic Charter. On the other hand, a *volte face* by Romania would be a devastating set-back to Hitler and that, they felt, was sufficient justification for trying to persuade her to surrender to the Russians, whatever the consequences to herself.

Negotiations for an armistice were complicated by the cumbersome administrative machinery – in particular communication between Novikov and Moscow – which made quick tripartite decisions impossible. Agreement among the Allies had not been reached on one point before other requests were coming in from either Antonescu or Maniu on which further tripartite agreement was required. The head of Southern Department of the Foreign Office felt that the obvious solution would be to move the negotiations to Moscow: 'This, however, is impossible as Maniu would not allow Ştirbey to proceed to Moscow for this purpose, his main idea being to contact ourselves and the Americans.'[14]

Then, on 4 April – a Tuesday – the American air force carried out their first raid on Bucharest. It was a heavy raid, intended to help Antonescu make up his mind. In our opinion, it did what conventional bombing almost always does – it stiffened civilian resistance. It also disrupted the W/T communications we had just established between Antonescu and Cairo; after this first raid, Reginald was off the air for ten days.

Chapter 18

Antonescu Says 'No' to the Allied Powers

On 4 April the alert sounded at about 1.45 p.m., while we were playing three-handed bridge. We heard the fighters go up, but took no notice; ten minutes later the first stick of bombs fell in the direction of the Gara de Nord. We watched through our windows until the telephone rang and the NCO was told to take us to the shelter.

This first time, we stayed downstairs for only forty minutes. It was not a real shelter, only a corridor below ground level. Women were sobbing in a corner, convinced that their families who lived in the station area had already been killed. The guards were keen to go out to see what was happening but were forced to stay with us, and since we prisoners were in the same boat Chas played his harmonica and we chatted about the war, guards and prisoners alike rather excited by this break in routine. Meanwhile, a lame man hobbled about opening windows and trying to keep people in order. Whenever the bombing moved away the civilians complained about the draught and the windows were closed again.

Since this first raid occurred shortly after a full-scale ARP exercise, few people had taken refuge in time. The station and railway workers' houses near it were badly hit. The trains were packed with refugees from Bessarabia and Bukovina and casualties were high. Bombs fell on a nearby German barracks which had been strengthened against rumours of a *coup*. A corner of the Ambassadors' Hotel – German military headquarters – was damaged. The Splendid Park Hotel – Gestapo headquarters – received a direct hit, though unfortunately, our informant told us, most of the staff had been out at lunch. The cigarette depot was hit and the firemen had a hard time with inadequate water pressure and the blinding, poisonous smoke to cope with. There was a run on cigarettes and within hours the kiosks were cleaned out. Orin Mogoşoaia, which Chas said was one of the biggest oil depots in Europe, burnt for twenty-four hours; we could see the glow all night.

The raid had an immediate effect on our way of life. Lunch was held up till 4 o'clock. Water was cut off for several days. We were given *mămăligă* instead of bread with our dinner and next morning the black bread the soldiers ate instead of our usual insipid white rolls.

Next day there was a raid on Ploeşti. According to Cristescu a smoke screen had been put up over the town, so most of the bombs missed the oil installations. With Cristescu one never knew how much to believe, but in this case he was telling us the truth.

During the Ploeşti raid we only spent an hour in the shelter and the officers, NCOs and men 'all talked with us very amiably'. Only once did a civilian turn on us during a raid, but that was after Bucharest had been subjected to months of day and night bombing, and more and more families were counting their dead. The others told him to control himself: this was war; we were not responsible for what was happening and he should learn to behave in a civilised way. When the soldiers threatened him he finally stopped.

From our windows we watched the beginning of a great exit of vans and carts piled high with household goods. An edict prevented shopkeepers and other essential people leaving town. The Marshal referred to 'a small, noble, unambitious people destroyed in this beastly way'. Şeicaru wrote a sob article which contrasted sharply with the gloating ones that had appeared in *Curentul* when London was being bombed in the autumn of 1940.

We encoded a second telegram from Antonescu about the military situation, together with a brief message from Chas which we hoped would go unnoticed under cover of the rest. This suggested that in his reply to Antonescu's first rather pathetic message the C.-in-C. should assure the Marshal that the UK and USA had underwritten the Molotov declaration on non-interference in Romania's domestic affairs. (We did not realise that they had done no such thing). He should go on to stress the need for early anti-German action. 'Saw Maniu Sunday . . . Please send latest directives and nature, kind, extent of military support available. If you persuade Maniu collaborate with Antonescu [Chas had presumably tried on Sunday], it would accelerate the finish. Secrecy essential. Cairo security suspect here. All well.'[1]

On the 7th, a Friday, Chas gave Vasiliu the encyphered messages, and next day Mihai Antonescu handed these to Maniu. They were taken to Rica Georgescu in his prison near the station – probably by Lygia – and then by Alecu Ionescu to Turcanu for transmission as soon as he was back on the air. Rica recognised Chas's handwriting. Maniu complained to Cairo that Ica had asked him to send 'through our secret W/T set a message encoded by de Chastelain without my knowing the contents'.[2] Cairo commented cheerfully to London that the Romanian authorities had clearly not yet located Reginald.

On Saturday, 8 April, Novikov unexpectedly produced the Soviet armistice terms. Lord Moyne commented to London: 'Less than three weeks ago they affected to consider Ştirbey as of no consequence whatever. Now they seem willing to go to any lengths to bring off a *coup*.'[3]

The terms provided for a Romanian *volte face* against the Germans. Bessarabia and North Bukovina would go to Russia. Romania would pay reparations. Although the country would not be occupied Soviet troops must have unrestricted freedom of movement. The Soviet Government would conduct operations with Romania for the return to Romania of all or the major part of Transylvania[4].

Churchill felt that reparations in the case of Romania were too onerous. The reference to Transylvania, which should rightly await the peace conference, he considered justified in the interests of prompt action by the Romanian Government. However Molotov, at his request, accepted the addition of the clause 'subject to confirmation at the Peace Settlement',[5] and Washington were keen to have this safeguard written in. Reginald suddenly came back on the air, and the amended terms were transmitted to Antonescu and Maniu on 13 April.

By the same radio contact Cairo received the Marshal's first telegram and de Chastelain's comment. Lord Moyne confirmed to the Foreign Office that our telegram embodied the secret security check carried in de Chastelain's head and that, following Chas's recommendation, Ştirbey would press Maniu to collaborate with Antonescu. Air Marshal Slessor would also be asked to lay off Bucharest until it was known that Antonescu had received the armistice terms. 'It has been too bad,' Moyne said, 'to be out of touch these last ten days.'[6]

On 8 April, the day Novikov produced the armistice terms, the trams were running again in Bucharest but there was still no water. We received cigarettes from the Romanian Red Cross with a reminder that it was Easter in Western Europe. I sent a letter to my brother, Eric, and had news from home. The BBC announced that if Romania did not capitulate, Bucharest would be bombed again within a week.

Next day we were taken for another drive. Some bombs had fallen accurately, some wide of military targets. We did not know at the time that by 'target' was meant 'target area'. On the 10th we saw no one, and Odessa was evacuated. On the 11th we again saw no one. On Wednesday, the 12th, Chas saw Colonel Teodorescu, who told him that public feeling was running high against the continuation of Antonescu's policy, and that the time had come for the opposition to act. 'I told him,' Chas wrote in his final report, 'he was in a very favourable position to help us communicate with the outside world, but he refused.'[7]

At about eleven o'clock on the 13th, Chas was called downstairs and given a cyphered telegram – the reply, we assumed, to the Marshal's message. We began work on it and soon discovered that it was from Ştirbey and contained the armistice terms offered to Romania by the Three Powers. Things were at last moving, and we worked until well after midnight deciphering, correcting and recorrecting the cumbersome code.

Next day, according to my diary, 'Chas and I up early and had a boiled egg' – its way of reminding me that we had had cyphering to do. We received the rest of the message and finished decoding it, and Chas gave the completed telegram to Tobescu. We were optimistic. In the circumstances the terms seemed extraordinarily lenient. I felt strongly that we should make sure that Antonescu realised the advantages of accepting these terms. He might never be given another chance. That night Chas and I wrote a four-page memorandum addressed to the Marshal. We pointed out that if these terms were turned down, Soviet occupation would follow. If they were accepted Romania would have an opportunity to contribute to the Allied war effort and could expect better treatment at the peace settlement. We went to bed feeling very cheerful.

What neither London, Washington, Cairo nor, of course, we prisoners knew was that the Russians had for some months been secretly establishing a direct line to Antonescu through Madame Kollontay*, their Ambassador in Stockholm. On Boxing Day Frederick Nanu, the Romanian Minister, had been sitting in his study with a children's party going on in the next room, when suddenly he had found a member of the NKVD at his door. The Russian had told him that Moscow preferred to deal with the Romanian Government rather than the opposition and that Antonescu should not interpret 'unconditional surrender' too narrowly.

When Nanu had reported this meeting to Bucharest he was told to pursue his contacts with the Russian Embassy in 'a dilatory' way. The government preferred to negotiate with the Western Allies and, in any case, Maniu's envoy would shortly be leaving to negotiate with representatives of all three powers.

On 12 April Madame Kollontay had told Nanu that Moscow took these talks in Stockholm very seriously. Strict secrecy must be maintained; Bucharest must leave it to Moscow to keep their allies informed. Next day the Soviet Embassy passed Nanu the armistice terms which differed from those sent from Cairo in only one respect – the Anglo-American clause referring to the peace settlement was missing.[8]

Assuming that Nanu immediately telegraphed this text to Bucharest, Antonescu (and presumably Maniu) would have it before the tripartitely agreed text which we had decyphered. The textual discrepancy could have been seen in Bucharest as a sign of discord among the Three Powers, and a reason for pressing for better terms. Maniu would take the absence of any reference to a peace settlement in the Soviet text as a further indication that, if Moscow had her way, Romania's future would be settled by

---

* Madame Kollontay and Stalin were the only leading Bolsheviks surviving from the time of the Revolution.

military means, and that a peace settlement, if there was one, would be no more than a rubber stamp on a Soviet *fait accompli*.

Sunday 16 April was Orthodox Easter. *'Cristos a înviat'*, we hailed the guard when we woke and the guard grinned back with *'Adevărat a înviat'* – 'truly, he has risen'. Yet we were not as joyful as we should have been. It was already two days since we had sent the armistice terms with our memorandum to the Marshal. Antonescu, it was true, was spending Easter at the front – he was always happiest with his troops – but on such a vital matter we had hoped for at least some hint of his reaction before now. Tobescu brought us *cozonac*, an Easter cake, and told us that RAF night bombing of military targets, to which no one objected, was more accurate than USAF high-level, daytime bombing. Our talk was interrupted by the alarm; this time the University, the Cartea Românească book shop and the Capşa restaurant were hit – all familiar and loved places.

The raids did not prevent people going away for Easter. The trains were packed. There was a holiday atmosphere in the nursing home. Two nurses came on to the balcony to practise their recorders and were shouted at by the anti-aircraft post on our roof. 'During air raids some of the nurses put on blue trousers and run around as pleased as Punch. Patients are always carried into the shelter.'

On Easter Monday, while Chas was downstairs, I mended my own trousers which had already been showing signs of wear when we came to Romania. I read some Odobescu: *A Few Hours at Snagov*, beautifully written though a little precious. I was coming to appreciate the Romanian language more and more. I then opened Vicki Baum's *The Grand Hotel* in German – how very different it seemed. But all the time I was listening for Chas.

The news he eventually brought could hardly have been worse. The Marshal had discussed the armistice terms with Maniu, and both, according to Vasiliu, had come to the conclusion that they were unacceptable. Vasiliu could be misrepresenting Maniu but not Antonescu. 'If Romanians continue on present line,' my diary says, ' they are likely to lose all Transylvania and bring about bolshevisation of their country – the two things they dread most.' I added that since we had finished our real coffee we had been trying local *ersatz*. One called Aroma was not bad, but our present one, Lydia, was very bad. 'My attempt to heat the plates over our electric stove succeeded. I tried on ten. The last one cracked.' I seem to be feeding my diary trivialities to cover the deep disappointment we really felt.

My mood comes through, however, in a reply to Tobescu about a rumour that Cairo were preparing to repeat our mission. My note was written in Romanian and the last sentence reads, 'I do not believe that at a time when the Russians are already on Romanian soil and when Romania has definitely linked her fate with that of Germany, the British command would squander personnel and material on a second mission which would prove equally useless.'

On Tuesday, the 18th, I saw a cart drawn by a horse; on it were three coffins, probably the victims of a single bomb. A man sat by the driver holding a wooden cross covered with black paper and the family walked behind. The weather was now quite warm and doves were cooing somewhere nearby. German trucks, I noted, were very good about giving their people a lift; they almost always pulled up at the tram stop if someone in German uniform was waiting.

Next day, Wednesday, 19 April, when Chas asked Tobescu and Cristescu for the text of Antonescu's reply to the armistice terms, they said he was giving no answer. However, in their view (which was, of course, the Marshal's) the terms were unacceptable, because to place lines of communication at the disposal of the Soviet army was tantamount to occupation. Chas, who felt strongly that some reply should be sent to Cairo, drafted a message then and there and was given permission to encypher it. This telegram of 19 April, which was to cause great trouble, read:

> Antonescu informed of terms by Maniu.* Do not know their reactions but those officials with whom we are in contact indicate
>
> (a) lack of faith in Soviet;
> (b) impossibility of collaboration between Roumania and the Red Army;
> (c) conviction that placing of lines of communication at the disposal of the Allies equivalent to occupation by the Red Army;
> (d) disillusionment that terms made by the Soviet and not the three Allies with whom Roumania effectively at war since air raids began. Although they admit German Army not defending Roumania east of the Carpathians they consider dishonour not fight Reds to the end. They do admit the country wants peace but they not willing to start new fight against Germany. They convinced Roumania abandoned to Soviet as we have lost initiative and supremacy. They believe the Red Army will not stop before Bosphorus, Adriatic. They infer attitude would be different if Anglo-American troops approached Roumanian territory. Hope have Maniu reply in day or so.[9]

As I remember, this telegram was an attempt, in a very cumbersome cypher, to make sure that our people knew the real reason for Romania's

---

* A telegram sent via Reginald would reach Maniu before Antonescu.

prevarication. It was written hastily, under considerable strain and disappointment, and was meant for British and just possibly US eyes. Chas never dreamt that it would be shown to the Russians.

Two days later, a stick of bombs fell in Ştefan cel Mare. A house behind Cioc's restaurant was hit. A bomb fell into the gendarmerie trench and killed a number of soldiers. The nursing home was lucky. A large hole was blown into the garden flinging earth and paving stones on to our roof and damaging a house opposite. An unexploded bomb fell against the wall of one of the wards. But the only real damage was to the small wooden mortuary.

I noticed a great improvement in the air-raid services. Within twenty minutes of the all-clear, damaged overhead wires at the tram junction were being repaired. The bomb disposal team reached the nursing home at about the same time, and not long afterwards the bomb had been made safe. On this occasion the trams, water and electricity seemed to be unaffected. According to the newspapers the men and women at the Otto Gagel bakery had refused to go to the shelter during the last raid, so saving 160,000 loaves. They had been given some kind of award.

On 23 April, the nurses were again playing their recorders but on a different balcony and we could not see them. During the last few days the leaves had come out, and the trees on each side of the *şoseaua* were now thick with greenery. We had been just four calendar months in Romania. When we came in, she seemed to be on the point of capitulating but here she was suffering terrible losses at the front, and bombed night and day at home, and still not surrendering.

Two days later I noted that at 12.30 I saw three drunken German soldiers in the street – the first I had ever seen. We were told by the duty officers that fighting had broken out between Romanians and Germans in the Crimea and that the Romanians were being disarmed before being evacuated.

On Friday the 28th I noted 'news of German troops crossing the river at Giurgiu which may mean some Allied move in the Balkans. This would make all the difference.' I added that Britain's relations with Turkey had improved now that she had stopped sending chrome to Germany. If we could use Turkey as an air base, a campaign into Romania would become feasible.

Next morning, Chas and I were again up early deciphering a personal telegram to Chas from Colonel Tom Masterson,* Ted Masterson's

---

* Colonel Tom Masterson, Political Adviser to the Mediterranean Section of SOE in London, was visiting Cairo. Previously, he had been Managing Director of Unirea. During the First World War he was awarded the DSO for his part in the destruction of the Romanian oil installations.

brother. It had been sent at Lord Moyne's suggestion because de Chastelain was 'so clearly out of touch with events'. 'All of us here,' Masterson said, 'have been surprised at the generous armistice terms,' which were unlikely to be improved and, if not accepted quickly, could be withdrawn; in that case total occupation would be inevitable. Fear of occupation under the terms offered to Romania 'by all three (repeat all three)' Allies was quite unwarranted. The bombing would continue. 'The Allies cannot allow themselves to be bluffed into relaxing their pressure on the pretext of negotiations which have shown no results after nearly six weeks. This is exactly what the Germans want them to do.' Masterson said he would like very much to know more about our working and living conditions. 'Marion and the children are well. Good luck.'[10]

The telegram made some good debating points but they were no longer of any use to us. The Marshal had moved from Bucharest to his house at Predeal in the hills, which seemed to give finality to his silence.

During the last few days of April two telegrams adressed to Antonescu and Maniu, which Lord Moyne had drafted and circulated to the three governments,[11] were approved and despatched. Antonescu's was a straightforward ultimatum though the passage referring to 'this last chance of redeeming yourself from the character of a common criminal . . . The Allies will pursue you relentlessly as such'[12] was omitted at the suggestion of the State Department. When agreeing to this amendment, Orme Sargent expressed the view that since Antonescu considered himself to be an honourable man such a personal attack would have the opposite effect to what was wanted.

Although worded differently, the telegram sent to Maniu was also in the nature of an ultimatum. Just before receiving it he had telegraphed Ştirbey to say that 'I cannot believe that the conditions of the Allies are absolutely unchangeable.'[13] Previously he had told Cairo that he was ready to negotiate on the basis of the terms 'presented by the Allied powers' together with his own suggestions. However these negotiations would be made more difficult by the fact that the Allied proposals included some which 'by their nature, belong more to a Peace Treaty than to an Armistice Convention'.[14] That same point had worried Churchill and Washington, but some five weeks before Orme Sargent had minuted that 'our object is to get satellites to revolt against their German masters rather than to conclude armistice with them.'[15] The telegram Maniu now received reprimanded him for his arrogance. His 'elaborate proposals' could not be entertained from a defeated country; he must accept or reject the Soviet terms as they were and let the Allies have immediately 'a final and definite statement of your attitude to . . . and of your intentions for implementing them'.[16]

Yet the incorrigible Maniu seemed never to learn; he continued to treat the armistice terms and the peace settlement as matters for serious concern. He obstinately refused to jeopardise his country's future in the interests of the Three Powers. While waiting for his two telegrams to be cleared for despatch Lord Moyne had commented to London, 'I have all along felt that the possibility of a successful *coup* as distinct from a mere suicide gesture, was exceedingly remote,'[17] and again 'Maniu's failure to play is' due to 'the fundamental inability of a worn out Roumanian politician to screw himself up to the point.'[18]

For Maniu there were two forms of suicide – a badly prepared *coup* against the Germans, and a successful *coup* against the Germans leading to Russian, as distinct from Allied, occupation. He refused to commit either. However, he clung obstinately to a third kind of suicide – the illusion that his commitment to democracy gave him a special relationship with the Western Allies.

He now planned to send out Constantin Vişoianu, whose journey to Cairo had been postponed after the news of Ştirbey's mission had been leaked. Vişoianu was a protégé of Titulescu's, and Titulescu's policy had always been to promote better understanding with the Soviet Union. He was, Maniu felt, the ideal man to tackle the British and Americans about these vital political and legal points on which, he still believed, Romania's future could depend.

As Ştirbey had foreseen,[19] by the time Vişoianu reached Cairo neither he nor Ştirbey had any mission left. Britain had withdrawn from the Romanian scene, and since the Americans tended to play second fiddle to us on Eastern Europe, the way seemed to have been cleared for an undisputed Soviet takeover.

Chapter 19

Molotov's Little Bombshell

During the first ten days of May 1944, after our bitter disappointment with the Marshal, my diary reflects a hardening of attitudes towards Romania. We decided to lower our sights, and concentrate, like all good prisoners of war, on escape. We did not know that, at the same time and largely on our account, London were also trying to wash their hands of Romania. Had SOE had the means, they would have instructed us to stop sending telegrams and to lie low – which was precisely what we had ourselves decided to do.

Prison life dragged on. Silviu had seen the first swallow on the 13th, but winter was still with us. On Sunday, 30 April, it was cold and it rained all day. I watched while the shoemaker's family on the other side of Ştefan cel Mare abandoned their home. They took with them all that was left of their furniture on a hand-cart, plus a goose in a basket.

One day the guards were excited about a Russian girl parachutist working in the garden. She was dressed like a boy, they said, and had told them that Russian parachutists often jumped without any training at all.

For the first time, my diary mentioned the Tudor Vladimirescu Division of Romanian prisoners, trained in Russia for internal security work. When the Red Army occupied Romania they would, I noted, help to install a Communist government.

But during the first ten days of May, air raids occupied most of the diary. On Friday the 5th, the end of a spell of bad weather, they started again in earnest. Ploeşti was successfully hit and Tobescu told us that bombing of railway stations at Bucharest, Piteşti, etc, had delayed the movement of troops and equipment to the Russian front by about ten days.

There were four types of alarm – one as the planes left Foggia, one as they crossed the frontier and, if Bucharest was their target, a third fifteen or twenty minutes later. The fourth was the all-clear. In May was instituted an hourly air bulletin so that, what with one thing and another, people seemed to be kept in a permanent state of anxiety.

The newspapers exhorted women taking refuge in the country not to patronise the peasants but rather to repay their hospitality by providing some practical advice on hygiene. They were reminded not to wear trousers or sunbathe, which would shock the peasants. This puritan trend was strong in Romania during the war. Women cyclists had to clip their skirts to the frame of their bicycles, a practice which led to many minor accidents.

Tobescu told us that although US pilots were always relieved to be told that they had bailed out over Romania, if machine-gunning of civilians continued the mood of the people might change. The gendarmerie were already being alerted to protect parachutists if the local population became nasty. In his report of September 1944, de Chastelain wrote that:

> Public opinion was seriously affected by the machine-gunning of civilians and, while I have no proof of this, nor do I know whether it was intentional or incidental to attacks on military objectives, I have no reason to doubt the numerous reports which I, personally, saw from outlying gendarme posts which were responsible for the collection of information on each raid immediately after it occurred.[1]

According to my diary, our easy relations with the duty officers suffered on account of the raids. Duţa dropped in at two one morning to say, 'Well, you really are our enemies, after all, you see.' Rocescu while always polite declined to sit down with us, 'standing beside the table with a cigarette in a holder which he has lit in the NCO's room before coming in'. Ionescu sulked. Diaconescu, recently promoted major, avoided the subject 'because his sympathies are really with the Allies'. 'Balzac [our name for Tobescu] comes up covered with medals and takes a seat at the table and has the door closed and is usually very friendly. He had to flee to Yugoslavia during the Iron Guard régime and is now really shaken by what is happening and is going to happen to his country'.

On 9 May I wrote:

> Afraid I had a rather heated argument with Chas at lunch because he supported Balzac's statement that Rumania expected and should have preferential treatment. I would have agreed a fortnight ago but now, although strongly condemning this type of bombing, see no reason why Rumania should be treated any differently from Hungary and Bulgaria. She is, in fact, giving Germans more voluntary support than either of these countries and must now be considered Germany's most important ally in Europe. In 1940 she was in most difficult position and was forced into an unholy alliance. But the government have had opportunities since then to break away.

On the last day of April while it rained all day in Bucharest and Chas and I were feeling particularly depressed over our failure with Antonescu, they had a warm day at Chequers. The weekend party consisted of Field Marshal Smuts and his son Jan, the Prime Minister of New Zealand and

Mrs Fraser, the First Sea Lord and Lady Cunningham. Colonel (Bill) Hudson of SOE, just back from Yugoslavia, came to lunch, as did Mary Churchill. The Smuts and Cunninghams left after tea, and the Prime Minister, who was showing signs of tiredness that weekend, worked for a while. After dinner, during which Mr Fraser told some rather boring stories, there was the usual film – *Half Way House*, a ghost story. The night before it had been *Fanny by Gaslight*. But

> the evening was marred by the arrival of an offensive telegram from Molotov who quite unjustifiably claimed we were intriguing behind the back of the Russians in Roumania. This set the P.M. off on his gloomy forebodings about the future tendencies of Russia and as he looked at his watch just before 2.00 am and dated the last minute awaiting his signature, he said, 'I have always not liked the month of May; this time I hope it may be all right.[2]

Molotov's telegram was offensive in both tone and content. Autonomous was 'a semi-official British mission with the Antonescu Government' with its own radio station which it used for cypher correspondence with the British representatives in Cairo. 'It is likewise known that the Romanian representative in Cairo, Ştirbey, uses the same radio station and ciphers for communication with Maniu and Antonescu.' The lively political correspondence which was conducted with the help of Autonomous between Bucharest and Cairo 'bears witness to the fact that the Antonescu government co-operates with it in this activity. Such a position could not exist otherwise than as a result of a definite agreement between the British Government and the Government of Roumania.'

The presence with Marshal Antonescu of a British mission 'whose purposes are unknown to the Soviet Government' would in no way contribute to hastening the capitulation of Romania and the acceptance of the Soviet armistice terms. 'The Soviet Government expects an explanation from the Government of Great Britain on this question.'[3]

Churchill drafted a reply before going to bed. He was not at his best that weekend – the morning before he had slept in until half past eleven, which was exceptional for him. He was upset by this further evidence of Soviet bad will and particularly the impugning of his own good faith. His emotional draft reply was sent to the Foreign Office who next day submitted the following amended telegram.

> Your message of April 29th about Roumania shows clearly that you have got hold of a mare's nest. The Ambassador is being sent instructions to give you a full explanation.
>
> Let me make it clear at the outset that in all this Roumanian business we are trying to work with you and Stalin. In spite of the

[unproletarian] demand for indemnities we have accepted as an agreement between us your terms of surrender as offered to Roumania with the amendments we suggested.

There have been physical difficulties about agents and about wireless communications, all of which are being explained to you in detail. What I am astounded at is that you should have imagined for one moment that we are in any intrigue with the Roumanian Government or anybody in Roumania, or that we have any evil interest in Roumania to the detriment of your operations and of the common cause, or that we have any secrets with Roumania to which we will not make you partners at any moment. The fact that you should harbour these thoughts shows how difficult it is working together, even when the greatest combined military operations in the world are impending. [What advantage do you think you get by saying these sort of things to people who are acting in good faith with you? You only build up barriers against yourselves in the future.] I must remind you that I send all this correspondence as it flows out to the President and the State Department of the United States.

I have already said we consider you our leaders in Roumanian policy on the basis of the surrender terms we have arranged, subject to the comment about indemnities. Of course if you do not believe a single word we say it really would be better to leave things to run out as they will. But considering the tremendous business we have in hand together, I trust that you will [send us an] *consider carefully your* answer [which will not have to be handed back to your Ambassador] *before you send it.*

W.S.C.
2.5.44.

The amendments shown here were made by the PM in pencil before he intialled the telegram for despatch.[4] He has crossed out the nonsensical word 'unproletarian' which, if it meant lack of compassion for the Romanian worker, was either ironical or demonstrated Eden's ignorance of Stalin's ruthless attitude to the proletariat. He has erased Eden's appeal to Molotov not to compromise the future of Anglo-Russian relations and has toned down his own ending.

The day after Molotov's bombshell arrived, Southern Department prepared a background memorandum which must have been put together in a great hurry. Not surprisingly, it contained inaccuracies. One was picked up by our Ambassador in Moscow before he saw Molotov – namely the suggestion that since our mission was purely operational there was no need to inform the Russians of it beforehand.[5] Autonomous had, indeed, started as an operational mission but when London learned that Maniu was to send out an emissary it had become almost entirely political. We were, it is true, specifically told not to undertake any negotiations with Maniu though, here again, if we had succeeded in contacting him it is unlikely that we would have had no influence on Maniu's replies to the telegrams he received from Cairo.

On 5 May Clark-Kerr gave Molotov the Prime Minister's message – the interpreters, of course, had great trouble with 'mare's nest' – and then went over the Autonomous mission in detail. The British Government had repeatedly offered to put the Soviet Government into touch with Maniu direct. The Soviet Government had always declined the offer but had raised no objection to our own contacts with the Romanian opposition. As soon as the Autonomous party had been caught, Novikov had been informed. London had little information about these men; they might well have been in touch with Romanian official circles. All they knew for certain was that de Chastelain had seen Antonescu once. (This was incorrect.) The party had no W/T set of their own and no direct contact with their principals in Cairo, let alone Prince Ştirbey. All recent communications with Cairo had come through Maniu's secret wireless set, and all had been communicated to either Novikov or to the Soviet Government direct through our embassy in Moscow. De Chastelain had not been used as a channel for communicating the wishes of the Allies to the Romanian Government. (De Chastelain had cyphered and decyphered the messages for Antonescu and had – though not at the British Government's request – commented on them to members of the Romanian Government. The material in Colonel Tom Masterson's telegram to de Chastelain was specifically intended for use with Romanian officials.)

After this explanation Molotov seemed unsatisfied. He thought that there was something peculiar about the position of Colonel de Chastelain and his fellow prisoners. He referred to what he called a 'combination' to which de Chastelain had been party, in that he had been used to cypher a 'vile' message insulting to the Soviet Government and flattering to Britain. He referred several times to this message of 19 April, and Clark-Kerr formed the impression that it was this above all which rankled. Finally, Molotov said that he would 'ponder over Churchill's message' and send him a reply.[6]

The reply received on 10 May denied that the Ambassador had given him any explanation and claimed that the PM's message 'in spite of all ingenuity was unconvincing'[7]. Next day Churchill told the Cabinet that he could not continue to correspond with Molotov, whose attitude led him to despair of the possibility of maintaining good relations with Russia.[8]

In a minute of 7 May Churchill asks Eden:

> Why were these two . . . important oil men [*sic*] picked? It does
> seem to me that SOE barges in in an ignorant manner into all sorts of
> delicate situations. They were originally responsible for building up

the nest of cockatrices for EAM in Greece . . . It is a very dangerous thing that the relations of two mighty forces like the British Empire and the USSR should be disturbed by these little pin-pricks interchanged by obscure persons playing the fool below the surface . . . Why should we be confronted with the descent of two oil men in Romania, in November,[*sic*] with vague powers who immediately tumble clumsily into the hands of the enemy? What reliance can be put upon Col. de Chastelain's cypher when it is in the hands of the enemy and can be used by Maniu [*sic*] whether he is a free agent or not?[9]

Eden drafted a reply which he did not send, but on the 14th he set out for the Prime Minister the history of relations with the Russians over SOE contacts with Maniu. He thought that the Russians were far less upset by the fact that they had not been told before de Chastelain went in than by the German-inspired press stories that he carried a copy of a treaty which Germany was supposed to have proposed to the Soviet Union at Romania's expense. Hence, Eden said, the *Pravda* article in February about Britain's alleged peace feelers to Germany. He also thought that Molotov was less concerned by the presence of Autonomous in Romania than by its use as a channel for messages that had hurt Soviet *amour propre*.[10]

The importance of this whole episode lies, of course, not in Autonomous as such, but in the more general deteriorating personal relations between Churchill and the Soviet leaders. The Molotov reaction to Autonomous was yet another sign that Britain's policy of building up a good wartime relationship with the Soviet Union which would survive into the post-war era was collapsing. Even Eden's almost compulsive commitment to this policy seemed unable to withstand Stalin's paranoia.

We can only speculate about Molotov's reasons for provoking a crisis over Autonomous. His claim that these messages were being sent without the knowledge of the Russians was, of course, nonsense. Encouraged by the British in Cairo, Ştirbey had formed the habit of discussing his drafts with Novikov, who knew that the Reginald-Autonomous channel had been used to send the Soviet armistice terms to Antonescu and Maniu. However, Novikov would never dare put Molotov right, above all about 'fact'. Since the Marshal had not responded to the Soviet offer, and only the 'vile' telegram from de Chastelain had been received, Moscow may have felt that Autonomous had served its purpose.

Again, the Molotov attack could have been pre-emptive, anticipating the day when his Western partners would learn what he was up to in Stockholm. If so, his tactic succeeded, for when London finally heard of the Stockholm negotiations from Vişoianu,[11] reluctance to provoke another Molotov outburst did, in fact, deter them from complaining.

But it is also possible that Molotov believed some of his own accusations. On our arrival the Turkish press had announced that we carried documents for the Romanian Government. We had dropped blind and unarmed, and on being arrested we had asked to be put in touch with a senior Romanian official. The rumours circulating in Bucharest that we had been seen dining at the Military Club would certainly be known in Moscow. In some ways we had been treated more like guests than POWs and we had been allowed to send cypher messages to the British in Cairo. Indeed at the time of Molotov's blast SOE were trying to send de Chastelain a second W/T set via a Romanian trade delegation. We had displayed initiative in the field – even contacting an enemy government – of a kind that would have been out of the question for NKVD agents. It is not inconceivable that someone in the NKVD, or even Stalin himself, saw Anglo-Romanian collusion at governmental level in all this. As for the idea that our people were showing them *all* operational signals from the field without any reciprocal arrangement, this though true might have been as difficult for some people in Moscow to swallow as it was for me when I eventually heard about it.

As for the 'vile' message, this was the telegram de Chastelain had drafted on 19 April giving SOE in Cairo the reasons for Antonescu's rejection of the armistice terms. If he had known that it was to be shown to the Russians he would, of course, have worded it differently or not sent it at all. Moscow already knew that the Romanians mistrusted them but never before had this been spelt out on paper – and by a British officer – in such blunt terms, and then given a wide circulation among Russia's allies. It was not the kind of treatment Stalin was used to from his respectful partners. Lord Moyne did consider withholding it from Novikov but decided that since the telegram was merely reporting a Romanian attitude it would not irritate the Russians against Britain. Nor did he want to be accused of suppressing anything, particularly if unpleasant, because to do so would only substantiate any possible suspicion of collusion with the Romanians. As it turned out, Lord Moyne commented ruefully, he and his people had fallen 'victims to our straightforwardness'.[12]

After the bombshell Lord Moyne told the Foreign Office that Antonescu was using de Chastelain as a tool. 'This we cannot prevent but we can and do ensure that we are not diverted from our main war aims by their manoeuvres.'[13] De Chastelain was not being used. It had been he, not Vasiliu, who had insisted on explaining Antonescu's rejection of the armistice terms to Cairo. Unfortunately his telegram could well have left the impression that, while regretting the Romanian attitude, de Chastelain nevertheless understood it – a sentiment which neither Molotov nor Moyne felt able to share.

The effects of the Molotov bombshell were considerable. Churchill, stung by the accusations of bad faith, blamed SOE. All SOE operations into the

Balkans were suspended and those into Romania were stopped. Churchill
suggested that the organisation be split between the Foreign Office and the
military. Although this did not happen, Molotov had certainly achieved a
major disruption.

On 12 May, the Foreign Office asked Cairo to instruct de Chastelain to
send no more telegrams, and our Moscow embassy so to inform
Molotov.[14] Moyne had to explain that he had no direct link with de
Chastelain; he could only send him a cyphered message through Maniu – in
other words, through Reginald. In any case, Reginald had been off the air
since 4 May and the instruction was eventually cancelled.

Lord Selborne, the head of SOE, who had not been consulted about this
instruction to one of his own men, wrote to Eden on the 19th:

> It seems to me that we have been taking too weak a standpoint. SOE,
> at the request of the Foreign Office, has undertaken the transfer of
> Russian agents into Germany, Austria, France and Italy and none of
> these countries can be considered as Russian spheres of influence.
> We have not questioned whether the agents we dropped were
> Communists or what was the purpose of the missions . . . I am sure
> that appeasement does not pay, even with one's best friends.[15]

When he received this letter Eden was furious; 'appeasement', he knew,
was meant to be insulting and he minuted 'It is gross impertinence'. In his
reply, he pointed out that the Russian armies would call the tune in
Romania. That was a hard fact and foreign policy had to take account of
hard facts. 'By doing so we can be firm where our interests, military and
political, are more vitally involved.'[16]

Eden was thinking of Greece where the Communist-led EAM-ELAS,
supported by Moscow, were giving the British a lot of trouble. When
Churchill appealed to Moscow for cooperation, Molotov replied at the end
of April that he could accept no responsibility for Greek affairs or for
British measures in Greece. At the Cabinet meeting of 11 May, Eden
suggested that the real object of Molotov's complaint about Romania
could be to establish a case for sending a Soviet mission to Greece. Since
Anglo-Soviet relations had deteriorated as a result of the two offensive
messages – one about Greece, the other about Romania – sent by Molotov
to Churchill within a few days of each other at the end of April, it is not
surprising that Eden made this association. On 4 May the PM had asked
him for a short Cabinet paper setting forth 'the brute issues between us and
the Soviet Government which are developing in Italy, in Roumania, in
Bulgaria, in Yugoslavia, and above all in Greece. It ought to be possible to
get this on one page.'[17] Next day while telling Gusev, the Soviet
Ambassador, about the replies he was sending Molotov on Romania, Eden
had also raised with him the difficulties he had been having in Greece. He

had then proposed a deal to Gusev: since Greece was in our theatre of command we were entitled to ask for help for our policies there, just as we gave it to them in Romania, which was in their sphere of command.

A fortnight later Gusev told Eden that his government agreed to formalising the arrangement, subject to US consent. Stalin had in mind, of course, American sensitivity about anything that smacked of spheres of influence in Europe. On 18 May, the Cabinet took note with satisfaction of Eden's rosy account of the Ambassador's reply and of his own assurance that there would be no trouble with the Americans. Eden was being over-optimistic. Churchill had repeatedly to assure Roosevelt that this was a purely wartime arrangement. There would be no question of post-war spheres of influence, but meanwhile someone had to play the hand. 'Neither you,' he reminded the President, 'nor we have any troops there at all,' and the Russians 'will do what they like anyhow'.[18] In fact the long-term implications of the proposed arrangement were clear to everyone concerned, though Roosevelt was finally persuaded to give it a three-month trial.

An agreement whereby Romanian affairs should be the primary concern of Russia and Greek affairs the primary concern of Britain – each government cooperating with the other in their respective countries – would be much to our advantage. Russia could still make trouble for us in Greece but with the Red Army on the Romanian frontier we could make little or none for her in Romania. For two years we had tried unsuccessfully to get Maniu to take some action. During the last six weeks a *volte face* by him or by Antonescu would have been of great strategic value to the three allies. We had provided through SOE the covert communications, had cajoled an unenthusiastic Soviet Government into offering armistice terms to Romania, including the leader of the pro-Western, anti-Russian, Romanian opposition. We had tried to persuade both Maniu and Antonescu to accept these terms. We had failed, and some of those involved had come away with a bloodied nose. In these circumstances, an effective Greek-Romanian barter agreement had two great advantages: it would enable Britain to get Romania, which had become a personal embarrassment for the Prime Minister, off her back; and at the same time it would provide for the withdrawal of Soviet support from Britain's opponents in Greece, a country which historically and strategically meant far more to us than did Romania.

Chapter 20

Escape Plans

When it became clear that Antonescu would continue to fight alongside Germany, de Chastelain told Tobescu that in future we wished to be treated as simple POWs. On 9 May he gave Vasiliu a letter to the International Red Cross, after which 'we devoted our time to communicating with the opposition through illegal channels and endeavouring to escape.'[1]

We had two reasons for wanting to escape: our fear of being taken to Germany during the general withdrawal and the need, now that Antonescu had failed us, to contact Maniu again. De Chastelain had asked Colonel Teodorescu to act as go-between with our friends in town, but he had refused and had not since been up to see us. Then Chas developed dental problems which, though partly genuine – costing the Romanian Government around 100,000 *lei* – were primarily intended to give him a chance to pass a message to the dentist whom we did not know, a Jewish man called Kahony, in the hope that he would have the courage to pass it on to whomever Chas indicated. The operation failed. Captain Ionescu, as might be expected, was arrogant and rude to Kahony, often arriving an hour late without a word of apology. I noted in my diary that he had been replaced on 27 May by Duţa, who was better behaved. But neither of them ever relaxed their security one jot. The girl assistants told Chas that they were being followed home in the evenings; Cristescu was taking special measures to ensure that messages would not be passed on by anyone working at the surgery.

On the 23rd a special Guards regiment replaced the gendarme soldiers: in their leather, instead of blancoed, webbing, they looked a great deal smarter. The two NCOs who were now permanently on duty spent much of their time in Chas's room making themselves at home with our wireless and books. One described how every night they had measured the progress of the American tunnelling operation at the Timis POW camp and how, when the prisoners finally emerged, they had only to shoot into the air to round them up again. He told a good story which we took with a pinch of salt.

On 12 May 1944, the three Allied Powers published a declaration to the German satellites which turned out to be virtually all stick and no carrot. A suggestion by Eden that unconditional surrender should not be applied to satellites since it would strengthen their will to fight to the finish had been accepted by the State Department but turned down by the President; Roosevelt refused to see that an East European country surrendering unconditionally to the USSR was in any different position from Italy surrendering unconditionally to the Western Allies. Later, what was meant to be a purely stylistic amendment by the British Cabinet erased from the declaration any reference to a satellite's independence and right to choose its own government after the war,[2] and the final text simply stated that the longer a satellite continued to fight alongside Germany the worse would be the consequences for her. Even this hint of a carrot was misleading. The extent to which an East European country had collaborated with Germany was to have little or no bearing on its post-war independence or its right freely to choose its government; Czechoslovakia and Poland would finish up in much the same boat as Hungary and Romania.

When Vişoianu reached Cairo on 25 May with news that Maniu would submit a new plan of action, he was wheeled straight into a meeting with the three representatives. He was not able to have a private word with a member of Lord Moyne's staff until the following day. He then asked, on Maniu's behalf, for some private assurance that Great Britain had not lost all interest in the Balkans; without some certainty on this point, Romanians would rather 'go down fighting under the Soviet flood'.

When the telegram reporting this conversation reached the Foreign Office, the desk officer minuted that he saw no reason why we should not tell Vişoianu that of course we had not disinterested ourselves in the Balkans and that this could be done orally. To the Head of Department, however, this was 'an attempt to drive a wedge between us and the Russians'. Orme Sargent regretted that the conversation had ever been allowed to take place. 'I think we ought to make it quite clear to Lord Moyne that he must not permit a repetiton. Meanwhile, Vişoianu should be told that there is no use his trying in this way to obtain assurances in respect of British policy as distinct from Soviet policy.' Lord Moyne should then give Novikov 'as full an account as he judges possible in the circumstances of these two conversations with a view to convincing him that we have no intention of carrying on separate negotiations with Vişoianu behind his back.' Cadogan agreed. Eden added, 'Please telegraph accordingly.'[3]

On another occasion Orme Sargent asked if SOE had any proof that messages from Maniu were not sent by the Germans, or that Vişoianu was not a German in disguise. It is indicative of the atmosphere in London that SOE thought it necessary to reassure him in writing on both points.[4]

Lord Moyne did not immediately grasp the full implication for Romania of Molotov's bombshell of 1 May. On 30 May an irritated Rose of Southern

Department minuted on a Cairo telegram: 'We have repeatedly told Lord
Moyne that he is not to take the initiative in these Roumanian negotiations.'[5] By early June, however, the penny had dropped, and Moyne was
proposing to his US and Soviet colleagues that negotiations with Maniu's
emissaries should be discontinued. To a suggestion that de Chastelain and
his party should be exchanged for a Romanian vice-consul interned in
Palestine he commented that since this would 'revive all the worst Russian
suspicion of collusion', de Chastelain should be left where he was.[6]

Not unnaturally, Foreign Service officers in Cairo found it difficult at first
to break the habit of taking the lead on Romania. However their
self-discipline, together with Novikov's disinclination ever to prod his own
government, meant that during the period between June and August, when
Maniu and King Michael were moving positively if belatedly towards a *coup*,
communication between Cairo and Bucharest had virtually ceased.

On Thursday 25 May, the day Vişoianu reached Cairo, I noted that 'Last
night Chas was called down to meet a woman who had the PM's (Mihai
Antonescu's) permission to see him – a pleasant change for him.' This was
Viorica, girl friend of the buccaneering Tozan, the Lufti Bey I had met in
Istanbul. Chas had great faith in Tozan and when Viorica gave him a
message – an escape plan – we were in high spirits. We were to make contact
by lowering a cigarette packet at certain hours after dark. We would use the
thread Chas had been given to make our parachute badges, and we tried to
estimate its length so that the container would be above eye level but within
reach of anyone standing below. When the hour came, two of us would keep
the guard riveted by animated conversation while the third carried out the
operation from the bathroom. We had hoped for a file and a rope; I was
nervous about the descent, since I had never learnt to control my speed
down a very much shorter and thicker rope in the school gym. Silviu, though
the oldest, would have undoubtedly performed best if anything had come of
the plan. But nothing did; the container always came back empty. Nor were
we able to contact our friends in town through the dentist or through any of
the duty officers.

Prison conditions grew worse after the armistice terms had been turned
down. Cioc sent a message that we could have no more *ţuica*, eggs or cheese
since we could not afford them, though Duţa, in this case, managed to put
things right.

When I asked for new trousers I was given the kind, lined with sacking,
that Romanian soldiers wore in winter. I had brought a decent pair with me
and felt that, like the American POWs, I should be allowed to wear them.
When we asked for permission to spend some time on the roof where it was
cooler, and this was refused, I wrote: 'What harm could we do? Jump off?
Put the ack-ack gun out of action? Signal to friends? We could do that
through our own windows if we had any friends.'

'I have asked for permission to buy a watch. The Colonel approved immediately. Then came the difficult part – the actual purchase. When the General is away, only he can issue the money. When the Colonel is away, only he can issue the money. So there it is – Ba e popa, nu e popa' [untranslatable though 'You can't win' would be something like it].

The bugs came out of the woodwork in the summer and kept Chas and me awake night after night. The colonel promised to do something about it and 'surprisingly enough, his promise was kept within twenty four hours.' In my diary I speculated that given the way things were going, Yugoslavia, Greece and Romania would become republics after the war, and Yugoslavia under Tito would probably be the leading nation in the region. Soviet would replace Western culture, and would prove particularly unpalatable to non-Slav countries. Czechoslovakia but not Germany would find itself in the Soviet zone. There was no mention of a divided Germany, or of extracting Greece from this scenario.

Yet the diary has its lighter and kinder moments. The soldiers of the guard brought us flowers from the gendarmerie garden; the colonel told us how one day, towards the end of the war, Hitler pulled off his moustache and hair and said 'I am Jack Jones of British Intelligence. I was sent here to destroy Germany and have now completed my mission.'

That same day I spoke to a woman for the first time in six months. I was watching the cars driving out of town when a nurse opened the window opposite and asked '*A sunat alarma?*' I replied '*Da, a sunat deja*' – 'Yes, the alarm has already gone' – and she smiled and disappeared. I noted this important event in my diary.

We had our first news of the Normandy landings before lunch on 6 June. The German radio was at first quite informative. The BBC concentrated on human-interest stories. Cristescu came up to say that, according to rumours circulating in town, the Allies had been thrown back into the sea, and Allied troops had landed in Piraeus. We no longer gave a damn what Cristescu said.

It took Goebbels just twelve hours to suggest that the invasion was 'probably big enough to satisfy Moscow'. 'Before long,' I noted, 'he'll be telling the world that Britain and America are sacrificing their boys exclusively for Russia; it is about the only line of propaganda left to Germany.'

As was to be expected, Romanian commentators saw the invasion almost entirely from a narrow Romanian point of view. Would it weaken Russia's plans for Romania? Would it stimulate Allied interest in Romania? This, Şeicaru wrote, was a time for clarification: 'In a month's time we should have a far better idea whether the Allies are going to be on a more equal footing with the USSR.'

PART FIVE

June 1944—August 1944

Chapter 21

Final Preparations for the Coup

For Maniu the Normandy landings signalled an early Russian offensive on the southern front; unless Romania acted quickly to break with the Axis she would miss the chance of becoming a co-belligerent. Antonescu did not agree. For him the Second Front provided an additional reason for holding out against the Russians until the balance of military power in Europe had swung towards the Anglo-Americans; that, he felt sure, was what the British really wanted.

We prisoners had put our hopes of a *coup* in Maniu and Antonescu. It had not occurred to us – nor to many people in Romania – that when Antonescu failed, and while Maniu still hesitated, King Michael himself would finally take the fateful leap in the dark.

Maniu though fifty years his senior had the greatest respect for King Michael. Antonescu had not. For years he had kept the King and his mother, Queen Helen, under virtual house-arrest. The idea that he should seriously consult this young man about anything seemed never to occur to the Conducator. A generation gap and a conflict of personality excluded frankness or confidence between them. But the conflict went further. By the summer of 1944, the King was no longer the teenager who had succeeded his discredited father four years before; he had become politically aware, feeling that Romania was heading for disaster and that neither the obstinate Marshal nor the traditional politicians with their legalistic quibblings and harkings back to the events of the Thirties (he had still been a boy when Tătărescu was supporting his father) seemed capable of saving it.

In his 1943 New Year broadcast, the King had called for peace, so enraging Hitler and Antonescu. A year later SOE was told that a 'Colonel Black' was preparing an anti-government army revolt in the King's name – unknown, according to the colonel, to the 'indecisive' political parties. Although nothing came of the revolt – for one thing the Allies could not provide the airborne troops Colonel Black required without depleting the Italian theatre – King Michael could well have had it in mind when he told de Chastelain on the night of 23 August 1944 that while the politicians had been lethargic, he himself had been ready to act since February.[1]

According to Pichi Pogoneanu, the King had pressed for action in the spring but had been advised against a *coup* at that time on the grounds that there were too many German troops in the country. The National Peasant Party based their estimate of German strength on the number of rations requested by the German authorities. Georgescu and intelligence agents in prison with him considered this to be a greatly inflated figure.

The King, being younger, was more impatient and flexible, readier to take risks than the older men. He had the support of his mother; of Baron Mocsony-Styrcea, the marshal of the court; of General Sănătescu, a cavalry officer whom Antonescu had made head of the King's military household in the hope of having at least one man in the Palace he could trust; of Niculescu-Buzeşti, the head of communications in the Foreign Ministry; and of his private secretary, Mircea Ionniţiu, with whom he had been at school. But he knew that when the moment came he, alone, would have to stand up to the Marshal – something that few Romanians of far greater experience and self-confidence than King Michael would have cared to do.

Maniu's relations with Antonescu were rather more complex. They were of the same generation. Maniu had always seen the Marshal as an honourable man who, having failed to consult either King or people before plunging the country into a disastrous war, would make amends if presented with reasonable terms of surrender. By the summer of 1944 Maniu had both the organisation and the backing of the people for a break with the Axis. But he had failed to obtain terms of surrender on which he was prepared to stake the future of his country.

Antonescu had always respected Maniu's electoral strength. He once told General Friessner that, having no popular following himself, he could do only so much in defeat. His decree of February 1941 forbidding all non-governmental political activity had never been enforced against the traditional parties. Maniu and Brătianu sent Antonescu a critical memorandum about once a month, which they then circulated to foreign missions under the nose of the Siguranţa. Whenever Hitler raised the question of Maniu's activities – Ribbentrop once told Antonescu that in Germany such a man would have been hanged by then – the Marshal doggedly refused to take any action against him.

Antonescu had put all his faith in Germany, and Germany had let him down. Maniu had put all his faith in the Western Allies and, in Romanian terms, they had let him down. Yet neither man would denounce the country to whom he had first committed himself – Germany and Britain – and they respected each other for this.

The *coup* would not have succeeded without Maniu's careful planning or the King's leap in the dark. But by the summer of 1944 another element had to be taken into account – the Romanian Communist Party. Though not essential to the success of the *coup*, Maniu hoped – as did Rose of the Foreign Office – that Communist participation would win Soviet support for his activities.

Formed in 1893, the Romanian Social Democratic Party had at first been led by intellectuals from aristocratic and middle-class families. By the turn of the century many of them had been disillusioned by the problems of applying Marxism in Romania and joined the Liberal Party.

During the First World War the socialist movement had advocated alliance with the Central Powers rather than one which would include 'imperialist Russia'. One of its leaders, the brilliant Rakovski, believed that, given the chance, Russia would repeat in Romania the ruthless russification of Bessarabia. After the Revolution he fled to Odessa where, on Trotsky's recommendation, he was made governor.[2] Romanian socialists were convinced that the Revolution had cleansed Russia of its imperialism, and Rakovski, now in the service of the Soviet Union, was soon advocating the incorporation of Bessarabia into the USSR, by force if necessary.

In Romania itself, the socialist movement split along familiar lines. In 1920, those in favour of affiliation with the Comintern formed the Communist Party, leaving the moderate parliamentary Social Democratic Party to represent the rest of the movement, though it never came to power. The Communist Party was made illegal four years later, and at the outbreak of the Second World War its membership was still only in the hundreds. Many distinguished members – Emil Bodnăraş, for instance, and Anna Pauker – had escaped to the USSR, where a Romanian section of the CPSU had been formed. Some had become Soviet citizens. All had been Soviet trained and were eventually to have considerable influence on the Party at home.

After the dissolution of the Comintern in May 1943, the Romanian Communist Party sought legitimacy by collaboration with other political parties. The party itself was not as homogeneous as we thought at the time. One group, led by the 'intellectual' Lucreţiu Pătrăşcanu, a Moldavian landowner, worked for an alliance with the two major traditional parties. But there were activists who carried more weight in the Party than Pătrăşcanu, men who had formed cells in their prisons with courier links to the outside world, and were prepared to work with less respectable political elements. In the autumn of 1943 such a group at the Tîrgul Jiu prison set up the National Patriotic Front, consisting of Communist, Socialist, Liberal and National Peasant political prisoners. The Front's clandestine newspaper, *România Liberă*, called on all anti-Hitlerite forces in Romania to unite, regardless of their party political views. It was possibly this group, rather than Pătrăşcanu's, which reached an agreement

with the dissident Liberal Tătărescu, whom Maniu and Brătianu had never
forgiven for his collaboration with King Carol. Mircea Ionniţiu, the King's
private secretary, remembers a meeting at which Maniu accused Pătrăşcanu of making this deal while Pătrăşcanu categorically denied the charge
and appeared to be telling the truth.

At first Maniu repulsed Pătrăşcanu's offers to collaborate, on the
grounds that Romania must be free of any foreign power and could not
abnegate her claim to Bessarabia and North Bukovina. But by the spring of
1944 both men knew that, with the approach of the Red Army, the
Communist Party's influence would increase out of all proportion to its
popular support. There was the possibility of a Communist government
being set up by the Russians in Iaşi. Support was in any case growing
among the war-weary workers. In March the Hungarian Minister reported
that the Communist movement 'has spread to an altogether unexpected
extent in Romania' and a month later the German Legation noted a
marked Communist attitude among the petrol workers.[3]

But it was the Normandy landings that gave the final push to the
formation on 20 June of the National Democratic Bloc, consisting of the
National Peasant, National Liberal, Social Democratic and Communist
parties. Its aim was to conclude an armistice, endeavouring to obtain the
best possible conditions for the country, and to withdraw from the Axis,
replacing the present dictatorship with constitutional democratic government. Maniu, who still mistrusted the Communists – and the Social
Democrats' ability to stand up to them – insisted on a clause binding all
signatories to work together for the urgent realisation of the Bloc's
objectives.

Even before the official formation of the NDB, Pătrăşcanu and Titel
Petrescu, the leader of the Social Democratic Party, were taking part in
secret preparations for the *coup* under the King's chairmanship. Ionniţiu
probably had Pătrăşcanu in mind when he wrote much later that all the
different political personalities who helped to plan the *coup* 'were working
honestly for their country'.[4]

The King usually spent the summer in Sinaia, but since opposition
politicians would have become conspicuous visiting him there, he came to
Bucharest as often as he could in 1944. He chaired a secret military
committee which planned to take over the state apparatus – the post office,
the broadcasting station, etc – and to defend Bucharest against a German
counter-attack. This committee recommended coordination with the
Allied Command in Cairo, and the use of Allied airborne troops to help
combat German forces.

A sub-committee under Colonel Dămăceanu drew up plans for the
defence of Bucharest. At one meeting Pătrăşcanu suggested that the

Communist Party's military representative, Engineer Ceauşu,* should attend since he could mobilise workers and put them at the disposal of the military command.

When Engineer Ceauşu appeared on the night of 13 June at a meeting held secretly in a house on Calea Moşilor, Mircea Ionniţiu was struck by the difference between him and Pătrăşcanu. A cousin of the Palace Master of Ceremonies, Pătrăşcanu looked rather like a schoolteacher, but in Ceauşu Ionniţiu thought he saw for the first time a really dedicated Communist ready for military operations.[5]

Ceauşu had arrived from Moscow to revitalise the Party and was now one of a ruling triumvirate which did not include Pătrăşcanu. Pătrăşcanu had invited Bodnăraş to attend this meeting in order to see for himself that the plans he was undertaking with the King and the traditional parties were serious. Bodnăraş was convinced, and a week later the Communist Party had joined the National Democratic Bloc.

Three days after the establishment of the National Democratic Bloc, Cristescu informed the Marshal that, in conversation with friends in Snagov, Maniu had named 15 August as the date for the *coup*.[6]

On 27–28 June, Cairo received Maniu's revised plan which Vişoianu had promised on his arrival. To be successful, Maniu said, the *coup* must be synchronised with Allied action as follows: (a) a massive Soviet offensive to be launched on the Romanian front within twenty-four hours of the change of government. Romanian troops would then be ordered to let the Russians through and to attack the Germans; (b) three airborne brigades with, if possible, an additional 2,000 parachute troops to be landed in the interior at the same time as the change of government. These could be either Anglo-American or Soviet. (c) heavy bombardment of communications with Hungary and Bulgaria.[7]

Lord Moyne commented to London that the plan so far as it went seemed reasonable and in parts even encouraging; 'acceptance of Soviet

---

* Emil Bodnăraş (code-named Ceauşu) had been court-martialled for desertion when an officer in the Romanian army. Colonel Radu Ionescu, the governor of Georgescu's prison, told Georgescu that he had been detailed by the court to defend Bodnăraş, and had obtained his release. Bodnăraş had then gone to Russia, where he had been active in the Moscow wing of the Romanian Communist Party. He returned to Romania in the spring of 1944. After the *coup* his Patriotic Workers were the only civilian group the Soviet Command did not disarm; during the Communist takeover they were used to intimidate Peasant and Liberal Party demonstrators. In 1945 Bodnăraş personally ordered Colonel Radu Ionescu's execution. In 1947, he became the Romanian Minister of Defence.

airborne troops is a definite step forward.'* Yet when McVeagh suggested a tripartite meeting to consider Maniu's plan, the British agreed with Novikov that this would be premature.[8]

In the second part of his message, received the following day, Maniu said that the opposition could not accept conditions less favourable than those offered to Antonescu. The Allies 'are warned against any illusions that an understanding is possible with Antonescu'.

Maniu's reference to 'conditions less favourable than those offered to Antonescu' related to the improved terms which Moscow, without telling their allies, had agreed with Nanu in Stockholm three weeks before. Under these, Romanian reparations would be re-examined. A district would be reserved for the seat of the Romanian Government and this would not be occupied by Soviet troops. Since Antonescu wished to 'play fair' with his ally, Moscow had also agreed that the Germans should be given two weeks in which to evacuate Romania before the Romanian army turned on them. In the unlikely event of the Germans leaving voluntarily, Romania could then consider herself neutral.[9] Although on paper these were far better terms than Cairo had offered Antonescu could not bring himself to accept them so long as he felt that there was any chance at all of reaching an agreement with the Western Allies. Maniu had not previously told the British and Americans about the improved offer. He either assumed that London and Washington knew of it from the Russians or he guessed the truth but did not wish to lay himself open to another charge of wedge driving.

The upshot of British inactivity and Russian preference for a bilateral deal with Antonescu was that when Maniu's plan – a very feasible one – was ready for action dialogue between Cairo and Bucharest had virtually ceased. Then in mid-July Nicolae Turcanu, Jockey's radio operator, was arrested and the plotters had to fall back on the slower and less secure link provided by Cretzianu in Turkey.

From his prison in Calea Plevnei, Rica Georgescu (Jockey) had been in contact with Sandu Racotta and Matei Ghica. Ghica had stolen a German plane with which to fly Vişoianu to Cairo, and when Vişoianu chose to go by train instead he himself had to flee the country. Ghica took with him Sandu Racotta, the Ştefan who had provided a landing place for Autonomous and who was now also in danger. They brought out what the US Air Force described as the best intelligence yet received from

---

*   Maniu's reluctance to depend on Soviet military help during the tricky few days following the *coup*, though considered in Cairo to be mere wedge driving, was justified in early August when during the tragic Warsaw uprising against the Germans the Red Army stood back from the beleaguered Poles and even refused to let the RAF drop them supplies.

Romania.[10] London, however, were so disappointed by the arrival of these 'nonentities' instead of a senior Romanian officer who would liaise directly with the Red Army and take Romania off their hands (Eden minuted 'fatuous'[11]) that they decided to authorise no further flights from Romania. After Sandu Racotta's escape his brothers and their wives were arrested and joined Georgescu in prison. At one point Georgescu arranged for all the prisoners – Romanians, Russians, Bulgarians, Belgians, Poles and four British – to walk to the shelter at the Gara de Nord during air raids, having personally undertaken that they would not escape. By July Rica knew that, apart from Cairo's silence, preparations for the *coup* were going smoothly. He was in good spirits until, on 14 July, he again lost radio contact with SOE Cairo.

A W/T operator in enemy territory could stay nowhere very long.. The Germans would soon recognise his as a new 'handwriting' on the air: they would then direction find (D/F) until they had a cross-reading. Under cover of a repair van they would cut off the electricity, street by street, house by house, until the transmission stopped and could be pin pointed. An operator could, of course, use accumulators but these were bulky and required prolonged charging which, in itself, could arouse suspicion by putting up the electricity bills. He could switch to batteries when the mains failed, but even if his transmission did not falter tension would show in his key work.

Not surprisingly, Turcanu had started to drink too much and would often have the gypsies strike up God Save the King in a restaurant packed with Germans. Costica Mugur, a member of the network who was trying to keep tabs on him, had a difficult time – and being of Jewish origin he ran an even greater risk of rough treatment if caught than some of the others.

While Turcanu was transmitting from the Protopopescus' flat his wife stood at the window watching Costica Mugur who was keeping a look-out for the German service van. If Costica blew his nose, Turcanu would sign off in the normal way, lever himself and his suitcase set into a motor-cycle side-car a few doors up the street, and be driven away by a police captain in uniform, who was a friend of Costica's. The manoeuvre worked smoothly for about ten months.

When Madame Protopopescu became pregnant she grew nervous about having a British agent in the flat and Turcanu moved elsewhere and eventually to Prince Ştirbey's house in Calea Victoriei. However the Siguranţa heard from the servants that at certain hours a man locked himself in one of the rooms. When Antonescu asked Maniu whether he had someone working in the Ştirbey palace, Maniu, who was told nothing of these operations, could truthfully say that he did not know. He then passed the warning on to Lygia, who told Rica. Antonescu of course knew that he was tipping off Maniu. Turcanu moved to a flat opposite the Royal

Palace – probably in the block where Reggie and Olivia Smith had lived. Although one entrance was watched by Alecu Ionescu's people, Siguranţa agents using another caught Reginald red-handed.

Colonel Radu Ionescu had replaced Colonel Velciu as governor of the Plevnei prison. Like his predecessor, he was a British sympathiser. As a result, when Turcanu was brought to the prison on 14 July Georgescu was able to arrange for the German escort to be out of the room long enough for Turcanu to unload on to one of Colonel Ionescu's agents his money and documents, including an *en clair* telegram which would have incriminated Maniu. Georgescu told Ionescu that Turcanu must at all costs be kept out of Gestapo hands; he knew too much. He persuaded the colonel to beat up Turcanu during the interrogation so that the Gestapo would feel that this particular British agent could be safely left in his hands. The colonel played his part so well that at one point Turcanu began to wonder whether he was really on his side; the Germans were convinced, and Turcanu and his transmitter remained at the Plevnei prison.

Throughout July, the King and his advisers got down to details. At a meeting on the 7th they decided that despite the lack of any response to their plan from Cairo, 15 August would be D-day; it was the date Maniu had mentioned to his followers a fortnight before. Three weeks later they changed this to 26 August, sticking to this date until, at the very last minute, it had to be brought forward to the 23rd.

At one of these meetings Maniu circulated the letter Churchill had sent him in 1940 assuring him that in return for an uprising in Transylvania Her Majesty's Government would do their best to guarantee Romania's integrity after the war. Although the uprising was now to be on a national rather than a Transylvanian scale at least one member of the committee, Baron Styrcea, thought that since the letter had been written before Romania's invasion of the USSR, which had led to a state of war between herself and Britain, the undertaking might no longer be valid. Maniu asked for his letter to be kept in the King's private safe but, in case the *coup* did not succeed, the meeting agreed that after it had been shown to 'old Antonescu' it should be hidden elsewhere.

The British were still pressing for a senior Romanian to cross the lines in order to negotiate directly with the Soviet High Command. Bucharest was unenthusiastic; the last thing they wanted was sole contact with the Russians. The King accredited General Aldea* to perform this mission, but when General Sănătescu carried out a reconnaissance of the

* General Aldea, a senior army commander, was in the King's confidence about the *coup*.

front, disguised as an 'inspection of the armed forces', neither he nor friendly local commanders could find a secure crossing place for the Romanian delegate.[12]

One question which was settled was how the Antonescus should be detained. The military advised against involving the army in a political operation and the police and the gendarmerie could not be trusted, so it was decided that all the political parties should jointly provide a temporary guard. In the event only Pătrăşcanu found any volunteers. According to the King's private secretary, there was never any question of executing Antonescu; when it became clear that all the warders would be Communists, Pătrăşcanu gave his word that the prisoners would be treated in a dignified and humane manner while in their hands.[13]

The King planned to have a decisive audience with Antonescu at the Peleş Palace in Sinaia, which was easier to defend than the building in Calea Victoriei. Should Antonescu decline to sign an armistice he would be dismissed, and a government of the NDB appointed. Should he accept the armistice terms – and there were still some who thought this possible – the plan would be modified accordingly.

On 5 August Maniu sent a message to Cairo about his plan. 'Nobody can understand how such a definite offer of collaboration can remain unanswered for five weeks . . .'[14] On the 20th he informed Cairo that he had decided to act without waiting any longer for a reply. 'Let us know what you can give us . . . We would prefer that you should tell us that you cannot give us all we have asked rather than to be left in ignorance which is completely paralysing.'[15]

Led by King Michael, the Romanian opposition fixed the date for their *volte face* at least six weeks before the Soviet offensive. They then waited for the 'go-ahead' from Cairo which never came. They were completely in the dark as to what to do. They could either act without waiting for a reply and risk an operation which could benefit neither the Allies nor Romania. Or they could wait for a reply which could arrive too late. The Soviet offensive of 20 August finally persuaded them to take a chance without any certainty of external help, but it was luck, courage, and their careful planning that made the *coup* a success.

Chapter 22

Antonescu's Last Visit to the Führer

We prisoners heard of Maniu's understanding with the Communist Party on 13 June, less than a week after Cristescu had reported it to the Marshal.

By then the bombing was having its effect. People were becoming jittery. The Prefecture of Police reminded them that 'any sound is forbidden that might affect the calm of the public – over-amplified wirelesses, motor horns, revving of engines etc.'

Although the V2 had reduced the propaganda effect of the Normandy landings, we were nevertheless much better treated after 6 June. Food from the new restaurant was brought warm in containers. We had ice for our wine. Our laundry was returned in forty-eight hours instead of ten days. The general's own adjutant came up twice a day to see if we needed anything. Things would improve even more, we felt, when the Russian offensive began.

Here we were mistaken. The Russians kept their promise to open an offensive to coincide with the Western invasion, but this was not, as everyone had been led to expect, on the southern front. The real plan was known only to Stalin and five officers. Orders were hand-written. Only low-powered radios were used, and none within fifty kilometres of the front.[1] The offensive when it came in the third week of June was not in the south, but in two great movements to the north: one against the massive German concentrations of the central sector, the other with the object of knocking Finland out of the war. On 22 June I noted that Vyborg had fallen, and the Russians were driving north and westwards towards Helsinki: and on the 26th, only four days after the beginning of the central offensive, that Vitebsk had fallen. By July, the German army centre had been smashed with 57,000 prisoners taken, including generals. So whenever I complained in my diary that the offensive had still not started, I was referring to an offensive on the Romanian front – one that would directly affect us.

Sunday 16 July. 'Rădulescu was up this morning and we talked about Romanian art. He hopes that Russia will still break with the Allies, which would put Romania on our side. I told him I thought Russia would in future be a great world power and that the Soviet tyranny of the last twenty years – which one would expect to follow any revolution of that dimension – would now be moderated.' I cannot remember whether I believed this; I suspect it was part of a general hope that my fears about the future would be proved wrong.

The papers announced that on 1 July a court martial had condemned to death *in absentia* certain men who had 'fraudulently crossed the frontier'. They included Captain Matei Ghica and Alexandru Racotta.

On Friday 21 July we had news of the attempt on Hitler's life. Telephone lines had been cut between Sweden, Switzerland and Germany. Berlin was under martial law. Many German generals had failed to send Hitler congratulatory telegrams and no telegram from Antonescu had been published.

On Thursday 27 July we had the long-awaited visit by representatives of the International Red Cross. They were both Swiss. Their office, they said, had asked London if they could be of any assistance but had received no reply. It was a fact that they could do little for us in our rather special circumstances. However they gave us a copy of the Geneva Convention which confirmed that we were certainly not being treated as prisoners of war. That day the flat was cleaned thoroughly, water ran all day, and Ionescu produced some sandals, which were a great blessing in that temperature. It was not a wasted visit.

On Saturday 29 July my diary reported that something was stirring. According to Ankara radio Hitler, suspecting a Romanian betrayal, was holding Horia Sima, the Iron Guard leader, in readiness to take over the government on Germany's behalf. The duty officers had already told us about this.

> There has been considerable activity at Sinaia during the past week. The King has given audiences to Tătărescu and Maniu. It is said that Antonescu will be asked to resign very soon . . . The Germans pretend to have found a booklet called 'Irregular Warfare' and have quoted sections on unarmed combat. Eden has denied its existence and Germans have given the Press photographs of it. Supposed to have been taken from an officer in Yugoslavia.

At the end of July, one of our best friends, Dobrojan, who was off to the front, came up early one morning to say goodbye. Later, we heard that a German general had gone to see Madame Kollontay in Stockholm to negotiate peace terms with the Soviet Union.

On 2 August Chas and I were called down to see Tobescu. He told us that although he could not be sure, he thought we would be free by 15 August. (He had presumably picked up the date from Cristescu's reports on Maniu's conversations.) That day Turkey had broken off diplomatic and commercial relations with Germany; the future looked decidedly brighter.

The day before, Marshal Antonescu had left Bucharest for a small watering place, Olăneşti-Vâlcea, about two hundred kilometres or one hour's flight from the capital. His doctor had suggested that since the Romanian front was so quiet he should take a twenty-day cure. One of his aides, Colonel Magherescu, had served him since the days of the Iron Guard revolt and, though he was probably not in the Marshal's confidence over political questions, was a very devoted officer.[2] Magherescu was unhappy about this proposed holiday. Unlike Hitler or Stalin, the Marshal, he felt, could not rule in absence – the generals and the Palace clique would plot in peace with the Marshal away. Nevertheless, the Marshal took his doctor's advice and went to Olăneşti with his wife, Mihai Antonescu, the doctor, Colonel Radu Davidescu, head of his military cabinet, and some of his aides.[3]

Three days later his cure was interrupted by an invitation to Hitler's East Prussian bunker at Rastenberg and the Marshal returned to Bucharest to prepare for what could be a very sticky interview. According to Magherescu, Mihai Antonescu was in a state about going to Germany. Since the attempt on Hitler's life the Germans were trigger-happy and Ica knew that the man they trusted least in the Marshal's entourage was himself. For the last eighteen months he had been putting out peace feelers to the Allies and now he felt sure that if the Marshal broke with the Axis Hitler would hold him responsible. He even consigned certain papers to a friend with the request that, if he did not return from Rastenberg, she should hand them to the King.

On the evening of 4 August, Tobescu told de Chastelain that at 6 a.m. the following morning, Antonescu would leave for Germany with Mihai Antonescu and General Şteflea, the chief of staff. They were due back at noon on the 7th. Later we learned from Colonel Teodorescu that the government had decided to accept the Soviet armistice terms – presumably the improved ones offered through Madame Kollontay at the beginning of June. Memoranda had been prepared listing Germany's failure to respect her military and economic undertakings, and these would be the Marshal's main brief for Rastenberg.

Tobescu said that measures had been taken to stop the Germans staging a 'Budapest' while the Marshal was away.* An extra 7,000 gendarmes had been drafted into the capital to strengthen the guards on public buildings – railway stations, ministries, broadcasting stations, etc – and a number of regiments had been moved from the provinces to the vicinity of the capital. Chas heard Tobescu giving orders by telephone to some of the unit commanders; 300 extra men, it seemed, had been allocated to our building alone.

* The Germans had taken Budapest over while Horthy was in Berchtesgaden.

On the 6th, Tobescu told us that, contrary to plan, the Marshal's party were returning from Rastenberg at 4 p.m. that day. The military talks planned for the following morning must, he thought, have been cancelled. He was optimistic. This time the Marshal might really have broken with Hitler, in which case we hoped he would be allowed to return home safely.

Antonescu's plane had taken a roundabout route to the east of Germany. Over Warsaw they saw what looked like a battle taking place below them; it was the Warsaw uprising. Keitel met them, apologised on behalf of Hitler who was still not well, gave each member of the party an arm-band and an identity card, and escorted them to the bunker. Hitler was waiting on the terrace. He shook hands with his left hand since his right was bandaged and in a sling. He looked tired and the atmosphere was strained. No one in Antonescu's entourage was allowed to carry arms or briefcases in Hitler's presence; the damage to the building and Hitler's bandaged arm were constant reminders of the 14 July plot.[4]

While the leaders had their discussions, Magherescu and the rest of the Marshal's party were entertained by German officers. In the evening Himmler appeared briefly and the Germans grew suddenly tense. He looked at each of them in turn and left.

At the crucial meeting between Antonescu and Hitler[5] the Führer first spoke with a wealth of detail about the attempt on his life.[6] He had expected it for six years and was glad it had now happened for it had given the German people a chance to close ranks around him and for him to clean up the army. He reviewed disloyalty in the army over the years, sometimes speaking calmly, sometimes with great agitation. He went so far as to blame the June disaster, when the Red Army had attacked the central instead of the southern front, on the defeatism of his own generals. Antonescu defended Kleist and Mannstein and said that he was sure an investigation into the summer *débâcle* would provide quite other explanations.

There would be no more plots, Hitler said. Himmler was now investigating the army. Nor would there be any trials as in the Soviet Union – merely executions. Those who did not agree with the German conduct of political and military affairs would be liquidated – they and their families. Then, looking the Marshal straight in the eyes, the Führer asked whether Romania and in particular the Conducator himself had decided to stay with Germany to the end. What had the Marshal in mind to do?

Ion Gheorghe describes the Marshal's answer as being potentially decisive. Everything hung on it including not only his own life but the fate of Romania. 'Unfortunately,' he says, 'the Marshal was not up to the historical moment.'[7]

But it is only fair to let the Marshal speak for himself. In a note dictated to Colonel Davidescu a few days later he says that he was

taken completely by surprise by this question which was certainly a
calculated one coming as it did after a description of the drastic
measures . . . taken against those in Germany who did not agree with
Hitler's conduct of affairs. I tried to gain time by expressing my
especial regret about the *attentat* and describing my views on the
situation in the east, the danger for Romania and the difficulties I had
to overcome on account of the enemy bombing.[8]

Returning to the critical question, which he now realised was the reason
for his invitation to Germany, Antonescu told Hitler that he would require
answers to various questions before he could reply. What were Germany's
intentions for the southern front? Romania could not undertake to go to
'total destruction' alongside Germany. When Hitler protested that the
front would be held, Antonescu reminded him that Romania had received
similar assurances in the autumn of 1943 and again in March, yet the
Russians had displayed superiority of forces, technique and manoeuvre. In
the end Hitler admitted that the front could not in all circumstances be
held. Nor could he offer any help against the Allied bombing which he did
not deny could become 'catastrophic' if the Allies obtained Turkish bases.
Although Hitler referred to a new weapon, the V4, which could
revolutionise the war, in effect he could give no assurance on Antonescu's
points – the front, the bombing, the threat from Turkey and Bulgaria. Only
on Transylvania did he repeat that this would be returned to Romania after
the war. But the three Allied Powers, who were far more likely to win the
war, had already promised to revoke the Vienna Diktat so, in effect, Hitler
had offered nothing.

Finding himself on the defensive, Hitler now accused Romania in violent
terms of dragging her feet economically, saying that he suspected either
outright maliciousness or passive resistance. Hitler must have known that
an accusation of duplicity against a man who had done so much for him was
likely to arouse Antonescu. The tactic succeeded: according to Gheorghe,
the Marshal's outburst was greeted with indulgent smiles on the part of the
Germans present.[9]

According to Paul Schmidt, Hitler's interpreter, the Führer warned
Antonescu that the Russians would never allow the British to make a
landing in the Balkans. He said that his promise to save the Crimea, where
so many Romanian troops had been lost, had been made in good faith but
the weather had been against him. He would not let Romania down.[10]
Antonescu seems at that point to have decided to end what had been a
pretty rough session for both men on a note of goodwill. He did not, he
said, doubt Hitler's ultimate aims and wanted to emphasise that Germany
had no ally more loyal than Romania. Romania would remain on
Germany's side and would be the last country to quit her; Antonescu was
aware that Germany's end would also be Romania's.

After a few personal remarks the Führer then brought the conversation to a close. Schmidt adds that he was so exhausted that he asked Ribbentrop to make his excuses at the dinner arranged for that evening.

Later, alone with his own delegation, Antonescu called the Germans 'gangsters'[11] and Hitler a *'nebun furios'* – a raging madman;[12] at the interview, he said, they had had him by the throat. He had failed to make the break with Hitler; on the other hand he must have given the impression that he knew he had very good grounds for doing so if ever he could bring himself to the sticking point.

It must have been a macabre dinner. Antonescu resented the Führer's absence. The 'slimy' Mihai Antonescu (as Guderian described him) was at loggerheads with Ribbentrop. Guderian was a constant reminder that his predecessor as chief of staff had been arrested. Only Himmler seemed to be enjoying himself. After dinner, Guderian made the situation report, and Hitler was present for this. 'During the conference,' Guderian wrote later,

> Antonescu showed that he fully grasped the difficulties of our situation and the need for reforming, first of all, Army Group Centre's front and then for re-establishing contact between Army Groups Centre and North. The Marshal himself proposed that Moldavia be evacuated and that, if the common interests of the allied powers should make such a withdrawal desirable, we withdraw to a line Galatz–Focşani – the Carpathian Mountains. [This was the narrow gap between the mountain range and the Black Sea which formed one of the best defensive positions in Europe]. I immediately translated this magnanimous offer to Hitler . . .[13]

Guderian was pleased that his French proved good enough to handle the discussion without an interpreter; over-confidence in his linguistic powers might possibly explain the contradictory accounts of the meeting left by Guderian and Gheorghe.

According to Gheorghe, the Marshal accepted the arguments for the redeployment of German troops following the summer disaster, but insisted that they should be either replaced or brought back in good time to meet a Soviet offensive in the south which, according to his intelligence, would occur quite soon. The Marshal, Gheorghe said, was not satisfied with the conditions under which Romania was being asked to conduct the war. Lying awake in bed that night Gheorghe remembered that to the question of what should be done when the Moldavian front collapsed the Marshal had replied 'with a weary gesture'.[14] He had no longer wanted to hear of withdrawal to his favourite Focşani–Nămăloasa–Galaţi line. Antonescu believed, according to Gheorghe, that if the front in northern Moldavia could not be held then an end should be made to the war.

Whatever the truth about this briefing, there is no doubt that General Friessner, the new Commander of the Army Group Southern Ukraine, recommended that the line should be withdrawn to the Focşani–Galaţi position; and that Hitler, who had seemed indecisive since the 14 July plot, would not agree without hard evidence that a Soviet offensive was planned in the southern sector. Evidence of this was not forthcoming until 20 August when the offensive itself had begun and even then the German High Command did not believe it to be more than diversionary.

At Hitler's headquarters Romanian loyalty was being reassessed. Von Killinger and Hansen continued to send back reassuring reports, but Friessner was far less confident. Ribbentrop himself was now sufficiently disturbed to ask Hitler to transfer a panzer division from Yugoslavia to Bucharest. But again Hitler could not make up his mind, and nothing was done.[15] If Hitler had agreed to this the Romanian *coup* might not have occurred or, if it had, would most likely have failed.

We prisoners had seen the Marshal returning to Bucharest from Germany on 6 August. We were being taken on one of our drives around the capital and were near the Baneasă airfield when his plane, a Heinkel, touched down with its fighter escort. We saw a small group around the plane and recognised Vasiliu and Tobescu. On our way back to gendarmerie headquarters we noticed that the special guard which always turned out for Antonescu was not lining the road and decided that he must have driven straight from Baneasă to report to the King in Sinaia. We were still hopeful that he had broken with Hitler, though the absence of any rumours of such a dramatic event worried us.

Two days later, Tobescu told us what he knew of the visit, and it was not encouraging. The government as such had been told nothing; Cristescu had had to pick up the following snippets of information from National Peasant circles who were, of course, in touch with the King. According to these sources, Hitler had demanded an immediate rupture of relations between Romania and Turkey; assured Antonescu that the seven or nine armoured divisions which had been removed from the Romanian sector and transferred to Lemburg would shortly be replaced; and assured him that the eastern front was now firmly under control and that he possessed sufficient reserves in the Reich 'to liquidate the entire Anglo-American forces between the Loire and the Seine'.

The new German chief of staff had been very optimistic, speaking of some new weapon which could change the whole course of the war. He had given what seemed to be a frank assessment of the general military situation but had used falsified figures to reassure Şteflea about the Romanian sectors of the eastern front.[16]

If one takes into account Gheorghe's version of the meeting, it seems unlikely that either the Marshal or his chief of staff were really taken in. More likely Antonescu's relations with the King were so strained that he could not bring himself to admit what he really felt about a situation for which he himself was mainly responsible.

Antonescu had, as we thought, gone straight to see the King. According to Tobescu, he had then driven to Olăneşti where he refused to see any member of his government, except Ica, for five days. Ica busied himself with his diplomatic contacts in neutral countries. He seems to have been collecting funds for a quick getaway, one day shocking Madame Antonescu and her secretary by walking into their room followed by a valet carrying a box, which he then unlocked, pouring gold coins over the table.[17] Ica was the exception; none of the other leading figures in the story – the King, the Marshal, Maniu and his close collaborators – had made any provision to send funds abroad. One wonders why Antonescu put up with a confidant who had so little in common with him.

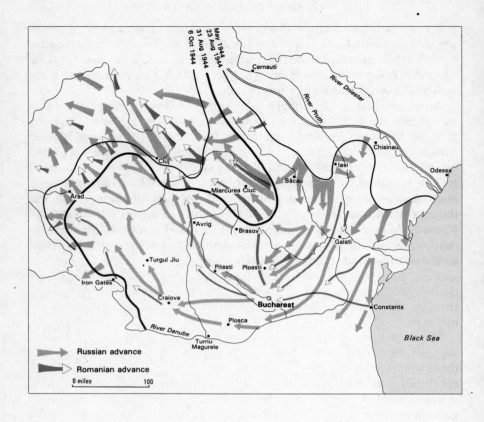

May 1944
23 Aug 1944
31 Aug 1944
6 Oct 1944

Cernauti

River Dniester

River Pruth

Chisinau

Odessa

Iasi

Bâcau

Cluj

Miercurea Ciuc

Arad

Avrig

Brasov

Galati

Turgul Jiu

Pitesti

Ploesti

Craiova

Bucharest

Constanta

Iron Gates

Plosca

River Danube

Turnu
Magurele

Black Sea

Russian advance

Romanian advance

0 miles   100

Chapter 23[1]

The Coup: I

Marshals

By the beginning of August Generals Malinovsky and Tolbukhin were ready for the offensive on the southern sector. Malinovsky would break through north-west of Iaşi and then proceed towards the Bǎcau–Vaslui–Felciu line – the Romanian Fourth Army headquarters were at Bǎcau – thus encircling the Iaşi–Cernǎuţi enemy concentration. His next objective would be Focşani, and so through the narrow gap between the Carpathians and the Black Sea into Romania proper. Meanwhile, Tolbukhin would destroy the concentration of forces in the Cernǎuţi area, approaching through the swamps of Kitskan, a manoeuvre which the Germans would not expect.

The final form of this operation was incorporated in a directive of 2 August, three days before Hitler assured Antonescu at Rastenberg that there would be no offensive in the southern sector. At the time Hitler was on the edge of a nervous breakdown and Antonescu in a state of deep depression. Had they taken General Friessner's advice and withdrawn in good time to the Focşani line they might well have held the superior forces of the Red Army for a time at least. As it was, the commander of the Romanian Fourth Army was not even allowed to withdraw to the line of the Prut so as to secure the passage of Romanian troops in Bessarabia.

After his Rastenberg visit the Marshal continued to follow the course of the war from his villa in Olǎneşti. On 15 August, Allied troops disembarked between Toulon and Cannes and, in western France, the decisive battle of the Falaise was fought. The King went to Bucharest, officially on his way to the Danube delta for the opening of the duck-shooting season, unofficially for a meeting in the Palace with his collaborators. However, the meeting had to be cancelled. Between the 15th and 17th there were almost continuous day and night raids and if – for example – Maniu and Pǎtrǎşcanu had had to go together to the Palace shelter, which was used by the public, people might have wondered what the leaders of the Communist and National Peasant parties were up to.

It was at about this time that Colonel Teodorescu, the Romanian military attaché in Ankara, attended a meeting in Bucharest and brought

Antonescu up-to-date news of the Cairo negotiations. The Soviet offer through Madame Kollontay was still on the table, but the Marshal could not bring himself to accept any terms – however good on paper – without being sure that Anglo-American troops would be available at the time of the *volte face*. Teodorescu could not have given him any such assurance. Antonescu sent a message back with him appealing to the Western Allies not to miss this last opportunity of playing a military part in the Balkans.

Meanwhile, in the Palace preparations for the *coup* were proceeding. The Marshal had approved a plan for the defence of Bucharest's key installations – the telephone exchange, the radio station, etc – and Colonel Dămăceanu reckoned that under cover of a practice exercise he could put his brief into reverse and take them over. A Romanian engineer was ready to cut German lines passing through the Romanian central switchboard. Emil Bodnăraş, alias Engineer Ceaşu, the Communist leader, could raise 2,000 men to free anti-fascist prisoners and to arrest Antonescu and other senior members of the Romanian and German administrations. There were, however, military objections to this plan. Ceaşu's men would require small arms, which were in short supply. The Romanian regular army might itself open fire on a gang of armed civilians. The committee decided to concentrate instead on strengthening regular Romanian forces in the capital and – no doubt to Maniu's relief – dropped Ceaşu's paramilitary operation.

The Communists would, of course, have preferred an armed uprising led by 'patriotic workers'. They complained about 'prevarication' by the traditional parties, and the King was sometimes inclined to agree with them. Bodnăraş may well have had detailed instructions from the NKVD in Moscow, even though on the day after the *coup* Molotov told the British Ambassador that his own ministry had no idea of what was going on in Romania.[2]

Maniu resisted pressure from the King and Pătrăşcanu to lead a coalition government of political parties, which he knew would have to include Communists in important posts. He argued that the armistice should be signed if not by Antonescu, who had brought the country to this pass, then by a government of technicians led by a soldier; the time for political government would be after a constitutional free election had been held.

The Palace also had encouraged Antonescu to conclude an armistice with the Allied Powers. Had the Marshal been ready to accept Madame Kollontay's terms earlier, the King would have supported him. As D-day approached and their plans became firmer, the Palace group were probably less inclined than Maniu to urge the Marshal to do the deed, yet they always felt that the King must give Antonescu a last chance to save himself. If the Marshal again refused, except on conditions that would jeopardise the *coup*, then they should detain him and go ahead as planned. Their success would depend on the loyalty of the army, the prompt disruption of German communications, and the ability of local troops to hold the capital until those at the front could reinforce them.

Meanwhile Ştirbey and Vişoianu in Cairo had formed the clear impression that the USSR would now prefer a straightforward conquest of Romania without any help from the opposition. After much conscience-searching they sent the King a telegram urging him to put a stop to military operations against the USSR without waiting any longer for a reply from Cairo regarding the Romanian plan.[3]

In mid-August the German High Command began to take the possibility of a push in the southern sector a little more seriously, and Friessner asked for German troops to be ordered back to the line. On Saturday the 19th, Antonescu abandoned his cure and set off for the capital. He and his wife spent the night at their Predeal house.

The diary notes that on the 18th the Romanians repelled an attack near Tighina. On the 19th there was more fighting south-west of Tighina and in the region of Iaşi. Timoshenko took up his position at Forward Command Post on Height 195. At dawn on the 20th, after a terrific artillery barrage, Timoshenko and Malinovsky attacked with 90 divisions and some 1,750 planes. Friessner opposed with 27 divisions, including 400 tanks and 800 planes, and the Romanians with 20 divisions, of which only one was armoured. On the first day of the attack Malinovsky penetrated deep into German defences north-west of Iaşi and the Romanian foot infantry began to crumble.

That morning the Marshal drove from Predeal to Snagov, from where he took a plane to the Fourth Army Headquarters at Băcau. Arriving at about mid-day to find the command indecisive, he ordered counter-measures to give the Romanian army time to stabilise. Some members of the Marshal's staff blamed the 'defeatist generals', men like Sănătescu, head of the King's military household, for the demoralisation of Romanian troops. This seems very far-fetched. The Romanian soldier was no fool. He had been in retreat for over two years, and had been treated badly by his German allies, particularly in the Crimea. He had never had adequate anti-tank or air protection, and now he saw his lines strung out to defend the territories for which Romania had gone to war, with forces and equipment that were clearly inferior to those facing them. He was outclassed and he knew he was fighting a lost war. He did not need Sănătescu or any other general to tell him that.

The Palace staff telephoned the King at Sinaia to say that the front south of Iaşi had been penetrated by powerful tank units and that the chances of stabilising it were problematical. The King immediately drove to Bucharest in the sports shirt and flannels he happened to be wearing at the time and that evening he had a meeting with his closest collaborators and military advisers.[4] The political parties were not represented. Styrcea began by describing conditions at the front, and it was agreed that the change of government must be made before a large part of Romanian territory had been occupied. The King asked Colonel Dămăceanu how long he needed to have his part of the plan ready. Five days was the answer so the *coup* was confirmed for Saturday the 26th at 1 p.m. The Marshal and Mihai Antonescu would be invited to lunch, to be followed by an audience to discuss how best to proceed. If the Marshal refused immediate negotiation with the Allies the King would dismiss him and appoint a new government according to a list still to be drawn up by the political parties. This government would invite the German armies to evacuate Romanian territory, and would empower its representatives in Cairo to sign the armistice. A telegram should be sent immediately to Ştirbey and Vişoianu bringing them up to date.

A telegram should also go to General Wilson asking for the bombing at 1 p.m. on the 26th of German barracks and airfields on the outskirts of Bucharest and certain Hungarian railway centres, followed the day after by the bombing of communication centres between Hungary, Bulgaria, Yugoslavia and Romania. After so many weeks of silence from Cairo no one really expected a response to this telegram. Nevertheless, they worked late pinpointing map references of the German barracks to the north of Baneasă airport, deciding which points of entry into the country the Germans were likely to use when they counter-attacked.[5]

By the following day, the 21st, Romanian positions between Iaşi and Târgul Frumos had been smashed, and the Russians were proceeding down the valley of the Prut with the remnants of the Romanian army in full retreat. The German positions at Iaşi had been outflanked from the east and west. Tolbukhin's mechanised forces were then only twenty miles from the Prut, cutting off the German line of retreat. Yet the German High Command still considered the offensive as no more than a supporting attack. The Marshal ordered withdrawal to another line and sent officers from his headquarters to help. They returned with news of disorganised troops, many cut off from the main body. Romania's only armoured division had suffered heavy losses; the fate of the Romanian and German armies in Bessarabia was not known.

That evening the procedure and draft telegrams agreed by the King with his Palace advisers the evening before were approved by the representatives of the National Democratic Bloc at their last plenary meeting before the *coup*. It was attended by King Michael, Iuliu Maniu, Constantin Brătianu, Lucreţiu Pătrăşcanu, Titel Petrescu, Grigore Niculescu-Buzeşti, Ion Mocsony-Styrcea, Constantin Sănătescu and Mircea Ionniţiu. Pătrăşcanu produced a draft proclamation and draft political amnesty for the King's approval. The only point of disagreement was on the composition of the post-*coup* government. Pătrăşcanu and Petrescu still argued for a government of political parties led by Maniu, to make it clear that this decisive change in Romania's affairs had the country behind it. Although Brătianu, like Maniu, was in favour of a government of specialists, he was not opposed to Maniu as premier. Maniu again refused. A government of specialists and technicians, he said, could better handle the difficult issues which would arise from the signing of the armistice and the arrival of the Soviet army. The matter was relegated to a committee of two, consisting of Maniu and Pătrăşcanu, who were asked to produce a government list by noon on the 23rd.[6]

At that time, Ionniţiu explains, the composition of the government seemed less important to phase one of the operation than the military aspects of the *coup*. The probable response of the Romanian army to an order to cease fighting alongside the Germans, as well as German reactions, had to be assessed. As Turcanu was now in prison, the telegrams to Ştirbey and Vişoianu and to General Wilson would have to await Cretzianu's next schedule, at 7.30 p.m. the following evening. Dămăceanu would complete his preparations. The politicians should disperse and go about their ordinary business, keeping their heads down until the 26th.

That night, during the early hours of 22 August, Ionel Styrcea drove to Snagov with the two telegrams approved for despatch to Cairo via Cretzianu in Ankara. He handed them to Pogoneanu, who was in charge of cyphers at the Foreign Ministry's Communications Centre at Snagov. Pogoneanu, like Buzeşti, was in the King's confidence. He would cypher the messages and make sure that they were sent by the 7 p.m. transmission. Cretzianu would decypher them and hand them *en clair* to the SOE representative in Turkey, who would then re-encypher them and transmit them to SOE Cairo. It was a cumbersome process.

Styrcea decided on an early morning swim in the lake before returning to Bucharest and so, quite by chance, he received news that meant an immediate change of plan. Ştefan Davidescu, a Secretary General of the Foreign Ministry, was fishing from a rowing boat on the lake. Styrcea swam over to him, and during their brief exchange learned that Antonescu, who was expected back from Băcau that evening, would be returning to the front on the 24th. This meant that he would probably not be in Bucharest on the 26th when the *coup* was to take place.

Styrcea dressed quickly and drove back to Bucharest. During a quick lunch with Buzeşti, Styrcea and Ionniţiu, the King decided that he could not now wait until the 26th and that Maniu should be told of this new development. He knew that Antonescu might well ignore an invitation from himself to come to the Palace. However Mihalache of the Peasant Party and the Liberal Gheorghe Brătianu, Dinu Brătianu's nephew, a professor with pro-German leanings, had reasonably good access to the Marshal and might persuade him that in these decisive days it was important for him to meet the King before returning to Bǎcau. Anyhow, they must try. After lunch Buzeşti looked for Maniu and when he failed to locate him left a message with one of his people. In the evening it was agreed with Maniu that the *coup* must be brought forward to the next day, the 23rd.

The King had already discussed Palace defences and the possible arrest of Antonescu with Colonel Ionescu, who was in charge of the Palace guard. During the last month or so, soldiers had been discreetly transferred to Sinaia, where the *coup* was originally to have taken place, and the guard in Bucharest hd been depleted. Now it was happening at the Casa Nouǎ, the four-roomed house King Carol had built in the Palace garden for his assignations with Madame Lupescu. The drawing room with an adjoining dining room were on the ground floor. Across the hall was the King's study and a bedroom. The large safe, two and a half metres deep, in which the Marshal and Ica could, if necessary, be locked up, was on the first floor. The King personally showed the sergeant-major of the guard how to open it and they fitted it out with two chairs and a small table brought from the bathroom.

That morning, Bǎcau had news of Soviet advance troops approaching Roman, only forty miles away. In the afternoon, Antonescu visited Friessner at his headquarters and agreed on a withdrawal, by stages, to the Focşani–Nǎmǎloasǎ–Galaţi line. When Friessner referred to unrest in Romania the Marshal reminded him that when, in 1939–40, Germany had pledged Bessarabia and northern Bukovina to the Soviet Union and had then forced Romania to give up not only these territories but also the Dobrugea and northern Transylvania, she had demoralised her best ally. Yet instead of joining Germany's enemies Romania had remained loyal to the Reich. The Allies had undertaken to return the Transylvanian territory Germany had taken from her: was it surprising that there was unrest in the country? He, the Marshal, had no political party behind him. There was a limit to what he could do.[7] After this frank interview Antonescu returned to Bucharest where he was met at the airport by, among others, Ica, Cristescu and Piki Vasiliu.

An hour later we prisoners were partly brought into the picture. According to de Chastelain's report, written about a month later:

At 8 pm on August 22nd I was called by General Vasiliu, Inspector General of the Gendarmerie and Under-Secretary of the Ministry of the Interior. He explained the position on the Russian Front in so far as it concerned Roumania. At this stage the Russians were 50 kms. South of Iaşi and had attacked at Cetatea Albă. The General explained that the Roumanians had only one armoured division against an estimated six or seven Russian armoured divisions South of Iaşi, and that there could, therefore, be no question of further resistance. In face of the attack in the South the Roumanian High Command had previously planned a withdrawal, and Roumanian troops would, therefore, retreat towards the Danube in the South and the Galaţi Gap in the West. The General described the position as very grave and added that fortunately the Prime Minister, Mihai Antonescu, had a 'more flexible outlook' than the Marshal. The former had decided that the time had come to make peace with the Allies. I was asked if I would be willing to proceed at short notice to Cairo with the Prime Minister and replied that, although in principle I was willing to do so I should have to insist upon certain conditions being fulfilled before leaving. The General was satisfied with this reply and left to report to the Prime Minister, it being understood that I should provide him with the conditions the following morning.[8]

According to my diary the Marshal had returned from the front at 7 o'clock that evening 'a disillusioned man'. Ica, Vasiliu had said, was to have full powers to negotiate an armistice, and he and de Chastelain would fly to Turkey – the first lap of the journey to Cairo – on the morning of the 24th. Although de Chastelain had no great faith in Ica he was ready to go along with any plan that had a reasonable chance of bringing Romania into the war on our side.

During the drive from the airport Ica put the Marshal in the picture. Antonescu had already spoken to him twice from Băcau but Ica, on his own reponsibility and without waiting for him to return, had tried to force the pace. He had called in the Turkish chargé d'affaires, and through him he had asked the Turkish Government to inform the Allies of Romania's desire to sign an armistice, requesting as a first step a ceasefire. Whether he also told the Marshal of his plan to go in person to Turkey, accompanied by de Chastelain, is not clear. When Vasiliu put the proposal to de Chastelain an hour later he inferred that Ica was acting independently of the Marshal. Later that evening Ica sent a telegram to the Romanian Legation in Ankara, again asking Saracioglu for diplomatic help for himself or anyone coming to Turkey in Romania's name. He wished Turkey to act as an intermediary for the conclusion of an armistice; and wanted to know within twenty-four hours which of three alternative procedures the Anglo-Saxons preferred. He seemed to have learned nothing from all the rebuffs he had received from the Anglo-Saxons over the last eighteen months.

The Marshal had three important interviews that evening. Two were the direct outcome of the working lunch at the Palace. Firstly, Ion Mihalache called on Maniu's behalf. They agreed on the need for an armistice, and discussed the possibility of Anglo-American military intervention. Then Gheorghe Brătianu called on Constantin Brătianu's behalf, and promised to see the Marshal next morning at Snagov with concrete proposals in the name of both parties.

Antonescu also saw Clodius that evening. He reminded him that Germany's undertaking to hold the Moldavian line had not been kept. Unless he received prompt assistance from Hitler he would be forced to conclude an armistice with the Three Powers. For Antonescu, who did not wish to take up arms against his old ally, this was his way of obtaining Hitler's agreement to his pulling out of the war.[9] According to a German report sent to the Foreign Ministry in Berlin on the 24th, the Marshal told Clodius that he would now throw in his last reserves in an effort to stop the Russians, and that if he failed he would have to recover his freedom of political action. Clodius had understood that the Marshal wished to be free to pull out of the war only if the front collapsed.[10] Since the German Military Command apparantly believed the Soviet attack in the south to be purely diversionary, this might explain why Berlin were not alerted immediately of the Marshal's *démarche*. Earlier that day Hitler had held a meeting at his headquarters to discuss the Balkans. He had expressed concern about the danger of a Greater Serbia but had made no mention of Romania.[11]

After the meeting with Clodius Ica sent a courier urgently to Stockholm instructing Nanu to inform Madame Kollontay of the Romanian Government's readiness to conclude an armistice. Then the Marshal, Madame Antonescu, Ica and the aides left for Snagov where they had the use of Prince Nicolas's house, arriving after one in the morning when the lake in summer is at its most beautiful.

Early next morning, Ica told Antonescu that the party leaders would be seeing the King in the afternoon. They wanted to sign an armistice jointly with the Marshal. He urged Antonescu to meet the King as well. Madame Antonescu supported him: 'Look, Ionel, wouldn't it be better to do as Ica says and make an armistice with the opposition? Why continue to take all the responsibility yourself?'[12] Although Antonescu was far from convinced, Ica seems to have taken matters a step further by waking Mircea Ionniţiu with a telephone call to say that he and the Marshal requested an audience for that day. Mircea – who slept in the King's study in the Casa Nouă on these visits to Bucharest – rubbed the sleep out of his eyes, gave the good news to the King, and let Ica know that the King would see them that afternoon.

In prison we, too, were up early that morning. Chas expected to be called down at any minute to plan his journey to Turkey with Ica. He had his list of conditions ready: before leaving he must have an interview with Maniu and an exchange of confidential messages in his own cypher with Cairo, and Ica's party must include a military expert able to provide the Allies with the entire German and Romanian battle orders in Romania. The night before, Chas had already obtained an assurance from Vasiliu about the safety of Silviu and myself if he left the country.

Having heard nothing from Vasiliu by ten o'clock, he asked to see him and was told that the general would not be available until 5.30 that evening. De Chastelain then sent his conditions to Tobescu, at the same time expressing his surprise that in present circumstances there should be such a long delay. In his final report he added, 'I received no reply to my letter and no reference to the conditions, and saw neither General Tobescu nor General Vasiliu again.'[13]

At ten o'clock that morning Vasiliu was in fact at Snagov attending a restricted Cabinet meeting called to analyse the position after the Soviet break-through. He had arrived at about a quarter to along with Pantazi, the Minister of War, Cristescu, Şteflea and Colonel Elefterescu, the Prefect of Bucharest. After examining the military and political situation they agreed that the government should be evacuated to Haţeg in Oltenia. The following rather confused account of part of what the Marshal said was circulating in Bucharest a few weeks later.

> The Gentlemen of the Opposition have seen fit to form a bloc and to treat for peace over the government's head. I recognise that this is a courageous act, but the responsibility lies with Marshal Antonescu – the only one with the right to decide on the question as to whether or not an armistice should be signed with the USSR. These men and their accomplices, the King and the Sinaia clique, have no right to mingle in these things. Marshal Antonescu has no need to be saved, he is strong and a patriot.
>
> Gentlemen, so that you will not consider me obstinate, I shall offer Russia an armistice. I will also warn the Germans and as I am sure that they will refuse to discuss the matter with me, I shall have the task of leading this war to the last man, right to the end, (shouting) until the final victory of the Axis.
>
> At this point, Mihai Antonescu informed the Marshal that the King wished to see him and the Marshal is said to have replied 'Let him leave me in peace. Tell him I have other work to do than to go to the Palace.'[14]

This over-dramatised version might in substance be roughly what the Marshal did tell his Cabinet. From evidence given at his trial he is

supposed to have warned Vasiliu and Cristescu privately after the meeting
that he had decided to sign an armistice jointly with Maniu and Constantin
Brătianu. But that was after seeing Georghe Brătianu.

Early that morning a meeting had taken place at Constantin Brătianu's
house at 16, Calea Dorobanţilor, at which Maniu and Brătianu – I believe
Titel Petrescu was included – charged Gheorghe Brătianu with making a
last appeal to the Marshal. Maniu wished the armistice to be accomplished
with 'a kind of national understanding'. He believed that an armistice
concluded with the collaboration of the government and in particular that
of Antonescu who had the necessary control and moral authority in the
army, would be achieved more quickly and more easily. 'Next morning,'
he said later, 'I asked Mr Gheorghe Brătianu, who had easier access to the
Marshal, to convince him to conclude the armistice since all of us without
exception would stand behind him. We put all our political and social
power at his disposal.'[15]

Gheorghe Brătianu arrived in Snagov at about 10.30. Antonescu sent Ica
out to talk to him, but later left the Cabinet meeting himself to join them.
Brătianu told him what he had been authorised to say. Antonescu listened
silently, remaining standing. He knew very well that the opposition wanted
him to admit his guilt by signing the surrender himself and Ica and his
friend Gheorghe Brătianu began to lose hope. Then, quite suddenly,
Antonescu agreed; he asked only for a 'letter of guarantee' from Maniu
and Constantin Brătianu confirming what Gheorghe Brătianu had told
him. Brătianu promised to return with this letter by three o'clock and
suggested that the Marshal should ask right away for an audience with the
King. Colonel Davidescu, the head of the Marshal's military cabinet, then
telephoned the Palace to ask for an audience at four o'clock, which was
agreed. Mihai Antonescu obtained a separate one for 3.30.

Before returning to the Cabinet meeting the Marshal asked Ica to set out
the government's position on the armistice terms in a memorandum which
could be sent to the Russians after his audience with the King. Mihai
Antonescu's document was little more than an expansion of a memorandum Nanu had already handed to the Soviet Embassy in Stockholm two
months before, to most of which Moscow had already agreed in the terms
offered through Madame Kollontay.

Late that morning, after the Marshal and Mihai Antonescu had asked to be
received by the King, the King had a meeting with General Sănătescu,
General Aldea, Styrcea and Niculescu-Buzeşti. They decided that the
confrontation with Antonescu, which could lead to his arrest, must take
place that afternoon. Buzeşti and Styrcea then went into town to bring
Maniu and Pătrăşcanu up to date. Buzeşti could not find Maniu, but left a
message with his aide that he and Brătianu were required urgently at the

Palace. Neither turned up. Styrcea saw Pătrăşcanu, who promised to come with Titel Petrescu, but only after dark. So much, Ionniţiu commented at the time, for the confidence of the political leaders in the success of a *coup*.

At one o'clock the Marshal received a signal from the Fourth Army Commander to the effect that the front was collapsing. That day five German corps were trapped in the fighting about the little town of Huşi on the Bessarabian border. Soviet troops cleared Tighina, to the south-east of Cernăuţi and others were racing south for the Focşani gap. At 1.30 the Cabinet meeting broke up and the Marshal had lunch and a short siesta. In Bucharest Cristescu called a meeting of his senior officials and hinted at the collapse of the Antonescu government. Meanwhile, Gheorghe Brătianu could find neither Brătianu, who had gone to his country house at Florica, nor Maniu. Just before three o'clock he arrived disheartened at Snagov. The letter, he said, would be forthcoming, but would take a little time to draft; the Marshal could, of course, refer to it in his interview with the King. But the Marshal was furious. Brătianu had come back with *vorba* – nothing but words. Mihai Antonescu could now go to the Palace alone and offer the King the Marshal's apologies.

In the Palace, all details were being checked. Colonel Ionescu was prepared to defend the building with his fifty-two soldiers. If the Marshal was held then his escort must be arrested and the cars removed from view of the Calea Victoriei. To reduce the chances of immediate counter-measures the Marshal's closest collaborators should also be detained. The most important of these were General Pantazi, General Constantin (Piki) Vasiliu, General Gheorghe Tobescu and Eugen Cristescu.

The temperature rose to 38°. The streets were melting. In the Palace all the shutters were closed against the sun. They had hors d'oeuvres for lunch, and ran over their plans yet again. Mircea Ionniţiu was ready to warn the telephone engineer, who had promised to cut the telephone lines from German headquarters to Germany and German units within Romania. The audience would take place in the yellow drawing room of the Casa Nouă. Aldea, Buzeşti, Styrcea, Ionniţiu and Ionescu were to wait in the King's study, and Captain Anton Dumitrescu and three NCOs in a corridor behind.

It grew even hotter after lunch. Then, just before 3.30 Mihai Antonescu, the Foreign Minister, arrived and was escorted to the Casa Nouă by Colonel Ionescu. The King, with General Sănătescu, received him in the drawing room. Ica said that the Marshal had asked him to present his excuses and to explain that he had to leave urgently for the front. It was not the first time that Antonescu had been off-hand with King Michael, but on this occasion the future of the country depended on the Marshal's attendance in person. While the King and Ica discussed the situation at the front, Sănătescu went to the telephone and told the Marshal that he had plenty of time to come to the Palace before going back to the front, and, moreover, the King knew it. What was the point, he asked, of insulting the King, of chopping off the last branch that might in the end support him?

Sănătescu may not have liked deceiving his old friend but there was much more at stake than his personal feelings. The Marshal changed his mind and said he would come.

We know from what Vasiliu had told de Chastelain that Mihai Antonescu had a plane standing by to take him to Turkey. We do not know whether he offered his services to the King – probably not when he learned that the Marshal had changed his mind and was coming to the Palace after all. According to Colonel Emilian Ionescu, however, Ica asked for plenipotentiary powers to negotiate an armistice in Ankara, which the King refused. The King would not change horses at this stage – particularly with a man as unreliable as Ica.

The Marshal arrived soon after four o'clock. He was tense and completely exhausted and missed his step on the way in. He felt that the party leaders had let him down by failing to confirm their offer in writing. He had been talked into coming to this house where no one – except possibly Sănătescu – liked him, and even Sănătescu did not agree with him. He had nothing but bad news for the King, and he certainly did not need his advice. He wanted to get back to the front where he was respected and might still do some good. And he had just driven from Snagov, in uniform, in a car which, in those days, was not air-conditioned.

Colonel Ionescu escorted him to the drawing room, where he found Sănătescu in civilian clothes, his Foreign Minister in a morning suit and the King in the sports shirt and flannels he had been wearing when he drove down from Sinaia three days before. That, in itself, would have annoyed the Marshal.

For the King, who was by far the youngest of the four men present, the meeting that was about to take place was a personal ordeal: could he stand up to a man who had grown used to authority and had bullied him for years? So much depended on today's interview and in that it differed from all its predecessors. On the other hand he had a solid brief, and the backing of the political parties and probably the army. The risks were considerable, and knowing that would in itself act as a spur.

The head of the King's military household, General Sănătescu, was a distinguished soldier, still as slim as a young cavalry officer. With his soft Moldavian voice, which he never raised, he always seemed to calm any disagreements within the Palace. But now he had to witness what amounted to a showdown between his old army friend, with whose political ideas he could not agree, and the young King to whom he was devoted. He was also worried that Maniu would not change his mind about accepting the premiership after the *coup* and that the job, for which he felt himself quite unsuited, would fall to him.

Ica no doubt felt rather too warm in his formal clothing – even though it would have been of the best lightweight English cloth. He may well have been thinking that if only Ionel was less obstinate and irascible there could still have been a way out of this mess for both of them.

As for the Marshal, he knew that he was always at his most unreasonable and peremptory when faced by the 'Palace clique'. He considered none of them trustworthy except Sănătescu: none had been to the front; they would all like to get rid of him but did not dare.

Colonel Ionescu, who was standing behind the thick curtain which divided the drawing room from the dining room, said later that the Marshal gave a fairly detailed account of the situation at the front. He explained the measures he had taken to stop the Soviet offensive. If need be, he said, he would conclude an armistice when the front had been withdrawn to the fortified Focşani–Galaţi zone but only after obtaining Hitler's consent. To this end he had already had an interview with Clodius. He could not agree, even in principle, to a truce until he had had the Führer's reply. He then spoke on the lines of Ica's memorandum: he would require guarantees that the country would not be occupied, and that frontier questions would be dealt with later at a peace conference.

When the King remarked that 'it is too late for us to start to haggle', the Marshal repeated that without guarantees he would continue to fight alongside Germany.

The conversation then became more lively. The King insisted that the military situation – about which, he said, he was already informed – was far too serious for further prevarication. The front had been broken and part of the country was already under Soviet control. An armistice should be signed immediately. At this point Ica and Sănătescu joined in to try to persuade the Marshal, and when Antonescu saw that everyone, including his own Foreign Minister, had turned on him he began to lose his temper. When the King asked him whether he would give way to someone who was prepared to contact the Allies he replied, 'Never.'

According to Nicolette Franck, he warned the King that he, Marshal Antonescu, would never put the country 'into the hands of a child'. The King seemed to control himself with an effort but, as he said later, 'I knew at that precise moment that the business would only really be settled between him and me. I had hoped that a solution would come from him. It did not happen. It had become clear that in his view if he had to fall Romania must collapse with him . . . Hitler who was mad had involved this man in his madness.'[16] When he spoke to de Chastelain later that day the King was still shocked by Antonescu's state of mind. The Marshal had asked Dr. Filderman, the leader of the Jewish community, to persuade American and British official circles to send missions to Romania in the event of a Russian occupation. Antonescu was a close friend of Dr Filderman, but to think that the latter could influence the policy of the Three Powers on such a matter seemed to indicate how divorced he was from the real world.

The King then made some excuse and crossed the corridor to his study, where he told the others that the moment had come. The guards were alerted. The King drank a glass of water and returned to the drawing room, where Ica and Sănătescu were still arguing with the Marshal. After listening for a moment the King used one of the phrases he must have rehearsed to himself before the meeting: 'In that case, Marshal, I must take account of the wishes of my people as expressed through the four democratic parties. I must take measures to pull the country immediately out of the war and save it from disaster. To this end I have decided that you should this very day conclude an armistice and if you refuse I shall order your resignation right now.'

When the Marshal said that he took orders from no one the King replied that if that was his answer he was dismissed and there was nothing more to discuss. He left the room and motioned Colonel Ionescu to make the arrest. Ionescu, in his turn, signalled the guard, and Captain Dumitrescu and his men entered the drawing room. Antonescu was taken completely by surprise. He looked, puzzled, towards Sănătescu who simply shrugged. For a moment no one seemed to know what to do and there was a chance that the Antonescus would escape. Then Ionescu pushed aside the curtain and shouted 'Execute' – meaning 'execute the order you have been given' – at which the Marshal, perhaps misunderstanding what was meant, said to his old friend Sănătescu, 'You can't treat me like a bandit.' But the spell had been broken. The captain walked up to the Marshal and told him he was under arrest. The Marshal turned and spat on him. Antonescu and his Foreign Minister were then led up the stairs, Ica looking pale as a sheet. When the Marshal turned and saw the King's staff in the hall, holding pistols behind their backs in case the business degenerated into a shoot-out, he shouted, 'You'll live to regret this. Tomorrow you will all hang in Palace Square.'[17] They were silent for they knew that, without a great deal of luck, the Marshal could well be right.

The King returned to his study and drank another glass of the spring water he kept in his room. Although his personal ordeal was over, he knew that things could still go badly wrong. According to Antonescu, Clodius and therefore Berlin had been warned that the Marshal was toying with the idea of surrender. The Germans might at that very moment be preparing to occupy the country. He could well find himself and his colleagues under arrest and on their way to Germany before the day was out. While they were discussing what to do next Mircea Ionniţiu heard a dull thud upstairs and knew that the safe door had been shut. He looked at his watch; it was just five o'clock.

Chapter 24

The Coup: II

The young King had looked in vain for Maniu's moral support that afternoon. Instead of going to the Palace Maniu had dropped in on an old friend, a radiologist called Dr Ionel Jovin, where he happened to meet another old friend, Rica Georgescu.

Rica had been attending Dr Jovin for treatment after damaging a ligament playing hand-ball with the Racottas in the prison yard. That afternoon he had arrived with his escort at three o'clock, as usual, but was immediately taken to a room behind the surgery, where he found Maniu sitting next to a telephone. At about five o'clock Buzeşti rang to say that the arrests had been made. Georgescu urged Maniu to reconsider his attitude to the premiership: he was the obvious man to lead the new government; the whole country and the Allies – particularly Great Britain – would expect it of him. The old man listened politely, as was his way, and thanked Rica for his advice, but his mind was made up.

Maniu had all along argued that an administration of technicians could best handle the problems arising from the armistice and act as a caretaker government until elections could be arranged. It was a valid point of view. Maniu also hesitated to head a government which would include Communists and would surrender unconditionally to the Russians. Mistrusted by the Russians for his commitment to Western democracy, yet rebuffed repeatedly by the Western Allies, he may well have wondered whether he was the best man to lead his country at this particular time. Whatever his reasons, he refused to head the post-*coup* government and stayed away from the Palace while it was being formed. Had the Gestapo, as was their habit, been watching the leader of the National Peasant Party for indications of a Palace insurrection that afternoon, they would have been badly misled.

At eight o'clock Maniu left Dr Jovin's surgery; five minutes later Rica set out with his escort for Colonel Radu Ionescu's office, which was not in the prison building. The prison governor's first reaction to the news was, 'So that's why that bastard Cristescu has kept me waiting.' After discussing the situation with Colonel Ionescu, Rica went to a delicatessen to buy food and drink for a prison celebration. In July Cristescu, at the request of the

Germans, had ordered Lygia Georgescu to go to Sinaia on the grounds that
she was seeing too much of Juliu Maniu, so she celebrated in the mountains
without Rica. At about midnight, General Manolescu, her uncle, called at
the prison to take Rica to dinner. But first they gave Colonel Ionescu a lift
home. Then they left a message at Maniu's house asking him to join them
when he could. On the outskirts of the city, near the turning off to the golf
club, they came on a Romanian road block. Manolescu, who was driving
fast and without lights, could not stop in time, and a soldier shot the
Director of the National Theatre, who was sitting next to him. Instead of
celebrating they spent most of the night at the hospital where their friend
died; after which a saddened Rica returned to prison.

Immediately after the arrests Niculescu-Buzeşti sent a telegram to
Pogoneanu in Snagov for transmission to Cretzianu who would inform the
Allied Powers that the *coup* planned for the 26th had already taken place.[1]
The King had assumed the full prerogatives of head of state, which had not
been possible while Antonescu was in power. A prime minister had to be
appointed to replace Mihai Antonescu who had been both Prime Minister
– though this had been a somewhat nominal function under the Marshal –
and Foreign Minister. Since Maniu was not available, Sănătescu, who had
the respect of the armed forces, was the obvious choice. Ionniţiu typed out
a decree, the King signed it, and Sănătescu put it into his pocket; after
which he set off for army headquarters in Strada Ştirbey Vodă. Some
months later he told Ionniţiu how he had felt as his car approached the
headquarters. 'I could have been arrested on the spot, Mircea, for I was
alone, in civilian clothes, and without an escort.'[2] Had that happened, it
could well have been the end of the *coup*. Luckily, Şteflea, the chief of
staff, was at the front, and he saw instead his deputy, who was a Maniu
man. He took the decree out of his inner pocket, unfolded it carefully and
handed it to the general, who read it through, stood up, saluted and
immediately put himself at Sănătescu's disposal.

For an hour they drafted and despatched instructions. Troops were to
concentrate in the Bucharest-Ploeşti region, drive the Germans out of
Romania and later push forward into northern Transylvania.[3] Not a single
general, senior officer or unit, disobeyed these instructions, which were
sent in the King's name; not one defected then or later in favour of
Antonescu.

By the time the new Prime Minister had returned to the Palace, the
operational centre had moved from the King's study to the larger offices of
the military household. Ionniţiu had already rung his friend at the
telephone company, and within minutes the German lines had been cut.
Most day staff at the German command posts had already returned to their
hotels where they remained incommunicado, and the posts were operating

on a reduced night rota. By 6.30 Dămăceanu's troops were in position and they proceeded to isolate both the command posts and the German High Command.

Marshal Antonescu's escort had been invited into the Palace, where they were offered a drink in the officers' mess and then detained. Their cars were taken to the garage. Not a shot was fired. Colonel Ionescu telephoned Pantazi and Vasiliu and asked them to come to the Palace; they did so, believing that the Marshal wished to consult them. Once they had been told what had happened, Vasiliu put himself at the King's disposal and, when he learned that Tobescu and Cristescu were hesitating to come in, he telephoned them in person. Tobescu agreed but failed to turn up; Cristescu, who had already been warned by his agents that something out of the ordinary was happening at the Palace, told Vasiliu that he would take orders personally from Marshal Antonescu. He then drove to the German Legation to warn von Killinger and seek shelter. He was still there when Romanian soldiers broke in four days later.

Since Maniu and Pătrăşcanu had failed to agree on a ministerial list and in any case Maniu could not be found, the new government had to be formed *ad hoc*. Niculescu-Buzeşti, a counsellor in the Foreign Ministry, was promoted to Foreign Minister and General Aldea became Minister of the Interior. Some posts were filled almost casually when a general walked into the Palace and was spotted by Sănătescu, and not always by the man best suited to the job. Since the new government had to be seen to have the support of the traditional parties the King, though unable to consult them beforehand, appointed the representatives of the four parties – Maniu, Brătianu, Petrescu and Pătrăşcanu – as Ministers of State without Portfolio.

Cristescu did not find von Killinger at the Legation: the Minister was dining with his secretary, Hella Peterson, at her villa at Săftica. However, Cristescu's news brought him back posthaste. He reached the Legation at about 7.30 and found General Erich Hansen, head of the German Military Mission, and General Alfred Gerstenberg head of the German Air Defences, waiting for him. Half an hour later he was at the Palace in full diplomatic uniform, accompanied by his counsellor. The King saw him immediately, with Sănătescu and Niculescu-Buzeşti in attendance.

Von Killinger asked about Marshal Antonescu and was told that he was unharmed. A new government had been formed, headed by General Sănătescu and supported by the political parties. Since Germany was clearly in no position to fulfil her undertakings to Romania the new government would take Romania out of the war. German troops on Romanian territory would not be attacked if the German authorities undertook to evacuate them in the shortest possible time. Sănătescu suggested that representatives of the German command should contact

Romanian army headquarters to make the necessary arrangements.[4] According to one version, von Killinger protested against the appointment of a government which Berlin did not recognise, and had to be reminded by Niculescu-Buzeşti that he was accredited to King Michael, not to the head of the former government.[5] Von Killinger, like Hansen, had repeatedly assured Hitler and Ribbentrop that, in spite of all the rumours, Romanians would never have the nerve to break with the Axis. He asked whether the King and his government had considered the grave consequences of this step and was assured that they had. He then left.

Although clashes with German soldiers could now be expected, Romanian troops were told to avoid any kind of provocation; the authorities wished to delay hostilities for as long as possible. News of the *coup* was given to Hitler at about nine o'clock that evening while he was drinking tea in his room at Rastenberg. His orders were to crush the insurrection, arrest King Michael and replace Sănătescu by a pro-German general.

Shortly after von Killinger had left, Lucreţiu Pătrăşcanu and Titel Petrescu arrived at the Palace. Pătrăşcanu had drafted the King's proclamation which was approved after some amendments by Buzeşti and Sănătescu. Pătrăşcanu had already arranged for it to be printed. He also brought with him two decrees granting an amnesty to political prisoners and abolishing the concentration camps in which many Communists and other political prisoners had been held. Pătrăşcanu pressed for the post of Minister of Justice. The King did not want to offend the other political leaders who had no Cabinet seats; on the other hand he probably knew that the moderate Pătrăşcanu needed every boost he could get within the Communist Party, so he offered him a compromise – Minister of Justice *ad interim*. The King and his advisers then drew up a decree reintroducing the 1923 constitution which King Carol had abrogated six years before. This would remain in force until a freely elected constituent assembly could prepare a new constitution.

In the midst of this drafting, General Hansen and General Gerstenberg were announced. Since their telephone had been cut they had simply turned up. The King asked Sănătescu and Buzeşti to see them.

After explaining the position, Sănătescu asked Hansen to disperse German troop concentrations south of Ploeşti, which were approaching Bucharest instead of withdrawing in the direction of Braşov. At this point Gerstenberg, who had been made responsible for carrying out the Führer's order, intervened to say that the German command had lost contact with German units outside the capital. He was ready to go personally to Ploeşti to prevent clashes with Romanian troops and arrange a German evacuation, but since Romanian troops had closed the Bucharest–Ploeşti road near Baneasă he would need a pass. To Buzeşti's alarm, the Prime Minister agreed to Gerstenberg having not only a permit but also a Romanian colonel to help him through the Romanian lines.

A Romanian lieutenant with a few soldiers had been ably defending the strategic bridge at Baneasă over which all traffic between Ploeşti and Bucharest had to pass. Unfortunately Sănătescu's trust in another cavalry officer's word now undid much of what they had achieved. As soon as Gerstenberg's car reached the German positions at Otopeni, he ordered the arrest of his Romanian escort and took charge of the German attack on the capital.

By then, however, German military telegrams were showing signs of panic. One, timed 22.30 hours, reported that 'Bucharest is in a state of alarm, the town is surrounded by Romanian troops. All ways into the town are blocked. One cannot foresee how the situation will develop. All members of the Legation have collected in the Legation building.'[6] The Germans had been led to believe wrongly that Bucharest was surrounded by Romanian troops because whenever they sent patrols forward they were wiped out – notably by the indomitable unit at Baneasă bridge. The Germans had about 30,000 troops in the Bucharest area but most of these were in barracks and since the telephone lines had been cut they were without orders.

According to the War Journal of the German Army Group South Ukraine:

> The fighting on the Front has been put into the shade by events in Romania . . . We should not fool ourselves that we are dealing with a small treacherous clique. Behind them is the whole Romanian people and in particular the whole corps of generals . . . Hansen, Killinger and Clodius are all agreed that our own forces are far too small to take control of Bucharest and remove the new government – any such action on our part will fail. We, therefore, strongly advise the withdrawal of the orders we have received.[7]

However, at 1.55 a.m. on the 24th the Führer's verbal order was confirmed by telegram.

The King, after several nervous attempts, produced a satisfactory recording of the proclamation which was then broadcast. For most people this was their first intimation that there had been a *coup* in Romania. At the Văcăreşti prison gate a doctor shouted to the Communist prisoners, 'You are free; an armistice has been concluded. Your Pătrăşcanu is at Justice. It was on the radio.'[8] Rica heard the King's broadcast in the delicatessen when he stopped to buy food for his prison party and we heard it in prison.

De Chastelain, who had been waiting to see Vasiliu since eight o'clock that morning, knew nothing of what was going on at the Palace. At 5.30, when Vasiliu should have been available for Chas, he was either on his way to the Palace or had already arrived and had been arrested. At ten o'clock we switched on the news bulletin and were told that an important announcement was about to be made: 'Attention, attention. Leave your wirelesses on after this bulletin. We will broadcast a communiqué of importance to the country.' After the collapse of Chas's plan to accompany Ica to Turkey, we were in no mood for another pep talk by the Marshal; like all Bucharest we were fed up to the teeth with them. The news bulletin at ten o'clock gave no indication of what had happened. The propaganda droned on: France was not even mentioned, though we knew from the BBC that the Paris police had revolted that day and Laval had left the capital.

Then, suddenly, we heard the King's voice.

> Romanians, in this most difficult hour of our history I have decided, in full understanding with my people, that there is only one way to save the country from total catastrophe; our withdrawal from the alliance with the Axis powers and the immediate cessation of the war with the United Nations.*
>
> A new government of national unity has been formed . . . The United Nations have guaranteed the country's independence and non-interference in our internal affairs . . . The new government means the beginning of a new era in which the rights and liberties of all citizens of the country are guaranteed and will be respected.

We prisoners had not known that the King was heading the resistance movement. Now he read out a list of the new government headed by a general we had never heard of – a General Sănătescu – and including the leaders of the three political parties, Maniu, Brătianu and Titel Petrescu plus a Communist, Lucreţiu Pătrăşcanu, who was also to be the *ad interim* Minister of Justice. There was no mention of Antonescu. It was fantastic.

The NCO came in to tell the guards but they already knew. They put their rifles into a corner and shook hands with us. Duţa rushed in, hit me on the back and told me I was free – more or less free, he added, laughing. I felt suddenly older, as if the last eight months had moved into place behind me. I started to pour wine with a new assurance into the glasses the soldiers were holding out.

At about eleven o'clock the Palace telephoned to say that we should be taken there immediately. We picked up our few belongings, said good bye to the soldiers, ran down the stairs and, accompanied by Duţa, Rădulescu and a motor-cycle escort, swept out of the gate and past the tram stop and the tobacco kiosk. But it was not until we reached University Square and I

---

* The term 'United Nations' was used at the time to denote the UK, USA and USSR.

saw the old, familiar building and caught the evening smell of melted tar that I suddenly realised I was free. We heard later that it was the King himself who, in spite of all that was going on that evening, had remembered us.

People were milling around everywhere. The Palace was illuminated for the first time in four years and as we approached it the crowd grew thicker. People were shouting 'Long live the King', 'Long live King Michael', 'Long live England', 'Long live the United States' and, in one corner of the square, 'Long live the Soviet Union'. When finally we could drive no further and had to get out, our uniforms were recognised and for a time the crowd's enthusiasm was turned on to us. I was embraced by both men and women. We were lifted shoulder high and cheered as we were carried towards a side door of the Palace. After eight months' imprisonment I was appalled by contact with so many people, and their voices were still ringing in my ears when the door closed behind us. A man approached us. He was about five years younger than me, and had a modest air and an intelligent, rather studious face. He welcomed us and said he was the King's secretary, and asked whether we needed anything. His name was Mircea Ionniţiu and I would grow to like him more and more over the next few years.

He took us into a large room. We met the Marshal of the Court, Baron Ionel Mocsony-Styrcea – a slim, athletic man with an aquiline face, who struck me as being very intelligent and spoke excellent English. He introduced us to General Sănătescu who chatted away as though this were an interval at the opera rather than a gathering of people involved in one of the critical events of the war. Not, of course, that I saw it that way at the time; for me this was an evening of liberation and excitement, and although I must have known at the back of my mind that I was taking part in an historic event, it is only the sheer happiness of being free that I remember now. When Chas asked about Maniu, the Prime Minister said that neither he nor Brătianu had yet appeared and he did not know where they were.

Titel Petrescu was there in his floppy tie – a kindly man who, I was to discover later, kept open house for anyone who wanted a talk. On that first evening he struck me as an intellectual, drawing-room kind of socialist. There too was Lucreţiu Pătrăşcanu, a Moldavian like Sănătescu, a landowner, and what was called, in those days, a 'national Communist', to distinguish him from the kind whose allegiance was exclusively to the USSR. Later I met his vivacious wife, one of the first women interior decorators of Eastern Europe. I remember thinking how odd it was to be meeting Petrescu and Pătrăşcanu at the Palace that night, but not Maniu, the politician SOE had always associated with the *coup*.

When the King came in through a small door people made way and we were presented. I remember him as a tall shy man to whom chit-chat did not come easily. But that evening he was full of the events of the afternoon. He spoke in private to us of the Marshal's obstinacy. Antonescu had refused to accept that Romania was beaten; he had still wanted to bargain with the Allies. He had maintained that Romanians could not trust the Soviet Union, but King Michael had argued that they had to trust her, and that he would take the responsibility for doing so. Once it became clear that Antonescu had not changed his policy he had decided to put him under arrest and to implement immediately the plan he had made for the following Saturday.

De Chastelain recorded later that the King

> was clearly not optimistic regarding the despatch of Anglo-American troops to Romania, but he certainly was relying upon the provision of small arms, anti-tank guns and bomber support. The King gives the impression of having matured considerably during the three years away from his father's influence. His conversation on the subject of Antonescu's policy was the most sensible I had heard from any Roumanian during the eight months I had been in Bucharest . . . Throughout our talks he was very calm, although worried as to the outcome of the decision he had taken. He said to me, in fact, 'I hope I have done the right thing.'[9]

The King had an immediate problem in that his radio communication with Istanbul had broken down. Anticipating that the Germans would block the road between Snagov and Bucharest, he had arranged for his W/T to be brought to Bucharest and it had been damaged en route. A break in radio communication with both Cairo and Istanbul could affect the whole operation, particularly the bombing of German positions on which he was counting. He took us to his wireless room, where the operator tried without success to raise Istanbul at midnight and 1.00 a.m. We, too, of course, had no way of contacting SOE, and when Chas suggested that he should fly to Istanbul, report what had happened, and make arrangements for radio communication with Bucharest to be restored, the King and Sănătescu jumped at the idea. They would send with him a Romanian staff officer, who could carry instructions to Cretzianu in Ankara and to Ştirbey and Vişoianu in Cairo.

Chas assured them that he would return in not more than four days. It did not occur to us that he would be called to Cairo for one debriefing and to London for another – and that for fear of reviving Soviet suspicions about Autonomous, Moscow's permission for him to return to Romania would never be requested.

De Chastelain travelled to Istanbul in a decrepit Lockheed, flying low to avoid German ack-ack. They pretended to make down the coast for Bulgaria and at the last minute turned out to sea. Istanbul had not been warned of their arrival, so they came in low and, instead of making the usual second turn which would have exposed them to Turkish gun fire, merely dropped on to the runway – and were lucky not to break a wing.

At about eleven o'clock, only half an hour after the King's broadcast, Romanians at the front started to carry out their new orders and the BBC made its first broadcast about the *coup*. About an hour later the Marshal, who was still locked in the Palace strong room, asked for paper and made his will. Mihai Antonescu, also in the strong room, asked to be put in touch with the King so that he could explain 'the important details of his negotiations with the Turkish Foreign Minister'. When this was not granted he wrote a long memorandum which he later tore up.[10]

Bodnăraş then arrived with a group of armed workers wearing arm bands carrying the letter 'P' – Patriotic Front – and took over the Marshal and those senior members of his government who were imprisoned in the Palace. The prisoners were kept at a secret address in the Vatra Luminoasă suburb. They were handed over to the Soviet army when it entered Bucharest and were then taken by train to Moscow.

Sănătescu and de Chastelain had strongly advised the King to leave the capital, which might still fall to the Germans. At two o'clock that morning a convoy of five cars, one driven by the King himself, set off on the long journey to a village in the Transylvanian Alps and was not to return to Bucharest for seventeen days. An officer also left for Sinaia, to take the Queen Mother, Queen Helen, to the same rendezvous; they arrived safely two nights later.

During the small hours the good-looking women of the Red Cross produced sandwiches and coffee in the Palace and asked me about life in prison. They all knew England well, and most of their brothers seemed to have been at school there. We talked for a while, after which I found a small drawing room and fell asleep on the sofa. On the table beside me were photographs of people who strongly resembled our own Royal Family. That must have been at about five o'clock; an hour later I woke to hear a plane overhead and the sound of machine-gunning from the direction of Baneasă and Cotroceni.

PART SIX

August 1944–December 1947

Chapter 25

The Vaults

The Palace was now being bombed systematically from Baneasă, three miles away. I counted a plane every five minutes, which roughly tallied with General Gerstenberg's report next day that 150 day and 40 night raids had been carried out on the Palace. It was, however, his only success. The oil fields had already been cut off by Romanian troops, and petrol workers were preventing tankers getting through to German troop concentrations. The German Legation and German headquarters in Bucharest had been surrounded.

I enjoyed a rather better coffee and roll than we were used to in prison before being told by an *aide* that Mr Maniu had walked down to the Palace that morning and would be glad to see me.

Maniu was sitting at a table with two of the people I had met the night before. Niculescu-Buzeşti, the new Foreign Minister, was a small, slender man, with an intelligent face and warm eyes that seemed interested in everything and I had liked him from the start. Pogoneanu, head of Foreign Ministry cyphers, was partly paralysed and was to show immense courage during the next few years. Maniu himself was a trim man with a small precise moustache. He was wearing a grey tie and one of those hard, narrow white collars my own father used to wear. He looked rather like a schoolmaster; he certainly did not look his seventy-three years. I conversed partly in halting Romanian – I had a large vocabulary but little speaking practice – or else Buzeşti interpreted.

Maniu began by asking whether we had been well treated in prison. He had told our headquarters that we were, and hoped he had not misled them. I assured him that, given the circumstances, we had been well looked after.

He had hoped, he said, to obtain our release. But Ion Antonescu was an obstinate man. He was not a traitor though now he would be treated as one. 'He is just too limited in his outlook to remain in power.' The Foreign Minister was looking to me for a reply but after such long isolation in prison I was feeling a little out of my depth. After a pause Maniu added that his emissary in Cairo could never speak freely because the Russian Ambassador was always present. That was to be expected, I replied. They were our allies.

When he said that he had asked the British for only two thousand parachutists and I commented that two thousand seemed rather a lot he asked me whether I meant too many to re-establish Western influence in Eastern Europe. With them, he said, Romania could have broken with the Axis while the Russians were still beyond the Prut. Two thousand men could have changed the history of post-war Europe. Now, it might be too late.

Before I could reply there was an explosion. The window shattered. My chair shifted. The Minister and I dropped our heads to the table. The lame man stretched out sideways and covered his face. Only Maniu did not move; when I came upright he was waiting for me to continue. I told him that it had taken two weeks to teach me to jump without breaking a leg. But to produce two thousand, fully trained, fighting parachute troops . . . I wondered whether there would be that many to spare in the whole of the Middle East.

He interrupted to say that he had understood. He thanked me and when he smiled I saw why this man had won such a huge following. Also he seemed to have taken my point immediately. If we had succeeded in contacting him the previous December, if Chas had been able to spend the last eight months at his side, the *coup*, I felt at that moment, might have happened much sooner.

Maniu nodded towards the window. The Germans were dropping small bombs, he said, but since they controlled the city's air defences they would continue until the building had been destroyed. This was Hitler's revenge on the King. The next forty-eight hours until Romanian troops could return from the front would be critical; the Germans, he concluded, could still turn the tables.

After meeting Maniu I went into the courtyard and saw that the damage was already quite considerable. Soldiers had been killed and the wounded were being taken down to the shelter. I gave a hand. Wounded were being brought in from the streets, too, and the nurses seemed short of equipment. In one corner of the cellar Sănătescu was holding a makeshift meeting – I noticed Buzeşti, Maniu, Styrcea and the new Minister for Economy and Finance. And then I saw Rica Georgescu – Jockey – or rather it was he who recognised me by my uniform, for we had never met. When he arrived at the Palace Maniu had taken him to a small room where footmen's uniforms were hanging in glass cases and offered him the post of Under-Secretary of State at the Ministry of Economy and Finance. The King, he said, had suggested Georgescu because of his oil experience; it was essential to bring refining capacity up from the low level it had reached after the raid of 18 August, when the Romano Americana refinery had been badly hit by the American air force. Rica was not looking for a political career, and had accepted the post on condition that he could be released once the oil economy was back on its feet. But I heard of this later. At the time I told him about his old friend de Chastelain and asked if there was anything I could do to help. I liked him immediately. I knew from his record with SOE and his long friendship with Chas that I could trust him — and for a young foreigner speaking indifferent Romanian, and finding himself in the middle of a major *coup d'état*, that trust was like an anchor. Rica, too, felt from the start that we were on the same wavelength, and so it has remained for us ever since.

Radio communication was the immediate problem. Rica thought there might be suitcase sets in the attics. We mounted an elegant staircase which had been slightly damaged; higher up, when we changed to a narrower one, there was so little left of the stairs that it became a pretty stiff climb. Up in the attics, it was like being on the roof – whole walls had been blown away. As we emerged, a plane was circling overhead, and we watched the bomb drop into the courtyard. We found a suitcase set but it was so wrecked that there was no point in taking it. The King's radio downstairs had not been hit, but it was still not functioning.

The Palace would soon be uninhabitable. One wing had already been badly damaged and the Casa Nouă completely destroyed. Word went round that we were to move to the vaults of the National Bank. I remember a long corridor to a side door, a car waiting for us there, an American voice calling to me – that of a Texan air force major called Jager. When the prisoners from Calea Plevnei had gone to the shelter in the Gara de Nord they used to pass the POW camp where Jager and other US pilots were imprisoned, and Rica would call war news to them through the wire fence. As soon as Jager and his colonel, Colonel Gunn, were released that morning they had gone to the Plevnei prison and told Rica that until they had contacted their headquarters in Bari they were at his disposal.

The first car that came to the door was machine-gunned from the air and put out of action. Next time there must be no delay. As the plane turned back to Baneasă another car appeared – Number 18 of the King's fleet, which was allotted to us during our stay at the bank. Rica and I carried Pogoneanu on to the back seat, and Maniu got in beside him. Rica sat beside the driver, the King's set on his knee, and I stood on the running board. When the car started with a jerk and began to gather speed I was nearer to a sudden end than at any time during the whole of the Autonomous operation. I banged on the window, Rica wound it down and I had a grip.

The governor met us at the door of the bank and made us as comfortable as he could in his vaults. He had cleared some of the shelves so that we each had a kind of bunk to sleep on. I examined the King's set but could do nothing with it; nor could the Americans. They then tried to get through to Bari and Istanbul on US air force frequencies on their own sets, but with no success. In the bank we felt safe but isolated. We did not know whether Chas had reached Istanbul.* We did not know what had happened to the King. We had only scraps of news about the fighting in the provinces, and could only guess by the direction and closeness of the shooting how the battle for Bucharest was going.

On the other hand, there was a wireless in the bank so we had news from the outside world. The BBC in its overseas broadcasts was commenting almost continuously on the *coup*, describing it as 'an act of great courage which could accelerate the end of the war'. It 'represented a far greater tragedy for Hitler than did even that in the Falaise pocket . . . Germany has lost her only source of petrol; Hitler's days are numbered.' According to the BBC, the Germans had announced the setting up of a puppet government led by Horia Sima, but this had met with no response from within the country. Radio Moscow confirmed Molotov's April assurance that the Soviet Union had no intention of changing the existing social system or in any way diminishing Romania's independence. We were left with the impression that Romania had made an important contribution to the war and would be rewarded. Yet that same day Cordell Hull had made a statement which came far closer to the true Allied position.

> Reports indicate that the Roumanians in the face of overwhelming force of Allied arms are abandoning their inglorious war at Hitler's side. They can now turn to the repentant task of helping to drive the Nazi invader from their country. Germany thus loses the first of her satellites. The Nazis must know that their hold on the Balkans is breaking.[1]

In the evening, General Sănătescu walked down to the bank to advise everyone to leave Bucharest; it was doubtful whether the capital could be held. Some ministers had left with the King, while others were now moving to the village of Bolintinul a few kilometres away. But Rica Georgescu and Niculescu-Buzeşti, the new Foreign Minister who was also in the vaults, decided to stay and I with them.

Before leaving for Snagov on the evening of the 22nd Ica had sent a courier to Stockholm. The courier had spent the night of the 23rd in Berlin. Since the German Government had released no news of events in Romania even to their own police, he was free to take a plane to Stockholm next morning. According to Nanu he burst into the room with 'Mr Antonescu agrees with

---

* De Chastelain had, in fact, sent a telegram from Istanbul to Cairo repeating the King's request for military help.

you. There were various reasons which held him up which I will tell you later . . . I am, therefore, bringing you instructions to see Madame Kollontay immediately . . . Marshal Antonescu is prepared to step out of the picture as soon as necessary and has given him a free hand to sign the armistice.' 'I am afraid you are twenty-four hours too late,' replied Nanu, who had been waiting for months to receive just such instructions.[2]

During the night of the 24th, Buzeşti woke Rica and suggested that they must try to reach army headquarters to obtain firm news of the fighting. They took the Palace car, and they got there without being stopped or shot at though under continual bombardment from the air. The guard halted them and brought out the duty officer. But like most other Romanians, he knew nothing of the people who had been working closest to King Michael. Although he did not recognise Buzeşti, who had no identification, luckily he remembered that the King had mentioned his name in his broadcast. He could tell them that there were some 2,800 Romanian troops in Bucharest and some 20–30,000 German. He could not, however, say how long it would take the Constanţa troops to reach Bucharest; for that they must go to the military liaison office at the Gara de Nord shelter. There an officer told them that the Constanţa troops should arrive next day, and those from Craiova by that evening. Meanwhile reports were coming in from all over the country of the surrender and disarming of German units.

All this was good news but without a radio link they had no way of knowing whether General Wilson had received the King's request for Allied bombing of German positions on the 26th or, if so, whether it would be met. That bombing, they felt, could tip the balance against the Germans.

Then Rica remembered that when Turcanu was arrested his set had been brought to the Plevnei prison. Perhaps it was still there. He woke up the prison storekeeper, who confirmed that it was, and talked him into letting him have it. Hurrying to reach the bank before daylight, he nearly had an accident that would have put paid to our radio communication with Cairo. A cartload of melons had spilled on the road; it was too late to stop; Rica shouted 'don't brake' and they went through them without even skidding. Turcanu came round from his flat in time for the morning schedule at 7.15. Even if Chas had not been in touch with them, I assured them that Cairo would be on the alert.

Half a dozen of us were watching while Turcanu transmitted then listened, transmitted then listened, fifteen, perhaps twenty, times and then held up his hand though there was not a sound in the vault except for the click-click of his key. All of a sudden the key spoke with a different rhythm and he was through. His fragile signal from this underground metal room had been picked up by headquarters a thousand miles away, and with their powerful transmitters they had blasted their way back to us.

We passed messages in my cypher to SOE Cairo. Some were from Maniu and the new government but, to begin with, most were military. The German bombing of Bucharest continued, but on land they were not doing so well. Captured German equipment was piling up. The officer whom Sănătescu had been tricked into sending with Gerstenberg had escaped and returned with useful intelligence. Gerstenberg had brought the several thousand German troops in the Ploeşti area to join forces with those he had at Otopeni and Baneasă. He was depending on further reinforcements from the Ploeşti area but these, and others who had joined them from the front, had been cut off by the Romanians. From his Otopeni–Baneasă positions, Gerstenberg sent patrols forward to test the Romanian defences, but these had been so systematically destroyed that he was deterred from making an all-out attack on the city. There was now a far greater concentration of German forces on the outskirts of Bucharest than there had been when the King had despatched his telegram on the 21st, and one of the first messages we sent to Cairo was to ask for bombing in the Otopeni–Baneasă area if possible within the next forty-eight hours.

Those few days in the vaults were extraordinary for Rica and me. The Prime Minister and most of his Cabinet were out of Bucharest and Maniu, who was staying in town with a friend, only dropped in from time to time. Rica and Niculescu–Buzeşti were each ministers of one day's standing and for a short time Rica, who had by far the greater administrative experience, was taking decisions about any problem that cropped up. For me, too, it was an unreal situation. I had no official position in Romania, yet in the eyes of Romanians I was representing Britain. I was invited to Bolintinul to attend part of a ministerial meeting in the village Sănătescu had moved to but can't for the life of me remember what it was they wanted to consult me about – a good sign, perhaps, if it meant that such unexpected honours did not go to my head.

On 26 August, only three days after the *coup*, the Communist Party made an appeal to the Romanian people – one of many which did not mention the King's part in the *coup*. They claimed that they alone had united all the 'patriotic, anti-Hitlerite' forces of the country. The Party, though supporting and participating in the Democratic Bloc, 'maintains its ideological, political and organisational independence and complete freedom of action in the solution of all problems of a social, economic and political nature in Romania'.[3]

Maniu must have seen in it confirmation of his fears. But most of us were concerned with the more immediate future. That morning some four hundred American bombers and fighters flew over Bucharest and dropped their bombs on the targets we had indicated. Five months before, General Wilson had told Maniu and Antonescu that massive air support would be available from his theatre and, at last, he had been given a chance to fulfil his promise. Inevitably, there were accidents. A Romanian Guards regiment had driven the Germans back at Băneasă, and themselves received many of the direct hits meant for the enemy. But the bombardment was decisive. That day Gerstenberg had been replaced by Lieutenant General Rainer Stahel, a specialist in repression who had come direct from Warsaw, yet he failed to destroy Romanian resistance. After the bombardment, the Romanians began to drive steadily westwards. As it moved through the country the Soviet army found that liberating Romanian towns often amounted to marching through streets of cheering Romanians with not a German in sight. After what they had been through they deserved this respite, though repeated BBC announcements that the Red Army had 'liberated' yet another Transylvanian town eventually began to get on our nerves.

By the 27th, the capital had been cleared (*deblocată*) of Germans. The Romanian army had taken thousands of prisoners, including Gerstenberg, and much military material. The German Legation was known to be running short of food and water. Sănătescu and his ministers returned from the country and at a Cabinet meeting held that day in the vaults Aldea, the Minister of the Interior, argued that since Bucharest was no longer threatened Bodnăraş's paramilitary troops should now be disarmed. Pătrăşcanu objected and nothing was done. Maniu insisted on respect for diplomatic and humanitarian usage; the Germans could be exchanged later for Romanian diplomats still in Germany. Again, Pătrăşcanu did not agree and the diplomats – except for von Killinger – were finally handed over to the Red Army along with Antonescu, his ministers and their families. When a Romanian detachment entered the German Legation Manfred von Killinger had already shot his secretary and himself.

Chapter 26

Post-Coup Euphoria

We left the vaults on 27 August. I was keen to set up a station as quickly as possible and to begin to send back information to Cairo. Rica found me an office in his new ministry on Calea Victoriei. Turcanu brought along the W/T. I asked Sylvia Placa, an English girl married to a Romanian – a good friend of Olivia Manning's and possibly the Bella of her trilogy – whether she would join my team. She agreed but forty-eight hours later decided that, with the Russians due to arrive, it was too risky. I then asked Annie Samuelli and she was game. Conditions were cramped. People were in and out of the office all day long and late into the evening – many simply wanted to shake hands with the British officer – and at first we found it difficult to get any work done. Rica's network now transferred to me. Their information went to Cairo under my symbol, DH88, instead of Jockey. I saw quite a lot of Niculescu-Buzeşti. We had links, too, with Romanian army headquarters and Rica, now a busy member of the new government, still found time to drop in with information and messages. I was also building up my own contacts. I remember in particular the journalist, Liviu Nasta, who continued to give first me and later, when he arrived, the Political Adviser objective reports, often quite critical of the bourgeois parties.

Rica and Lygia invited Silviu and me to stay with them at their house in Strada Grigore Mora, 14. We lived on the first floor, and Maniu had a flat on the ground floor. A Russian colonel called Grigorenko and his wireless operator, a girl lieutenant, were in the attics. A quiet bland man who had been in prison with Rica, Grigorenko used to sit with him in the Gara de Nord shelter during air raids and they had become friends. After the *coup* Grigorenko had been taken by the Communist Party to the home of Pătrăşcanu's nephew, but when Rica suggested that he might be safer with him until the Russian army arrived he had jumped at the offer. This was probably a mistake on his part – he already got on with Rica, a friend of Britain, far better than was good for him. Still, there he was in the house, and we all liked him and his lieutenant girl friend.

On 22 August, Friessner had reported that the Focşani–Galaţi line could be held. Two days later he reported that this was no longer the case. After the *coup* the nine Romanian battalions defending the Focşani–Galaţi zone dismantled their heavy armament and moved, as ordered, into the Bucharest and Ploeşti areas. Of the four German divisions holding the gap, two had to be withdrawn into Romania to help carry out the Führer's order. By then, however, German forces around Ploeşti were in a hopeless position, and in the Bucharest area many had been killed or made prisoner by the Romanians. More importantly perhaps, Romanian troops were keeping open the Carpathian passes for the advancing Soviet army.

During the last week of August Soviet forces fanned out and made for the central districts of Romania. Tolbukhin cleared south-eastern Moldavia, occupied Constanţa on 29 August and was soon at the Bulgarian frontier. Meanwhile, Malinovsky, once through the Focşani gap, made for Ploeşti and Bucharest, his Fortieth and Seventh armies swinging round towards Braşov in southern Transylvania, where the Romanians had taken up defensive positions against an invasion from Hungary. Malinovsky ordered Kravchenko, the Sixth Army commander, to use one tank corps on the Ploeşti operation and two for the capture of Bucharest, but on receiving a copy of the order the Soviet High Command, or Stavka, decided to hold back from an all-out thrust on the capital.[1] Ploeşti was 'captured' and three to four German divisions trapped. Bucharest had by then been cleared of Germans by the Romanian army.

Sănătescu approached Kravchenko at Ploeşti with the suggestion that the Romanians should be allowed to deal with German forces in the territory not already occupied by the Red Army. The Stavka turned down this request which would have kept Soviet troops out of Bucharest, the 'seat of government' – which according to the terms agreed by Madame Kollontay was to be free of Allied forces. They ordered Malinovsky to march into Bucharest from 10 a.m. on 31 August, a move designed to stifle the 'intrigues' of the 'internal and external reactionaries' – meaning, as John Erickson points out, to bring nationalists to heel and to forestall any Anglo-American intervention. As a result the Russian army made an organised and disciplined entry into the capital with divisional and regimental commanders on horseback and bands playing. The Romanian Tudor Vladimirescu division was included in the procession.[2]

The Romanians, as I remember, did not greet the Soviet troops with either enthusiasm or enmity. What struck them most was that many were Mongols, stripped to the waist, but wearing fur hats in the heat of August.

Two days earlier, Rica had arranged for Prince Bâzu Cantacuzinu, Romania's top fighter pilot, to fly the American Colonel Gunn to Bari in a Messerschmitt; Gunn was anxious to get the American air force ex-prisoners of war out of the country before the Russians arrived and possibly interned them. On the 31st, Liberators were taking the Americans out at one airfield while the Russians were landing a few kilometres away at another.

When the Stavka turned down Sănătescu's proposal, the First and Fourth Romanian armies in southern Transylvania came under Soviet control. Malinovsky now had twenty Romanian divisions, indifferently equipped but with infantry who knew the terrain. When the Soviet Twenty-Seventh Army closed with the Romanian First Army, some units went north to help the Romanian garrisons which were holding out in Arad and Timişoară on the Hungarian frontier.

Colonel Grigorenko had told Rica that when dropped into Romania part of his brief had been to ascertain which opposition group was doing most for the Allies. One night over dinner I heard him say to Maniu, 'You, Mr Maniu, and your people have done more for the Allies than anyone else during the war.' Most probably he said the same thing to his superiors. One day two Russian officers came to take him on what they described as a long journey, and when Lygia offered him coffee and sandwiches for the trip they said he wouldn't need them where he was going. There may, of course, have been nothing sinister about this, but the Georgescus never heard from Colonel Grigorenko again.

Another evening I became angry with Maniu, insofar as one could ever have an argument with that old inscrutable. Following the Romanian example, in mid-October the Hungarians attempted a *volte face* against the Germans and Maniu could not hide a certain satisfaction when his old enemies muffed it so badly that the Germans took over again within hours.

On one occasion I arrived back to find the house guarded by Russian soldiers. I indicated that I lived there and was eventually let in. As I passed the dining room I saw a Russian colonel, six other Russian officers and a Romanian civilian having dinner with Rica and Lygia. The colonel had come to tell Rica that the Russians intended to take over the Romanian railways. Rica had objected that this was a matter for his colleague, the Minister of Communications, but the Russian insisted that Rica had a reputation for getting things done. Although Rica Georgescu had been appointed Under-Secretary at the Ministry of Economy and Finance, the Minister, himself, had for political reasons had to resign, and Rica was left effectively in charge.

What happened then was typical of Russian behaviour at the time in that although they hardly ever dared to meet a foreigner alone, were suspicious of the most ordinary courtesy, and were discouraged from fraternisation, their natural conviviality sometimes took over. Lygia interrupted the conversation to ask if they would like a drink. The colonel looked at his watch. He had only ten minutes but, yes, he would like a drink. A little later Lygia looked in again. Why did they not all stay for dinner – she would be delighted if they could. Again the colonel glanced at his watch. Yes, but only if it were ready in twenty minutes. In the end, they stayed for two and a half hours and by the end of the evening the colonel no longer seemed to care what time it was.

Later, the Russians thanked Rica formally for the steps he subsequently took with his colleagues to ensure Russian communications, while keeping the railway system in Romanian hands. They invited him to Moscow but he declined.

The Georgescus were so hospitable that one felt one could stay with them indefinitely. However, as soon as I had found my feet in Bucharest, I decided to get a flat of my own. When the Russians began to requisition property this was not difficult. I moved to a small flat at the top of a house in Stradă Londra along which we had often been driven during the bombing. Above the living-cum-dining room was a round tower with a circular bench – an imitation of the original medieval *banquet*. From the bedroom window on my first afternoon, I watched Russian soldiers in the garden opposite putting up a rough target and then lugging out heavy boxes of ammunition and I realised why the rent of my flat had been set so low. Incidentally, until the Allied High Commission arrived, Rica's ministry advanced me funds.

I got on well with the local Russians without kowtowing to them. Although I spoke Romanian and had many Romanian contacts the Russians never asked for my withdrawal. I had inherited the motor cycle and side car which had been used to drive Turcanu and his transmitter away when the Germans were too hot on his trail. Its owner, a police captain and friend of Costica Mugur's, became my driver. It was safer in those disorderly days to identify oneself, so I attached a small Union Jack to the handlebars. One day some Russian soldiers tore the flag off while I was in the Athenée Palace Hotel. I called on the Russian commandant partly as a courtesy visit, and partly to complain about the incident. Western journalists had flown in from Istanbul soon after the 26th and Archie Gibson of *The Times* interpreted for me. The commandant was quite cheerful about my protest and promised it would not happen again; it must have seemed an unimportant event to someone just off the battlefield. Years later I came across a Foreign Office file on which someone had minuted that I had no legal right to be flying the flag, anyhow. In those days such considerations mattered far less to me than they did later. For instance, I made up a confidential bag of letters and reports, sealed it and sent it to Cairo with a visiting British journalist; I thought my people should see the material and, since there was no official courier within hundreds of miles, was prepared to take the slight risk of the journalist losing such a precious piece of luggage. I was told off for that. I have no idea whether Cairo guessed that Annie was doing most of the cyphering. Again, there was no one else, and I trusted her.

I still have a copy of a thoughtful report by Liviu Nasta which I sent to Cairo in the middle of September. Nasta referred to the unwillingness of the new government to take action against the Iron Guard or other German collaborators. Several of the generals holding ministerial posts were unable, in his view, to change with the times – one, Rica's minister, had even been a signatory of the declaration of war on the USSR. Nasta proposed for the Interior Ministry a General Rădescu, who had been given sixteen months in a concentration camp for writing a critical letter to von Killinger in the early days of the war. He pointed out that this man – who later became first chief of staff, and then Prime Minister – was in a position to get rid of the major German collaborators from the civil service and press without being suspected of favouritism towards any political party. Nasta had already put his finger on a weakness in Sănătescu's government, which was to be exploited to the full by the Communist Party and, with more justification – since the Communists had themselves absorbed a large number of the Iron Guard – by the Soviet authorities.

I met Anna Pauker, one of the leading Communist personalities of her day. She had been largely responsible for opening her party's ranks to anyone who wanted to join. Their strategy was in three stages – unrestricted expansion, achievement of power, followed by a purge and ideological purification of the Party. I have in my papers a rather glowing account of her which I wrote at the time. 'Of middle height, powerful face with her iron-grey hair worn short . . . combines intellect with practical fighting qualities.' She had studied in Switzerland and become a doctor, and joined the Communist Party when it broke away from the Social Democrats in 1921. She had escaped from a Romanian prison, and had been Maurice Thorez's mistress, an executive member of the Comintern, and a major in the Soviet army. When her husband was condemned to death as a Trotskyist she is said to have supported the sentence. When the British Mission arrived in September she told our Political Adviser that he spoke excellent French 'for an Englishman', which did not go down at all well with Ian Le Rougetel. While her ideological integrity was never in doubt, she was more intelligent, less rigid, easier to talk to than most of her colleagues. At one of our parties she was brought over to meet Rica Georgescu and congratulated him on his work during the war. What a pity, she added, that he was with Mr Maniu and the English, since it was the Communists who would now be in power. 'With a party of only 800 members?' Rica asked. 'Yes,' she replied, 'with a party of 800 members which, while the Red Army is convalescing in Romania, will grow by thousands and tens of thousands.'

At some point during the first few weeks after the *coup*, Frank Wisner arrived with an OSS mission. OSS was the precursor of CIA, and Frank had a far better equipped set-up than mine. But I had the contacts and more practical experience and was, I think, able to help him in those early days. I was to become a friend of Frank and Polly Wisner in Washington ten years later, by which time he was a senior member of the CIA.

Chas wrote to say that he had been delayed. Although I knew that he would be ten times more valuable in Romania than I was, those weeks on my own were some of the best I can remember. I acquired relatively more responsibility with less bureaucratic constraint than I had ever had before. I was answerable only to an identification symbol at the end of a wireless wave. My only guidance was to stick to collecting intelligence and to avoid being used as a link between the Romanian and British governments. In a copy of a letter I sent to someone called Bill – possibly Bill Burland who had taken over the SOE office in Istanbul when Chas left – I say that the Russians were always very cordial, and that with Romanians I was taking the line that their only hope was to win the confidence of the Russian command as quickly as possible and without our help. Although I knew nothing of the Molotov bombshell or of Churchill's proposed trade-off of Romania for Greece, I seem to have picked up the atmosphere in Cairo fairly quickly.

But not quickly enough. My telegram Number 59 had dealt with the arrival of the Red Army and had described among other things the behaviour of battle-hardened troops who suddenly find themselves in an 'enemy' and, by their standards, luxurious country. As I remember it was purely factual. I was surprised, therefore, to be told that the Russians were our allies, and that the incidents of rape and pillage had been carried out by fascists dressed in Russian uniform. A friend – Bickham Sweet-Escott – wrote to explain that, though I could not have known it, my telegrams 'owing to the way we are set up at present . . . get a fairly wide distribution'. In other words, they were being shown to the Russians, who must have protested about Number 59. The Romanians who were working with me, and trusted me, were being compromised with the Russians by my own people. In fact, Sweet-Escott's letter seemed to turn what could have been a touch of naiveté on Cairo's part into double-think. The reprimand I had received had been classified, yet the Soviet propaganda it contained – which I knew to be false – had been served up as the truth without any gloss or attempt to put it into context. If this meant that Cairo's outgoing telegrams were also being self-censored and copied to Moscow, then we really were living in a world of distorting mirrors.

Apart from this one rather nightmarish experience, those were wonderful days. I worked hard and often late, and stayed up even later talking, eating, drinking, taking part – as we all were – in a period of change which started almost unnoticeably, and within six months had become a whirlwind. Later, my future father-in-law, A.T. Cholerton,* who had recently been a British correspondent in Russia and was now in Romania, told me how, stage by stage, the Communists would take over the country. At that time Stalinist tactics were new to most of us – surprising, fascinating and, for some, deadly. But during those early weeks of September we felt them as no more than a slight stirring of the air.

As often as I could I went for a swim at the Snagov villa, which I had known in 1939.† It was not half a mile from where Antonescu had had his last Cabinet meeting. There were Romanian rugs scattered about the floor of the living room and most of the wall space was taken up with books. The food was wonderful and was still plentiful if you were reasonably well-off. Even caviar from the Danube delta hardly seemed a luxury. And if I think back to that room I can still pick up snatches of conversation which are imaginary, of course, but to me, at least, ring true:

'We call caviar *icre* in Romanian,' my hostess is saying – she is a year or two younger than me – 'Try some of the black kind, *icre negre* . . .'

'Hemingway's realism . . .' from a corner of the room.

'You mean Americanism. It's no more real to get tight in a South American bar than to moon around the way Proust's people do.'

'Tell me why Romanians go on about the Russians so much,' I ask, changing the subject, less interested in Eng. Am. and Fr. Lit. than I used to be.

'Frustration,' from the other end of the room. 'We'd like to see the English and Americans here, so we take it out on the Russians.'

'I object to being raped by anyone,' says the Hemingway girl, gloomily.

'But with the Americans, of course, it wouldn't be rape.'

'Oh, shut up.'

'England must have changed during the war.' Someone else is changing the subject and I not liking what I see coming.

'Yes,' I reply carefully.

'But Churchill is a historian; he knows that his country's biggest asset is its reputation.' This from the clever one who has read Proust.

'So he wouldn't let a handful of Communists destroy the people who carried out the *coup*, would he?' my hostess asks me – and then to a girl who has just opened the door, 'Come in, chérie. Have some coffee.'

This time I do not have to reply. I am saved. But I know I shall not escape that question for long. It will be put to me over and over again until I begin to hate the people who ask it. And eventually, I know, I

---

* A historian and one-time Fellow of King's College, Cambridge.

† The step-sisters Josette Lazar and Eggie Heliad-Rădulescu held a kind of youthful salon at their Snagov villa.

shall come out with the brutal truth: 'Yes, the Communist Party, backed by the Red Army, will take over this country and you and your friends will disappear. And because there is no question of our going to war with Russia there is absolutely nothing we can do about it.'

The armistice was signed in Moscow on 12 September. Molotov presided. Harriman and Clark-Kerr, the US and British Ambassadors, were in attendance. Harriman's telegram to Washington describes how Molotov read out a clause, let the Romanian delegation have their say, ignored what they had said and passed on to the next clause. The Romanians, he said, seemed less concerned by the terms themselves than by the way they could be interpreted. It was true, he conceded, that the armistice gave the 'Soviet Commission unlimited control of Romania's economic life' and considerable influence in police affairs. 'The extent to which other political groupings are able to make their influence felt will depend, to quote a common Moscow phrase, on the understanding which they show for Russia's position.'

The Russians, Harriman said, seemed to see the functions of the American and British Allied Commissions as purely liaison though the British were challenging this energetically. He assured Washington that the Americans had gone along with the Russian desire to have a free hand in drawing up the terms and in 'the subsequent treatment of the Romanians'. The British, he said, had made themselves unpopular with the Russians by their various proposals – particularly in connection with reparations.[3]

When the British element of the Allied High Commission arrived in Bucharest two weeks later, Air Vice-Marshal Stevenson, our High Commissioner, saw me immediately. He asked about shooting in Romania; there were bears, he had heard, in the Carpathian mountains. Since I was now a member of his staff I must sever my radio and courier links with SOE. He assured me that my Romanian contacts and knowledge of the country would not be wasted. I should see him personally about important Romanian developments. He reminded me that I was now of field rank – I had become captain on landing in Romania, and, since the *coup*, had been promoted major and awarded a military OBE. Then he added with a great guffaw that my uniform was in a terrible state – not even regulation; my immediate duty was to order a new one.

AVM Stevenson was telling me, in the nicest possible way, that with Operation Autonomous over, I must now face up to the values of the real world again.

Chapter 27

Consequences of the Coup

To try to estimate by how much the Romanian *coup* shortened the war would be a hypothetical exercise. Romanian historians and the French press of the time have put it at about 200 days. It almost certainly did more than the Anglo-American landing on the French Riviera the week before, which the two emerging superpowers had forced on Churchill at the Teheran Conference. But I would prefer to mention a few military facts which will serve to explain why Hitler himself considered it decisive to his ultimate defeat.

Since the Soviet war machine relied on space in which to manoeuvre, German military experts believed that they could have held the the narrow Focşani–Nămăloasă–Galaţi line between the Carpathian mountains and the Black Sea. Once the Romanians had dismantled these defences and turned on the Germans, Soviet troops of the Second Ukrainian Front advanced into the Balkans at the rate of over fifty kilometres a day (motorised) and between thirty-five and thirty-eight kilometres (infantry)[1]; only logistical problems, rather than enemy resistance, prevented them from moving faster.[2] They crossed the Bulgarian frontier on 8 September, met with no resistance from the Bulgarian army and in a matter of weeks were at the Greek and Yugoslav frontiers. Again their main problems were logistical occasioned by their rapidly lengthening lines of communication.

In the week following the *coup* the Romanian army advanced westwards ahead of the Red Army, killing or capturing over 60,000 Germans, including fourteen generals, and driving the enemy out of an area the size of Belgium, Denmark, Holland and Switzerland put together. More importantly perhaps, by holding the Carpathian passes until the Red Army arrived, they transformed what might have become a series of Monte Cassinos into a way into Central Europe. Romanians continued to fight alongside the Red Army until the end of the European war. Their casualties amounted to nearly 170,000, of which over 111,000 were killed or severely wounded.

According to Albert Speer in an interview given in 1975, 'Beginning from June 1944 we could only count on 50,000 tons of benzine a month but after August, when our troops had to leave Rumania, the figure dropped to

20,000 tons.* It was clear then that we were heading for disaster.'[3] During the period that followed the *coup* the Germans were ordered to hold on to oil installations in the Prahova valley at all costs. This they failed to do. The Balkans also produced a high percentage of Europe's bauxite, antimony and chrome – all essential to Hitler's war machine.

The Soviet citation to King Michael's Order of Victory speaks of the decisive contribution that Romania made to the war 'at a moment when one could not say for certain that Germany would be defeated'. In 1944 German armament production was at its highest since the beginning of the war. With enough time and materials Hitler intended to mass-produce such advanced weapons as the rocket-equipped jet fighter – the Messerschmitt 262 – which could have influenced, if not the outcome, at least the duration of the war. The *coup* denied him both the time and the materials.

Post-war references to the *coup* have suffered from one of two distortions: in the West we have been inclined to give the whole credit for the Red Army's surge forward into the Balkans during the months of August and September 1944 to the Soviet Union – where, of course, most of it belongs. In Romania the *coup* is usually attributed to the Romanian Communist Party.

According to the British official history of the Second World War, 'The three weeks from 15 August to 5 September were among the most dramatic of the European war, equalling those of May and June 1940 . . . the Russians drove from the Rumanian frontier to Yugoslavia and into Bulgaria, destroying twelve German divisions and routing the Rumanian army.'[4] The only indexed references to Romania are to be found on page 377. After a brief account of the Tolbukhin and Malinovsky advances of 20–23 August, we learn that 'These successive blows were too much for the Rumanian Government. On 23rd August, King Michael arrested the dictator Antonescu, formed a new Government and pledged his loyalty to the Allies. On the 25th Rumania declared war on Germany.'[5] The Romanian Government, though much of its army was on the run, had not, in fact, succumbed to the Soviet offensive, which was why Antonescu had to be arrested. Had the Romanians not prepared their *coup* against the Germans months before the Soviet offensive, and timed it for August, it would probably have failed, in which case the Red Army's advance would have been far less dramatic. The Russians had been courageous allies and the Red Army had fought one of the greatest defensive wars of all time. Romania, on the other hand, had contributed substantially to Hitler's war effort, and had turned against him very late in the day. Yet without denying any of this, a little more credit should perhaps be given to King Michael and those Romanians who, against heavy odds, achieved a *volte face* which brought victory noticeably nearer.

* No oil was exported from Romania to the Reich after August 1944.

In Romania the events of 23 August are presented to Romanians who did not witness them as entirely the work of the Communist Party. The King, Maniu and the other people directly concerned in the *coup* are no longer credited with these events. For instance *200 de Zile Mai Devreme* gives an excellent account of the military aspects of the *coup* from which I have drawn freely, yet the following passage provides a thoroughly misleading account of the *coup* itself:

> On the 23rd August at about 17 hours, there began the revolt of the Romanian people which marked the start of the revolution for social, national, anti-fascist and anti-imperialist freedom in Romania. The political and military plan for this, drawn up with great historical responsibility for the destiny of the Romanian people by the Communist Party, was put immediately and faultlessly into practice.[6]

No one reading this would realise that the Romanian people first heard of their 'revolt' when the King announced it, and that they then cheered King Michael, Maniu and the Western Allies and not the Romanian Communist Party. Nor were the pro-Allied Romanian generals or the army as a whole fighting for Soviet occupation and the installation of a Communist government. Such an idea would have seemed ludicrous at the time. It was mistrust of Russia and fear of a Communist takeover that had delayed the *coup* for so long.

The Soviet offensive, followed by the Romanian *coup*, gave Stalin undisputed superiority in the Balkans. There was no obvious reason why he should put himself under the constraints of a half-formalised understanding with the British over Greece and Romania, which had never had American support. Whereas the Red Army now occupied Romania, including Transylvania, and Bulgaria down to the Greek frontier, Britain had only a small army in the south of Greece. Moreover the Greek Communist partisans were well equipped and active. Yet when Churchill saw Stalin in the Kremlin on 9 October he raised with him the need to harmonise their respective interests in the Balkans. Given the military situation this took considerable nerve and in his own dramatic account of the event Churchill does not hide his feeling of achievement.

> The moment was apt for business, so I said, 'Let us settle about our affairs in the Balkans. Your armies are in Roumania and Bulgaria. We have interests, missions and agents there. Don't let us get at cross-purposes in small ways. So far as Britain and Russia are concerned, how would it do for you to have ninety percent predominance in Roumania, for us to have ninety percent of the say in Greece, and go fifty-fifty about Yugoslavia?' While this was being translated I wrote on a half-sheet of paper:

Roumania
Russia 90%
The others 10%

Greece
Great Britain 90%
(in accord with USA)
Russia 10%

Yugoslavia 50–50%

Hungary 50–50%

Bulgaria
Russia 75%
The others 25%

I pushed this across to Stalin, who had by then heard the translation. There was a slight pause. Then he took his blue pencil and made a large tick upon it, and passed it back to us. It was all settled in no more time than it takes to set it down . . .

After this there was a long silence. The pencilled paper lay in the centre of the table. At length I said, 'Might it not be thought rather cynical if it seemed we had disposed of these issues, so fateful to millions of people, in such an off-hand manner? Let us burn the paper.' 'No, you keep it,' said Stalin.[7]

A paragraph deleted from the draft official record of this conversation gives the flavour of Churchill's buccaneering mood. As he handed over his 'naughty document' he stressed that he had consulted neither Cabinet nor Parliament. 'Marshal Stalin was a realist. He, himself, was not sentimental while Mr Eden was "a bad man." '[8] In his published account Churchill claims that he was thinking only of wartime arrangements, all larger questions being reserved for a 'peace table'. By the end of 1944, however, reference by Churchill or Eden to a peace settlement had become little more than a device for putting off the day when the British and American public would have to be told that all Stalin's territorial claims in Eastern Europe had been accepted.[9]

Soviet historians have never admitted that this discussion – which took the form of a kind of summit doodle – constituted an agreement. When the Prime Minister said that, to avoid shocking the Americans, it would be better not to use the phrase 'dividing into spheres', Stalin interrupted to remind him that Roosevelt wished Harriman to sit in at these talks. Churchill insisted that they stick to a *tête-à-tête* for the Balkans. Stalin went along with him, but seems to have been forthcoming on only one point – Britain's great interest in the Mediterranean, equivalent to Russia's in the

Black Sea, and, consequently, her legitimate interest in Greece. To all the other countries on Churchill's list, the 90–10 formula was subsequently applied in Russia's favour – including Bulgaria which, having a common frontier with Greece, was of particular interest to Britain.

Many Romanians thought, naively perhaps, that because of the great contribution the *coup* had made to the Red Army's advance they would be treated as allies. From the start the Russians treated them as a conquered people. Even before the armistice was signed they had taken equipment – including oil-field equipment and most of the merchant fleet – valued at around two billion dollars. The armistice had, in Maniu's view, moved the Focşani–Nămăloasă–Galaţi line to the gates of Budapest, giving the Soviet command the right to interfere in every aspect of Romanian life. He told the US representative in December that if he had known the armistice was to be applied by the Russians alone he would not have advised the King to accept it.

There were, however, three main impediments to an early Communist takeover. There was the electoral weakness of the Romanian Communist Party itself; in those days one could not hide the fact that the *coup* had been carried out by a popular young King and Maniu, backed by the great anti-Communist majority of the people. Then there was the Communist Party's revolutionary inexperience; according to Soviet political officers, it would take months before it was ready to carry out a *coup*. And, thirdly, there was the need for stability on Red Army lines of communication with the Central European front. Under the circumstances the Soviet Commission did rather well to install a People's Democracy within six months.

The Romanian Communist Party was now under the leadership of Moscow-trained people like Anna Pauker, Emil Bodnăraş (Ceaşu) and Vasile Luca, and of Romanian militants who had organised Communist cells in Romanian prisons – notably Teohari Georgescu and Gheorghiu Dej. Pătrăşcanu, although a government minister, was not particularly influential in the new Communist hierarchy. Under Moscow's tutelage this new leadership adopted what have since become familiar tactics. They used affiliated groups – the Ploughman's Front, for instance – to recruit workers and peasants who would have refused to join the Party itself. (The great majority of agricultural and industrial workers still stood by the National Peasant and Social Democratic parties.) They opened their ranks to anyone who found it expedient to be on the winning side, including the Iron Guard. Like King Carol II, they welcomed dissident National Peasants and Liberals: within seven months the unscrupulous Tătărescu had committed his ultimate betrayal of the Liberal Party and had joined Petru Groza's* Communist-controlled government as Vice-Premier and

---

* Petru Groza was leader of the Ploughman's Front, one of the Communist Party's front organisations.

Foreign Minister. They split and destroyed the Social Democratic Party and used their paramilitary group – the only civilians permitted by the Soviet Mission to carry arms – to break up opposition meetings and demonstrations. The Soviet Mission controlled the distribution of newsprint while the Romanian Communist Party forced printers – who had worked quite happily for Antonescu's press – to close down opposition newspapers. Given their overall lack of experience, the Party worked well, and Moscow needed to intervene obtrusively on few occasions.

General Sănătescu was quite at sea in this situation. His was a caretaker government, appointed to prepare for elections. But, with each week that passed, democratic elections seemed to become more remote. On 13 October a group of Liberals and National Peasants demonstrated for 'the King and Democracy' and were attacked by armed Communists. Next morning the Communist newspaper *Scânteia* falsely accused them of having provoked the Communists by shouting 'Long live Horia Sima' and 'Long live Juliu Maniu.' This association of Maniu with a known fascist was the first hint that Maniu would eventually be labelled a 'fascist'. Three days later a large National Peasant Party meeting was cancelled by Sănătescu in case it was broken up by Communist thugs, so giving the Russians a pretext for intervening directly. Maniu remarked, perhaps disingenuously, that 'it is incomprehensible that the most powerful party in the country should be prevented from getting in touch with public opinion.'[10]

Sănătescu resigned on 2 November and was asked by the King to form a new government. He now appointed a Communist Minister of Communications – one of the key posts for any group wishing to stage a takeover. Niculescu-Buzeşti resigned as Foreign Minister in favour of Constantin Vişoianu, and concentrated on preparing the National Peasant Party for the elections. Vişoianu impressed on the Soviet Mission the harm the Communist Party were doing to the war effort by their political and economic disruption; Moscow must already have accepted such disruption as part of the price they would have to pay to achieve their objective. Towards the end of November an incident occurred which gave the Russians an opportunity to get rid of Sănătescu altogether. A group of drunken Romanian soldiers opened fire into a suburban workers' dance hall because they had been refused entry. The Communist press screamed about 'Hitlerist Fascist bullets from automatic rifles of the Fifth Column supported by leaders of the National Peasant Party'. When Vyshinsky, the Soviet Deputy Foreign Minister, supported the calumny, Sănătescu resigned.[11]

On 2 December the King replaced Sănătescu by the energetic General Rădescu who had been mentioned in Liviu Nasta's article. Rădescu had been in concentration camps with some of the Communist leaders; the previous October, following considerable Russian pressure, Sănătescu had appointed him chief of staff, though he had had no recent active military experience. However, as Prime Minister he turned out to be a more vigorous exponent of constitutional democracy than his predecessor, and although his appointment had been strongly supported by Moscow, he clearly could not be allowed to remain in power long enough to be effective. Rădescu decided to run the sensitive Ministry of the Interior himself, and to appoint Teohari Georgescu as his Under-Secretary of State. The Communist Party had been waiting for an entry into this ministry; within two months Georgescu had infiltrated the police and secret service, and was appointing prefects in the provinces with instructions to ignore government briefs and to take their instructions only from him.

The Yalta Conference of 4–11 February 1945 committed the Allied Powers to allow the European peoples 'to destroy the last vestiges of Nazism and Fascism and to create democratic institutions of their own choice'. Two weeks later the Communist-controlled National Democratic Front organised a large demonstration, which at one point threatened the Ministry of the Interior where Rădescu had his office. Under orders the guards fired into the air to disperse the crowd. Some of the demonstrators were at the same moment shot by Communist *agents provocateurs*, and Rădescu was held responsible for their deaths. Although a mixed commission of Russian and Romanian doctors found that the bullets that were extracted from the victims were of a calibre never used by the armed forces, it made no difference. The provocation had been successful. Rădescu lost his temper, and in a broadcast that evening accused Anna Pauker and Vasile Luca by name. By now the Communist machine was working smoothly, and after a week of chaos Rădescu was forced to take refuge in the British Mission. This was the cue for Vyshinsky to return to Bucharest and to carry out his own *coup*. On 28 February he gave the King a two-hour ultimatum to appoint a Communist-controlled government under Petru Groza – a Communist front man – or risk Romania's disappearance altogether as a sovereign state.

With the arrival of the British Mission, I had been appointed Information Officer to the Mission's Political Adviser – Ian Le Rougetel – who had been Counsellor at the Legation in 1941. Ted Key, one of the nicest people I would ever meet, became Assistant Information Officer. Annie Samuelli was my personal assistant, Costica Mugur looked after the accounts and supervised the press cuttings. He was helped by Eleonora de Wied.* Later,

---

* Queen Elizabeth (Carmen Silva), wife of King Carol 1, was born Princess Elizabeth de Wied. Princess Eleonora de Wied was therefore a cousin of King Michael.

George Racziu worked with us and for a time Nadia Herescu,* a Bessarabian, was our Russian translator. We kept in touch with the Romanian and foreign press, and the information that came our way – though classified as 'intelligence' by the Communist Party – could mostly be obtained by simple observation.

At first the Political Adviser's Office knew nothing of the so-called 'percentage agreement'. Like our American colleagues, we worked actively for the restoration of parliamentary government, and wondered why our reports and proposals were not better received in London. Churchill became increasingly concerned about our activities. On 4 November he minuted Eden that Le Rougetel evidently 'does not understand that we have only a 10 per cent interest in Roumania and are little more than spectators'.[12] Three days later he was minuting 'Here are a new batch of telegrams showing the zeal with which Le Rougetel, Stevenson and others are throwing themselves into the agonising turmoil at Bucharest';[13] and, on the 10th, 'Have you or the FO at any time made our representatives in Bucharest aware of the broad balances we agreed to at Moscow? It seems to me they are behaving as if they were in Greece. WSC.'[14] Two days before a 'most secret' telegram had, in fact, gone from the Foreign Office to Bucharest (War Cabinet distribution) warning Le Rougetel of the Moscow understanding: 'We must, therefore, avoid the temptation of endeavouring to get the best of both worlds and proceed with the utmost caution.' The situation would, of course, be different if legitimate British interests were threatened.[15] This telegram would be given very restricted circulation in the Bucharest office. On 11 December Churchill again minuted, 'Considering the way the Russians have so far backed us up over what is happening in Greece, which must throw great strain on their sentiments and organisation, we really must not press our hand too far in Roumania. Remember the percentages we worked out on paper.'[16] Five weeks later he asked Eden why we were making such a fuss in Romania about the Russian deportations of Saxons and others.[17]†

Under these circumstances, Maniu, fighting for a democratic system of government and looking to the Western Allies for support against the Russians, must have seemed at his most irritating to London. When we reported on 1 December 1944 that Maniu had told us he would quite understand if the British Government wanted Romania to cast in her lot with Russia rather than the Anglo-Saxon powers, but would be grateful to receive word from them to this effect, the PM minuted to Eden, 'Surely we are not called upon to make such admission.'[18] Maniu begged repeatedly

---

* Known later in films as Nadia Grey.
† The Hungarians had introduced experienced settlers from the Rhine lands into Transylvania in the eleventh century. These became known as Saxons.

to be told the truth – had Romania been sold into the Russian sphere of influence, or had she not? – and each time the representatives of the Western Allies were instructed to deny this. Years later, Clark-Kerr, by then Lord Inverchapel, told Rica Georgescu at the British Embassy in Washington that one of the most distasteful things he had ever been asked to do was to lie to a man like Maniu.

By February 1945 the Communists in Greece had been crushed, and Churchill became more outspoken on Romania. When we thought that an attempt might be made to take Rădescu from the Mission premises we received instructions to prevent it by force if necessary. As soon as the Russians realised this, they climbed down. However, neither the so-called 'percentage agreement', nor the *coup d'état*, nor even the fact that Romania had taken part in the invasion of Russia can be held solely responsible for the communisation of Romania. This was not in much doubt once it had become clear that there would be no Western military presence in Eastern Europe. To expect Stalin to apply principles of government to occupied territories which he did not apply at home would have been as naive as to expect Hitler to do so five years earlier. Even when Bevin became Foreign Secretary, and we sensed a more robust attitude towards Moscow, we in Bucharest could do no more than slow down the process. Our advice to Maniu and the King was to compromise, to take another step, however small, in the direction Russia was pushing them. The opposition parties did not seem to realise that the British and US governments – even with Truman as President – could only exert diplomatic pressure, and the less realistic of them envisaged open political conflict at high level between the Western Powers and the Soviet Union. Wishful thinking of this kind led the opposition parties – including Titel Petrescu's followers – to maintain that they had been let down by the Western Powers.

In 1946 I joined the Foreign Service and moved to the political side of the Office which, following London's recognition of the Romanian Government earlier that year, was now a Legation. John Bennett, a friend of Sir Stafford Cripps, became the new Information Officer. Francis Bennett, who later had a distinguished career in Conservative Party politics, was the Assistant Information Officer. They made an excellent team.

A few of the younger Romanians looked for a military solution and made for the hills to organise armed resistance. Others produced outspoken opposition newspapers. Mihai Fărcăşanu, leader of the Young Liberals, edited a paper called *Viitorul* (*The Future*) – we called it Vitriol – until his presses were smashed, his printers beaten up and he and his wife Pia, daughter of the poet Ion Pillat and great-niece of Constantin Brătianu, were on the run.

Matei Ghica was back in the country, again helping people to escape. He arranged for the Fărcăşanus to leave from a small airfield at Caransebeş, near Timişoara in the Banat. They were to use an old bomber which had just been repaired and was returning to its base at Braşov. The government commission charged with preventing Romanians escaping by air arrived at Caransebeş the day before the Fărcăşanus were due to leave. The commission checked that the aircraft was carrying no illegal passengers and only enough petrol for the official journey to Braşov. (They failed to realise that the mechanic had fixed the petrol gauge.) Members of the commission stood in front of the building while the aircraft taxied to a point which was momentarily out of sight, and turned into the wind; as it revved its engines, Pia and Mişu leapt out of the bushes and climbed in. Since all the instruments except the altimeter had been dismantled, they had quite an exciting flight. Chased by Yugoslav fighters, they used up petrol hopping from cloud to cloud. They ran short of fuel while still over the Adriatic, and only just made it to Bari airfield.

Although only a Second Secretary, I happened to be temporarily in charge of the Legation and had a telegram about the Fărcăşanus ready drafted to send off the moment Bari notified their arrival. This was important, since there was always a risk of their being sent back. They almost were, only the RAF, who were rather impressed by their crazy landing, took them under their wing.

Under the circumstances, Romanians resisted a full-blown Communist Party dictatorship longer than one might have expected. By November 1946, when elections finally took place, London and Washington had weakened their hand by recognising the Groza government of Communist and Communist-affiliated groups. The opposition had pressed for an international commission to supervise the elections, but this had not materialised. Yet Paragraph 35 of the Legation's annual report which I drafted that year describes the remarkable obstinacy of the Romanian people in the face of enormous pressure on them to come into line:

> After this last effort on the part of the Government to prove the Opposition parties to be 'Fascist', the elections took place on 19th November. Apart from the abuses mentioned above it should be noted that there were widespread cases of Government supporters voting several times and of ballot boxes being filled with Government voting slips either before the voting opened or during the count, at which Opposition representatives were not present. On the morning of the 19th, a number of Opposition representatives were arrested and physical intimidation during the voting was reported from many districts. Normally after an election in Romania, the results are

announced by radio during the course of the night so that by about 2 o'clock in the morning, the public have a very fair idea as to who has been successful. On the night of 19th November, however, a few results were announced and then there was silence for three days. Telephone communication was cut with the provinces to prevent the Opposition obtaining district results and, it appears, these were so uniformly in the Opposition's favour that the Government soon realised that all their ingenious methods of falsification had failed. They were therefore ultimately compelled to falsify the official figures and publish what had been a crushing defeat for the Government as an overwhelming victory. As, however, the truth became known, it was clear that the Government had lost not only in the country as a whole, but even in the citadels of Communist activity. Many of their most ardent followers had clearly joined the Communist Party for personal gain only but when the moment came to express their will, had voted for the Opposition. Even the railway workers, from whom Communist shock troops were chosen, and the employees of the Ministries of Finance and War had failed to support the Government.[19]

After such a clear manifestation of the people's will, Moscow and the Romanian Communist Party were to wait another year before bringing Maniu to trial. He was arrested on 25 July 1947 and his trial opened on 29 October. He was charged with high treason and, on 11 November, condemned to solitary confinement for life. He was then seventy-five years old. All organised political opposition, which had been only brushed under the carpet during the régimes of King Carol and Marshal Antonescu, was now virtually stamped out.

Only one man still stood in the way of a complete Communist takeover – King Michael. The Foreign Office were impressed by the King's outstanding sense of duty, his attempt to work within the system, and his willingness to put up with humiliations and at least one assassination attempt rather than abandon the Romanian people. They urged the British Government to give him at least their moral support by letting it be known that London would take a serious view if he were to die 'accidentally', and by offering him and the Queen Mother a refuge in England if this became necessary. The Cabinet – largely, it seems, on account of Herbert Morrison, who distrusted the Foreign Office – did not respond.[20]

On 12 November, the day after Maniu had been condemned, the King and the Queen Mother left for London – the King, as usual, sharing the flying with his pilot. They were on their way to attend the wedding of Princess Elizabeth and Prince Philip of Greece. When the King returned to Bucharest on 21 December he was engaged to Princess Anne of Bourbon-Parma, and Moscow were faced by a new obstacle, the prospect of the continuation of the dynasty.

On 30 December Petru Groza, the Prime Minister, and Gheorghiu Dej, the Secretary General of the Communist Party, had an audience with the King and his mother; since Groza had said it was to do with 'family business', it was assumed to be in connection with the forthcoming royal wedding. Instead they were told that the time had come for the King to abdicate. Documents incriminating the King had been discovered before the trial of 'Maniu and his band of fascist traitors'. The government – and, it was implied, Moscow – wanted no trouble: only a smooth transfer from a Monarchy to a People's Republic. When the King referred to the Constitution, Groza exclaimed, 'The Constitution. But, you see, we've thought of everything.' He produced a document from his briefcase in which the King, recognising that the Constitution no longer corresponded to the need for 'speedy and fundamental change' and that 'the Monarchy . . . constitutes a serious obstacle to the development of Romania' would 'in the interests of the Romanian people' abdicate in his own name and that of his descendants.[21] While the King was out of the room speaking to his officials Groza, who was always inclined to play the clown, showed the Queen Mother a revolver he was carrying in his pocket, and told her with a grin that he had to take precautions after what Michael had done to Antonescu. When the King returned – realising by now that the Palace was surrounded by troops of the Tudor Vladimirescu division, and that the telephone lines had been cut – he again referred to the will of the Romanian people. They alone must decide. Groza told him that if he did not sign immediately thousands of people would be arrested that day; there could well be civil war and a great deal of blood would be spilled. King Michael abdicated at about three o'clock that afternoon, 30 December 1947.[22]

The brief resurgence and subsequent destruction of Romanian democracy after King Michael's *coup d'état* was to mark the beginning of a traumatic disenchantment with Russia in Western public opinion.

Militarily, the *coup* had proved invaluable. It had, without doubt, shortened the war. The Order of Victory with which Stalin decorated King Michael – the only other foreigner to be so honoured being General Eisenhower – was appropriately a military, not a civilian, order. Politically the *coup* must have been as unwelcome in Moscow as it was unexpected.

The Russians seem to have had two possible dictators in mind for Romania after the armistice – King Carol and Marshal Antonescu.

Madame Antonescu told Annie and Bobsie Samuelli, with whom she shared a prison cell for a time, that after his arrest her husband had been given VIP treatment in Moscow – he had been put up in a large house, with excellent food, visits to the ballet and so on. The Russians had urged him to head a Romanian government on their behalf. Even Field Marshal von

Paulus, who had been made prisoner at Stalingrad, had been called in to try to persuade him; only when Antonescu had repeatedly refused had he been sent back to Bucharest for trial and execution.

Assuming that Madame Antonescu was telling the truth, it seems possible that, had the Marshal accepted the Stockholm armistice terms in the summer of 1944, Moscow would have wanted him to head their government at least provisionally.

A more amenable candidate could have been King Carol. During the Stockholm negotiations the Russians had asked Frederick Nanu, the Romanian Minister, how he thought the country would react to the return of their ex-king, and in the autumn of 1947 they tried to reinstall Carol who was living in Portugal. They were outmanoeuvred by our Minister in Bucharest, Adrian Holman, and the Foreign Office who asked the Portuguese Government to use every means at their disposal to detain him.

Naturally, the Russians wanted to keep intact the machinery of dictatorship, for which they were indebted to Carol and Antonescu. Ideally it should have been achieved by an orderly transition from one dictatorship to the next, but if this were not possible they preferred that Antonescu fight on to the last man, until the country had been completely subjugated and occupied. In the general fray leading democrats could have been liquidated and would in any case have been rendered powerless by the complete breakdown of civilian order. But after the *coup* neither solution was possible. King Michael annulled his father's constitution of 1938 and reintroduced that of 1923, which would remain in force until a freely elected constituent assembly had prepared a new one. The line of dictatorship had been broken, and there would be stubborn resistance to restoring it. The democratic parties were functioning. The Romanians had set up their own government a week before the Red Army entered Bucharest. The Russians now faced what from their point of view was a messy interlude of semi-representative government, for which they rightly held the King and the traditional parties entirely responsible.

A proven constitutional monarch backed wholeheartedly by the army and by the traditional parties representing over ninety per cent of the country, King Michael could not be ignored. The democratic parties were hell-bent on free elections and the Communist Party was pathetically weak. There was no doubt about Moscow's ability to solve the problem, but she could not now avoid organised political resistance and, with the British and US Missions and Western journalists present, consequent publicity. As a result of the *coup*, Romania became a case study in Stalinist takeover methods, applied to a country in which Communism had hardly existed. It was to be an eye-opener for the British and American publics, which for four years had been shown only the rosier side of the Soviet Union.

When Russia was invaded in June 1941 Churchill, in spite of his reservations, had welcomed her as an ally; and when the Russian people showed by their outstanding courage that they could well be the decisive factor in defeating Hitler, loose talk about Bolshevism and Russia was discouraged. In future there would be only one enemy of democracy – Hitler. Had this been a purely tactical measure, without any element of self-deception, the Cold War might have been avoided. But nothing so clinical was humanly possible. To behave properly, even quite senior people in Britain and America had to convince themselves that Stalin was their friend, and that to think otherwise was a kind of treachery.

To the Western leaders Stalin was an enigma and in the circumstances they were inclined to give him the benefit of the doubt. After Stalingrad Russia seemed to become more traditional and less ideological. Stalin could not be expected to feel any sympathy for countries which had helped the Germans ravage his country but by the end of the war he would be economically in such a bad way that if only for this reason he might wish to maintain good relations with the Western Allies. Soviet respect for the Atlantic Charter could not therefore be entirely ruled out.

Other considerations influenced the attitude of the Western Allies to Russia during the war. One sometimes forgets that however fundamentally different they were, the early Bolsheviks and the Founding Fathers had a great deal in common – an evangelical urge, a conviction that their way of life was best for the whole world, and an intense suspicion of colonial Britain with its never-setting sun. Nor was this feeling altogether dead in Roosevelt's and Stalin's time. The State Department suspected the flamboyant Churchill of seeking spheres of influence quite as much as they suspected Communist Russia. Roosevelt flatly refused to believe that the USSR could behave anything but magnanimously towards any East European satellite country that surrendered unconditionally.

Britain's own assessment of the Soviet Union was influenced by the importance Churchill and Eden gave to their personal contacts with Stalin and Molotov, and by their inadequate understanding of Marxism-Leninism. Whenever the Russians smiled on them they felt a change of heart. They found it difficult to see through Stalin's eyes. Even the Foreign Office was inclined to believe that because the Communist Party was weak in Romania, the Russians would be forced eventually to hold free elections.

Not surprisingly, British and American leaders were slow to grasp the Soviet use of semantics. After the *coup*, 'democrat' in Bucharest came to mean anyone who supported the Soviet-backed régime; even Pătrăşcanu was shocked when Legionaries and other ideological opportunists were recruited in droves to swell the ranks of the lean Communist Party. 'Fascist', of course, included anyone who sympathised with Britain, the USA or parliamentary democracy. And since the Communist Party claimed to speak for all Romanian democrats, the requirement that a government should consult the people was already an otiose concept by the time of Yalta in February 1945.

So we find Churchill recording that:

> On the evening when I was speaking in the House of Commons upon the results of our labours at Yalta the first violation by the Russians both of the spirit and letter of our agreements took place in Roumania . . . I was deeply disturbed by this news, *which was to prove a pattern of things to come* [my italics]. The Russians had established the rule of a Communist Party minority by force and misrepresentation.[23]

British and American journalists were by then reporting the ideological pogrom which had followed the Romanian *coup*. Although at least one British newspaper instructed its correspondent to make no criticism of the Soviet Union in his Bucharest despatches, these events – followed by the suppression of non-Communist movements in Poland, Czechoslovakia and throughout Eastern Europe – shattered the benign wartime image of Uncle Joe. Four years of self-deception and misleading propaganda boomeranged. An uninformed American and British public overreacted to this surprising misbehaviour in a gallant ally to whom they owed so much. The common enemy which had bound their governments to that of the Soviet Union had been removed. The Cold War became inevitable.

By 1948 it was high time for me to leave. My Romanian experience meant much to me. In nine years I had seen three faces of dictatorship and was growing altogether too fond of those who, however unsuccessfully, had stood up to it. I knew that I would arrive in England a stranger and I badly needed to get back. In 1946 I had joined the Foreign Service. Two years later I was transferred from Bucharest to London and have never returned.

Epilogue

Most of those involved in the Romanian Resistance during the war survived the struggle against the Germans: during the ideological conflict which followed the *coup* the King was exiled and others either fled the country or were given long terms in prison, where many of them died.

King Michael went first to London and Washington, to inform Western leaders of the circumstances of his abdication. The US Government offered him a home, but he and his wife decided to live in Switzerland, where for many years now they have had a house near Geneva. They had five children. The King had made no provision for living abroad. For a time he earned his living as a test pilot for an American aircraft company. Later, after passing the necessary exams, he became a broker in Switzerland for a Greek firm based on Wall Street.

On leaving Romania Queen Helen, the Queen Mother, moved back to Florence, where she had been in exile during the reign of her husband, King Carol. She died in 1982.

After working for Radio Free Europe and the Voice of America, Mircea Ionniţiu, the King's secretary, became an engineer with a firm producing liquid rocket propellant engines. He lives in California. Though now retired, he is occasionally called back as a consultant. He also works with the American-Romanian Academy of Sciences and Letters.

Marshal Antonescu behaved with dignity at his trial in 1946. The prosecution tried hard but unsuccessfully to implicate Maniu and Brătianu in his policies. After giving evidence Maniu walked across to shake hands with the prisoner, and when the Communist President of the Court protested, he explained that Antonescu was a rival, not an enemy. Some of us saw this as a final gesture of thanks to the Marshal for having protected him and his Romanian and British collaborators from the Germans.

Although the Marshal refused to plead for mercy, King Michael insisted that all the sentences should be commuted to life imprisonment. At the last minute, as the condemned men were walking from the chapel to the place of execution, three of the sentences, including Cristescu's, were, in fact, commuted; but the Marshal, Mihai Antonescu and General Piki Vasiliu – our contact with Antonescu while in prison – were shot.

Bodnăraş is thought to have intervened on behalf of Eugen Cristescu. Cristescu was an outstanding intelligence officer with a remarkable memory – possibly the most valuable man the Communists inherited from the previous régime.

Maniu urged Constantin Vişoianu and Niculescu-Buzeşti to escape and represent the National Peasants, Liberals and Titel Petrescu's independent Social Democrats abroad. Gafencu and Cretzianu were already out of the country. Mihalache and other members of the National Peasant Party were caught trying to escape. Maniu himself refused to leave. Vişoianu became president of the Romanian National Committee and lives in Washington. Buzeşti and Cretzianu died in the States and Gafencu in Paris.

At his trial in 1947, Maniu was as courteous and composed as ever, and utterly immune to intimidation. Had he authorised his colleagues to flee abroad? the prosecutor asked. He had. Why? Because he thought that since free opposition and legal criticism were prevented at home, the claims of the Romanian people should be heard by the Western democracies who were still responsible for the situation in Romania. Did he intend to oppose the government? He would continue to fight for free elections, genuine political liberty and the restoration of elementary human rights. How? By every means open to him.[1]

There were nineteen defendants at this trial, some of them absent. Among those present was Pichi Pogoneanu, the paralysed civil servant Rica and I had carried to the Palace car on 24 August. When accused of having been in touch with traitors abroad he saluted the 'traitors' as patriots, adding that his only reason for not joining them was for fear his bad health should become a burden on their activities. Maniu and Mihalache were sentenced to life imprisonment with solitary confinement, the others to hard labour or solitary confinement for periods ranging from five years to life. Maniu died in Sighet jail on 3 February 1953.

Constantin Brătianu, leader of the Liberal Party, was arrested at about the same time as Maniu. Since he was in his eighties and of less propaganda value, he was not given a public trial. Nevertheless, he was condemned to life imprisonment and died in 1950. This was the old man I had watched dozing at his country house after lunch while children jumped over his legs. The only news the family had of him while he was in prison was from someone in an adjacent cell, who had heard him sometimes cry out on account of the rats. He was the last of the political Brătianus – one of the great European Liberal dynasties.

The deaths of Dinu Brătianu and Juliu Maniu were ironically enough announced in an interview with the *New York Times* on 21 October 1955 by Gheorghe Tătărescu, the politician they despised most. Tătărescu, the arch-opportunist, was, as might be expected, never tried, and died comfortably at home under house arrest.

Georghe Brătianu, who had carried messages from Maniu and Brătianu to Antonescu in Sinaia during the last-minute attempt to get the Marshal to sign an armistice, committed suicide in prison.

Titel Petrescu's Social Democratic Party was infiltrated by Communists and split on orthodox lines in 1946. Petrescu continued to lead the Independent Social Democrats until his arrest. He was released from prison in 1965 when he was known to be terminally ill and died the following year.

Early in 1947 Rica and Lygia Georgescu were invited to 'visit' the United States by the Board of Standard Oil (N.J.). Their children, Costa and Peter, aged twelve and seven, had to stay behind in Transylvania with their grandparents. At the zonal frontier in Austria the Georgescus' diplomatic passports and Russian *laissez-passer* would have been impounded by Soviet guards had they not been carrying dollars, Swiss francs and pounds with which to bribe them. In London they were entertained by Lord Selborne – the former head of SOE – at a lively dinner with Douglas Dodds Parker and de Chastelain. In the States a more formal dinner was given in their honour by General Bill Donovan, wartime head of OSS (the predecessor of CIA) who praised what they had done for the Allies during the war and called Lygia the 'Molly Pitcher' of Romania. Both became US citizens in 1952.

Rica was appointed Associate Coordinator of Standard Oil exploration and production activities worldwide. In 1957 he was made Associate Middle East Representative of Standard Oil, based in London. In 1964, when he was sixty, he retired from Standard Oil but continued to work as an oil consultant. He and his wife live in Geneva.

The fact that they had not been able to take their children out of the country was, of course, a personal tragedy. In 1953 a member of the Romanian Legation in Washington tried to blackmail Georgescu, but he refused to spy on the United States and informed the US authorities; within the year General Eisenhower had obtained the release of their two boys. Peter is now President of Young and Rubicam Advertising. Costa, after taking a PhD in Arabic History and Literature, works for the US Government in Washington. They have become integrated US citizens and like to annoy Lygia with 'Hi, folks' when they ring up their parents from the States.

During the war Georgescu depended for his radio communication with Cairo on two people in particular – Alecu Ionescu, who with his wife did the cyphering, and Nicolae Turcanu, the wireless operator. After the *coup* Ionescu was imprisoned for eighteen years, which left him a sick man. The

Foreign Office provided £1,000 with which he emigrated to Australia, where he died in June 1988. Turcanu was luckier. He escaped from Romania by boat and was able to continue his career as a ship's radio operator.

Annie Samuelli, Costica Mugur and Eleonora de Wied, all of whom had worked with me – I was described as 'the principal British spy' at their trial – were arrested in July 1949 together with Bobsie Samuelli who had worked at the American Information Office. They were charged with high treason and espionage. The usual Gestapo methods were used before the trial which began on 14 April 1950. Costica was sentenced to twenty-five years, Annie to twenty, and Bobsie and Eleonora to fifteen.

Costica's sentence was harsher because he had been part of Georgescu's network during the war. By 1950 the active 'enemy' was, in Communist eyes, not the Reich, against which Georgescu had been working, but the Western Allies with which he had been associated; and the new definition was being applied retrospectively. It was implied at the trial that my own unfriendly 'espionage' dated back to my anti-German activities with the Autonomous mission.

Costica was sent to a Transylvanian prison. Annie, Bobsie and Eleonora began by spending four years in a prison near Ploeşti. In the autumn they were joined by Madame Antonescu and Codreanu's widow, both of whom had been arrested as part of a drive in 1950 against the widows of important people. It was then that Madame Antonescu told them of her husband's experiences in Moscow. In 1954 the so-called 'national widows' were released, still without trial. The other three were moved to Miercurea Ciuc, a Transylvanian fortress built by Maria Theresa in the eighteenth century for Romanian rebels – Annie says that iron rings were still set in the stone floors. Princess Eleonora de Wied died there the following year. In 1956 there was a great influx of Hungarians and Romanians implicated in the Hungarian uprising.

Meanwhile the Foreign Office missed no opportunity to press for the release of those prisoners who had been employed by the British Government. By 1961 the political atmosphere had improved, and on 14 June the Romanian Government suddenly accepted the ransom offered for the Samuellis by an American relation; they had served twelve years of their sentences. Costica Mugur was released the following year.

The British Government granted Annie Samuelli, Costica Mugur and his wife Adela British citizenship for 'services rendered to the Crown', together with back pay and entitlement to a full social security pension. In the USA, however, such payments could only be made to US citizens and Bobsie had to rally sufficient Senate support for two private bills to be introduced and passed through Congress before she and other locally employed persons in her position could obtain what she considered to be their rights. In recognition of her courage and success, President Lyndon Johnson presented Bobsie with the pen with which he had signed these two laws.

Annie and Bobsie settled in Paris. Annie published a book about her experiences,[2] and now makes a living as a translator. Bobsie, who taught English, died in 1987.

Costica and Adela settled in Hampstead in a flat provided by the Foreign Office, who also found Costica a job. When he retired he took up painting and gave several successful exhibitions in London. Adela died some years ago, and Costica in 1987.

Lucreţiu Pătrăşcanu was purged in 1948 and brought to trial in 1954. Among the defendants were two other men who have appeared in this narrative. Baron Ion Mocsony-Styrcea, the Marshal of King Michael's court, had liaised between the King and Pătrăşcanu during the run-up to the *coup*. After a long and cruel interrogation he was sentenced to fifteen years' hard labour. He was always very fit and survived, and now lives in Geneva. Harry Brauner, whom I had introduced to Bonamy Dobrée at the Sinaia summer school in 1939, was condemned to twelve years' hard labour. He became a universally acclaimed folklorist and died recently in Romania. Also among the defendants was an A. Ştefanescu – quite possibly the Coates representative who had brought General Antonescu from his prison to meet Maniu and Brătianu in September 1940, and had later given Georgescu's illegal network some financial facilities. I did not get to know him until after the *coup*. He was condemned to life imprisonment.

Pătrăşcanu himself was accused, *inter alia* of nationalistic tendencies. When the ubiquitous George Tătărescu was introduced by the prosecutor Pătrăşcanu rose and shouted, 'Such scum of history are brought to this trial as witnesses against me, who am a Communist.' It proved, he said, the low level to which the Romanian Communist Party had sunk.[3] He was condemned to death and executed.

Anna Pauker, who replaced Tătărescu as Foreign Minister, was purged in 1952, and died a natural death at home eight years later.

Sandu Racotta returned to Romania after the *coup*. He left again before he could be arrested, and Shell – for whom he had worked in Romania – appointed him to Mexico. He died in the early Sixties. Matei Ghica also went to South America and he now lives in Caracas.

Gardyne de Chastelain was awarded the DSO. After the war he and Tozan – the Turkish buccaneer I had met in Istanbul – started an import-export company in London but in the commercial climate of the time could make no headway. Subsequently Chas worked in oil equipment enterprises in Canada and Australia. In 1967 he became adviser on oil, gas and minerals to the Bank of New South Wales. After his retirement at the age of sixty-five he and Marion returned to Canada, where he worked as private consultant in oil and related services until his death in 1974. His son, who was born at the nursing home next to our prison, is now Vice-Chief of Staff of the Canadian Armed Forces.

De Chastelain never quite got over a feeling that the people who had trusted him had been let down. Both he and Frank Wisner – the OSS representative – perhaps lacked that touch of ruthlessness which can be a great comfort in wartime. Frank, too, was deeply affected by his Romanian experience. In 1956 he was involved in another 'betrayal', the Hungarian uprising. Some years later, when already a senior member of the CIA, he shot himself in the woods behind his weekend house.

After serving with the British Mission in Bucharest, Silviu Meţianu returned to breeding poultry in Kent; he had a family of five.

Olympia Zamfirescu claims to have been completely apolitical and to have played no part in the Resistance. She was given eight months' solitary confinement for a crime which she never identified, then ten months' imprisonment followed by three years' internal exile for trying to sell a silver tray for a friend who needed the money for her sick husband. While banished to a village of mud huts not far from the Danube a new prisoner arrived who after a while trusted her sufficiently to tell her the following. Since it concerned Maniu, whose name was still a powerful force for freedom in Romania, he had not dared to reveal it to anyone before in case the authorities should hear of it and charge him with sedition.

> 'One night they moved me to another cell where I found a very old sick man. It was Juliu Maniu, or what remained of him. He was half paralysed and could no longer leave his bed. They had not tortured him but systematically let him die for lack of medical attention and under-nourishment. I nursed him. I cleaned him. I fed him till he closed his eyes. I expect you know that Maniu was a Uniat, and a very devout man.'
>
> I nodded.
>
> 'When he felt his death was approaching he told me: "When you are freed go to Rome and tell the Pope how deeply I regret that my political obligations prevented me from going to see him in Rome. Tell him also that I lived as a Uniat but that I want to die as a Roman Catholic."
>
> 'Then he said, "Absolution."
>
> 'I knocked on the wall of the adjoining cell. I had reason to believe that there was a Roman Catholic bishop there.
>
> 'Those of us who had spent months and sometimes years in prison had learnt to use morse fluently as a means of communication. The good bishop spelt out to me the Latin words of the prayers, the Pater Noster and the Ave Maria, and it was I, an atheist and a sinner, who gave the dictated last rites to this saintly man, and closed his eyes.'[4]

Notes

Many of the sources given in these notes are documents in the Public Record Office. Foreign Office papers are indicated by the prefix FO 371 or FO 800; the Prime Minister's papers by the prefix PREM 3 and Cabinet papers by the prefix CAB.

Documents on German Foreign Policy, *Documents on British Foreign Policy* and *Soviet Documents on Foreign Policy* are referred to as DGFP, DBFP and SDFP. *Akten zur Deutschen Auswärtigen Politik 1918–1945* are referred to as Akten. Some telegrams exchanged between the German Legation in Bucharest and Berlin about the Autonomous operation are published in *Memorii, Corespondenţă, Însemnari* (Revista de Istoria, Tom 35, No. 12, Bucureşti, 1982) which is referred to as *Memorii*.

Useful American, British, German and Romanian documents are to be found in *23 August 1944 – Documente*, two volumes, (Editura Ştiinţifică si Enciclopedică, Bucureşti, 1984), which is referred to as *Documente*.

I had no direct access to SOE papers but material provided by the SOE Adviser is shown as SOE Archives.

Sir Denis Wright's diary and the unpublished papers of Mircea Ionniţiu, King Michael's secretary, are referred to as D.W. and M.I.

Sources other than these are self-explanatory or refer to the bibliography.

Chapter 1

1 Frances Donaldson: *The British Council*, p. 60.

Chapter 2

1 Patrick Leigh Fermor: *Roumeli*, p. 217.
2 R.W.Seton-Watson: *A History of the Roumanians*, pp. 252–3.
3 Hannah Pakula: *The Last Romantic: A Biography of Queen Marie of Roumania*, p. 224.
4 R.W.Seton-Watson: *A History of the Roumanians*, p. 502.
5 Sacheverell Sitwell, *Roumanian Journey*, pp. 42–3.

Chapter 3

1 Olivia Manning: *Fortunes of War* Vol. 1, p. 565.
2 *Politics and Political Parties in Rumania* (London, 1936), p. 147.
3 Ghiţa Ionescu: *Communism in Rumania 1944–1962*, p. 26.
4 *Rumanian Communist Party: Lessons of its Youth*: George Schöpflin. BBC talk broadcast on 6 May 1971.
5 C.Z. Codreanu: *La Garde de Fer*, p. 210.
6 *Ibid* p. 282.
7 Hannah Pakula: *The Last Romantic*, p. 362.
8 *Ibid*, pp. 390–1.
9 Ghiţa Ionescu: *Communism in Rumania*, p. 50.
10 DGFP, Vol. D/V p. 209.
11 FO 371/22448 R716.
12 DGFP/D/V p. 249.
13 FO 371/22448 R716.
14 Hector Bolitho, *Roumania under King Carol*, p. 153.
15 *Ibid* p. 153.
16 DGFP/D/V p. 249.

Chapter 4

1 Maurice Pearton: *Oil and the Romanian State*, p. 219.
2 Norman Rich: *Hitler's War Aims*, Vol. II Note 59 on p. 482.
3 *Ibid*, Vol. I, p. 207.
4 DGFP/D/V p. 265.
5 *Ibid* p. 309.
6 *Ibid* p. 313.
7 FO 371/22445 R5380.
8 FO 371/22446 R8151.
9 FO 371/22446 R9168.
10 FO 371/22446 R9475.
11 DGFP/D/V p. 330.
12 DGFP/D/V p. 349.
13 DGFP/D/V pp. 354–5.
14 DBFP/3/V p. 315.
15 Maurice Pearton: *British Policy towards Romania (1939–1941)*, p. 530.
16 Richard Hoggart: *Speaking to Each Other* (London, 1970), p. 203.
17 DGFP/D/Vl p. 608.
18 DGFP/D/Vll p. 317.
19 Personal Notes.
20 *Ibid*.
21 Olivia Manning: *Fortunes of War*, pp. 78 et seq.

Chapter 5

1 DGFP/D/V p. 352.
2 Halifax papers (1938–1940) FO 800/322 Vol.14.
3 Maurice Pearton: *Oil and the Romanian State*, p. 249.
4 *Ibid* footnote 5 to p. 253.
5 D. W.
6 Maurice Pearton: *British Policy towards Romania (1939–1941)*, pp. 541–2.
7 DGFP/D/lX p. 165.
8 D.W.
9 Geoffrey Household: *Against the Wind*, p. 101.
10 DGFP/D/X p. 570.
11 D.W.
12 FO 371/24845 N6526.
13 This and other episodes involving John Davidson-Houston are taken from J.V. Davidson-Houston: *Armed Pilgrimage*.

Chapter 6

1 DGFP/D/Vlll p. 498.
2 DGFP/D/X pp. 33–34.
3 FO 371/29991 R 5638.
4 Personal papers.
5 DGFP/D/X p. 137.
6 *Ibid* p. 570.
7 Hoover Institution on War, Revolution and Peace. File R.B.Bossy roll l.
8 DGFP/D/X note to p. 566.
9 Hoover Institution on War, Revolution and Peace. File R.B.Bossy roll l.
10 DGFP/D/X p. 588.
11 FO 371/24984 R6897.
12 Clare Hollingworth: *There's a German Just Behind Me*, p. 62.
13 M.R.D. Foot: *SOE in France*. Chapter 1 deals with the origins of SOE.
14 Constantin Drăgan: *Antonescu*, Vol. I p. 75.
15 DGFP/D/Xl p. 22.
16 *Ibid* p. 63.
17 *Ibid* p. 870.

Chapter 7

1 DGFP/D/Xl pp. 136, 144, 279.
2 Personal papers.

3 DGFP/D/Xl p. 662.
4 Patrick Howarth: *Intelligence Chief Extraordinary*, p. 150.
5 SDFP Vol.lll. p. 470.
6 Paul Schmidt: *Hitler's Interpreter*, p. 214.
7 Winston S.Churchill: *The Second World War*, Vol. II, p. 518.
8 DGFP/D/Xl p. 1094.
9 Larry Watts: *In Serviciul Mareşalului*, Vol.I p. 31.
10 FO 371/29992 R80.
11 *Ibid.*
12 Personal papers.
13 Josif Drăgan: *Antonescu*, Vol. II p. 162
14 D.W.
15 *Ibid.*
16 FO 371/29992 R335/80/37.
17 Personal papers.
18 *Ibid.*
19 Larry Watts: *In Serviciul Mareşalului*, p. 58.
20 Personal papers.
21 *Ibid.*
22 *Ibid.*
23 Josif Drăgan:*Antonescu* Vol. II p. 161.
24 FO 371/29992 R614.
25 John Colville: *The Fringes of Power*, Vol. I p. 417.
26 Told by Olympia Zamfirescu.
27 DGFP/D/XI p. 1187.
28 DGFP/D/XII p. 171.
29 *Ibid* p. 230.
30 FO 371/29992 R943.

Chapter 8

1 FO 371/29977 R2612.
2 Told to author by Rica Georgescu.
3 DGFP/D/Xll p. 661.
4 FO 371/29991 R8466.
5 SOE Archives.

Chapter 9

1 SOE Archives.
2 FO 371/33257 R8293/G.
3 SOE Archives.
4 George Duca: *Cronica unui Român in Veacul XX*, Vol.III, Chapter XII.

5 Frederick Nanu: *The First Soviet Double Cross*, p. 238.
6 FO 371/37386 R9271.
7 FO 371/37386 R7346.
8 *Ibid* R9628.

Chapter 10

1 FO 371/32874 N108/86.
2 *Ibid* N109/86.
3 Isaac Deutscher: *Stalin*, p. 480.
4 R.W.Seton-Watson: *A History of the Roumanians*, p. 211.
5 FO 371/37031 N6684.
6 FO 800/302 Personal and Secret letter from Christopher Warner to J. Balfour of 25 January 1944.
7 Milovan Djilas: *Conversations with Stalin*, p. 106.
8 Liddell Hart: *History of the Second World War*, pp. 510–11.
9 Milovan Djilas: *Conversations with Stalin*, p. 105.
10 FO 371/33256 R213.
11 FO 371/29975 R4962/2/37.
12 PREM.3 399/6 PM to Eden. Minute of 16.1.44.
13 FO 371/37377 R9441.
14 FO 371/37377 R1039.
15 *Ibid*.
16 FO 371/33133 R216.
17 PREM 3 399/6 Eden minute to PM of 25.1.44.
18 George McJimsey: *Harry Hopkins*, p. 305.
19 CAB. 66/45 WP(44) 9 of 7 Jan. 1944.
20 FO 371/43993 R4028.
21 Josif Drăgan: *Antonescu* Vol. II p. 433.

Chapter 11

1 Much of the material used in the first part of this chapter was provided by Christopher Woods, SOE Adviser to the FCO.
2 *Documente*, Vol. I No. 456.

Chapter 15

1 CAB 65(41) pp. 42–3.
2 FO 371/43992 R3236.
3 *Memorii*, p. 1343.
4 Akten, No. 154. pp. 296–7. Von Killinger's tel. to Berlin of 31.X11.43.
5 *Memorii*, pp. 1341–2.

6 *Ibid* pp. 1342–6.
7 *Ibid* p. 1347.
8 Frederick Nanu: *The First Soviet Double Cross*, p. 243.

Chapter 16

1   FO 371/43992 R1696.
2   Personal Diary.
3   *Documente* Vol. II. No. 889. Report No. 1.
4   *Memorii*. p. 1347.
5   *Memorii*, p. 1340. Berlin tel. of 4 January to German Legation, Bucharest.
6   *Ibid* p. 1342. Bucharest tel. of 24 January to MFA Berlin.
7   *Ibid* p. 1349. German Security Service's tel. of 28 April to Berlin.
8   FO 371/44000 R8070.
9   FO 371/44002 R9433.
10 *Memorii*: p. 1349 Bucharest tel.No. 1689 of 15 Jan 1944.

Chapter 17

1   Josif Drăgan: *Antonescu*, Vol. II p. 434.
2   Alexander Cretzianu: The Lost Opportunity, pp. 115 et seq.
3   FO 371/43995. R 4965.
4   *Ibid*.
5   *Documente* Vol.II, No. 503.
6   FO 371/43999 R6642.
7   FO 371/43998 R5816.
8   FO 371/43995 R4794.
9   FO 371/43998 R5946.
10 FO 371/43998 R5947.
11 *Documente* Vol. 11, No. 889 Report No. III.
12 FO 371/43998 R6282.
13 FO 371/43999 R6646.
14 FO 371/43997 R5587.

Chapter 18

1   FO 371/43998 R5986.
2   FO 371/43998 R6150.
3   FO 371/43998 R5678.
4   FO 371/43998 R5666.
5   CAB 65(46) No. 8 WM(44)47th Conclusions of 11 April 1944, Minute 2.
6   FO 371/43998 R5946 and R5986.

7   *Documente* Vol.II, No 889. Report No. III.
8   Frederick Nanu: *The First Soviet Double Cross*, pp. 248–9.
9   FO 371/43999 R6514.
10 FO 371/43999 R6651.
11 FO 371/43999 R6487.
12 FO 371/43999 R6487.
13 FO 371/43999 R6819.
14 FO 371/43999 R6434.
15 FO 371/43993 R3912.
16 FO 371/43999 R6487.
17 FO 371/43999 R6436.
18 FO 371/43998 R5634.
19 FO 371/43999 R6878.

Chapter 19

1   *Documente* Vol. II No. 889 Report No. I.
2   John Colville: *The Fringes of Power*, Vol. I pp. 286–7.
3   FO 371/43999 R6882.
4   FO 371/43999 R4016.
5   FO 371/43999 R7215.
6   FO 371/43999 R7287.
7   FO 371/44000 R7556.
8   CAB 65/46 WM(44) 63rd Conclusions, Minute 1 of Confidential Annexe.
9   FO 371/44000 R7756.
10 FO 371/43999 R7829.
11 FO 371/44000 R8318.
12 FO 371/44000 R4338.
13 *Ibid*.
14 FO 371/44000. R7598.
15 FO 371/44000 R8070.
16 *Ibid*.
17 Winston Churchill: *The Second World War*, Vol. VI, pp. 63–4
18 *Ibid* p. 66.

Chapter 20

1   *Documente*. Vol. II No. 889 Report 111.
2   CAB 65(42) Conclusions for 27 April 44 p. 261.
3   FO 371/44000 R8341.
4   FO 371/44000 R7998.
5   FO 371/44000 R8396.
6   FO 371/44001 R8985.

Chapter 21

1 *Documente* Vol. II, No. 889 Report No. II.
2 Ghiţa Ionescu: *Communism in Rumania* 1944–1962, pp. 2–6.
3 *Documente* Vol.ll, Nos 484,494,496,544.
4 M.I.
5 *Ibid*
6 *Documente* Vol.II, No. 605.
7 FO 371/44002 R10114.
8 FO 371/44002 R10230.
9 Frederick Nanu: *The First Soviet Double Cross*, pp. 251–2.
10 FO 371/44003 R11015.
11 FO 371/44002 R9596.
12 M.I.
13 *Ibid*.
14 FO 371/44005 R12711.
15 FO 371/44005 R13108.

Chapter 22

1 John Erickson: *The Road to Berlin*, Vol. 2 p. 198.
2 In his interviews with Larry Watts and J.C.Drăgan, Colonel Magherescu gives us some interesting personal glimpses of the Marshal.
3 Josif Drăgan: *Antonescu*, Vol. I pp. 315 et seq.
4 Ion Gheorghe: *Rumäniens Weg zum Satellitenstaat*, p. 398.
5 For the meeting between Antonescu and Hitler we have three sources:
   a note dictated by Marshal Antonescu (Josif Drăgan: *Antonescu*,
   p. 321–332) a résumé by Paul Schmidt, Hitler's interpreter (Akten,
   Vol.VIII p. 307 *et seq*) and the more atmospheric account by Ion
   Gheorghe, the Romanian Minister in Berlin (*Rumäniens Weg zum
   Satellitenstaat*, pp. 391–401).
6 Josif Drăgan: *Antonescu*, Vol. I p. 322.
7 Ion Gheorghe: *Rumäniens Weg zum Satellitenstaat*, p. 398.
8 Josif Drăgan: *Antonescu*, Vol. I pp. 323–4.
9 Ion Gheorghe: *Rumäniens Weg zum Satellitenstaat*, pp. 400–1.
10 Akten vol.VIII. p. 307.
11 Ion Gheorghe: *Rumäniens Weg zum Satellitenstaat*, p. 401.
12 FO 371/44005 R12950.
13 Heinz Guderian: *Panzer Leader*, p. 365.
14 Ion Gheorghe: *Rumäniens Weg zum Satellitenstaat*, p. 403.
15 Heinz Guderian: *Panzer Leader*, p. 366.
16 Personal Diary
17 Josif Drăgan: *Antonescu*, Vol. I pp. 334–5

Chapter 23

1 This chapter draws freely from John Erickson (*The Road to Berlin*) for developments on the eastern front; from Josif Drăgan (*Antonescu*) for material on the Marshal and his entourage, and from Mircea Ionniţiu (*23 August 1944: Amintiri şi Reflecţiuni*) and other unpublished papers for the planning of the *coup* by King Michael and his collaborators.
2 FO 371/44005 R13197.
3 FO 371/44004 R12404.
4 Nicolette Franck: *La Roumanie dans L'Engrenage*, p. 24.
5 M.I.
6 *Ibid.*
7 Josif Drăgan: *Antonescu*, Vol. I p. 354 et seq.
8 *Documente*, Vol. II No. 889 Report No. II.
9 Josif Drăgan: *Antonescu*, Vol. I p. 435.
10 *Documente*, Vol. II No. 687.
11 John Erickson: *The Road to Berlin*, p. 360
12 Josif Drăgan: *Antonescu*, Vol. I p. 365.
13 *Documente*, No. 889, Report No. II.
14 Personal papers.
15 Josif Drăgan: *Antonescu*, Vol. I p. 489.
16 Nicolette Franck: *La Roumanie dans L'Engrenage*, pp. 33–34.
17 *Ibid* p. 36.

Chapter 24

1 Josif Drăgan: *Antonescu*, Vol. II p. 451.
2 M.I.
3 *Documente*, Vol. II, No. 670
4 M.I.
5 Nicolette Franck: *La Roumanie dans L'Engrenage*, p. 47.
6 *Documente*, Vol. II, No. 678.
7 *Ibid* No. 682.
8 Haralamb Zinca: *Şi a fost 'Ora H'*, p. 251.
9 *Documente*, No. 889 Report No. II.
10 M.I.

Chapter 25

1 *Documente*, Vol. II No. 696.
2 Frederick Nanu: *The First Soviet Double Cross*, pp. 354–5.
3 *Documente*, Vol. II No. 742.

Chapter 26

1 John Erickson: *The Road to Berlin*, p. 365
2 *Ibid* p. 365.
3 *Documente*, Vol. II No. 851.

Chapter 27

1 Ilie Ceaucescu et al.: *200 de Zile Mai Devreme*, pp. 132–3.
2 B.H. Liddell Hart: *History of the Second World War*, p. 613.
3 Ilie Ceaucescu: *200 de Zile Mai Devreme*, p. 165.
4 John Ehrman: *History of the Second World War*, Vol. V, p. 377.
5 *Ibid*. p. 383.
6 Ilie Ceaucescu: *200 de Zile Mai Devreme*, p. 57.
7 Winston S. Churchill: *The Second World War*. Vol. VI. p. 198.
8 FO 800/302 Meeting in Kremlin, 9 October 1944 at 10 p.m.
9 PREM 3 399/6 Eden to PM of 25 January 1944.
10 Personal papers.
11 *Ibid*.
12 PREM 3 374/13A M 1070/4 PM's Personal Minute to S.of S. 4 November 1944.
13 *Ibid*. M 1083/4 PM to S. of S. 7 November 1944
14 *Ibid*. M 1098/4 PM to S. of S. 10 November 1944.
15 *Ibid*. FO tel. to Bucharest No. 171 of 8 November 1944.
16 *Ibid*. M 1207/4 PM to S. of S. 11 December 1944.
17 *Ibid*. M 84/5 PM to S. of S. 18 January 1945.
18 *Ibid*. PM's minute of 2.12.44. on Bucharest tel. No. 247 of 1 December 1944.
19 FO 371/67233 R4150/46/37.
20 Victor Rothwell: *Britain and the Cold War, 1941–1947*, pp. 377–8.
21 Josif Drăgan: *Antonescu*, Vol. II opposite p. 449.
22 Nicolette Franck: *La Roumanie dans L'Engrenage*, pp. 232–5.
23 Winston Churchill: *The Second World War*, Vol. VI, pp. 368–9.

Epilogue

1 Ghiţa Ionescu: *Communism in Rumania, 1944–1962*, pp. 135–6.
2 Annie Samuelli: *The Wall Between*.
3 Ghiţa Ionescu: *Communism in Rumania, 1944–1962*, footnote to p. 156.
4 From the unpublished memoirs of O. Zamfirescu.

Select Bibliography

Arnold-Forster, Mark: *The World at War* (London, 1973).

Bacu, Nicolae: *Agonia României* (Munich, 1988).

Barker, Elisabeth: *Churchill and Eden at War* (London, 1978).

Barker, Elisabeth: *British Policy in South-East Europe in the Second World War* (London, 1976).

Bazna, Elyesa: *I was Cicero* (London, 1964).

Beamish, Tufton and Guy Hadley: *The Kremlin's Dilemma* (London, 1979).

Beza, George: *Mission de Guerre* (Paris, 1977).

Bolitho, Hector: *Roumania under King Carol* (London, 1939).

Ceaucescu, Ilie; Florin Constantiniu; Mihail Ionescu: *200 de Zile Mai Devreme* (Bucureşt, 1984).

Churchill, Winston S.: *The Second World War* (London, 1948–54).

Codreanu, C.Z.: *La Garde de Fer* (Paris, 1938).

Colville, John: *The Fringes of Power* (London, 1985).

Conte, Arthur: *Yalta* (Paris, 1964).

Crankshaw, Edward: *Putting Up With the Russians* (London, 1984).

Cretzianu, Alexander: *The Lost Opportunity* (London, 1957).

Davidson-Houston, J.V.: *Armed Pilgrimage* (London, 1949).

De Porte, A.W.: *Europe between the Super Powers* (Yale, 1979).

Deutscher, Isaac: *Stalin* (London, 1966).

Djilas, Milovan: *Conversations with Stalin* (London, 1962).

Donaldson, Frances: *The British Council* (London, 1984).

Drăgan, Josif: *Antonescu, Mărturii şi documente coordonate şi îngrijite de J.C. Drăgan* (Venice, Vol. I 1986, Vol. II 1988).

Duca, George: *Cronica unui Român in Veacul XX* (Munich, 1985).

Ehrman, John: *History of the Second World War*, Vol. V, *Grand Strategy* (London, 1956).

Erickson, John: *The Road to Berlin* (London, 1983).

Fees, Herbert: *Churchill, Roosevelt, Stalin* (Princeton, 1957).

Foot, M.R.D.: *SOE in France* (London, 1966).

Franck, Nicolette: *La Roumanie dans L'Engrenage* (Paris-Bruxelles, 1977).

Gheorghe, Ion: *Rumänienis Weg zum Satellitenstaat* (Heidelberg, 1952).
Ghyka, Matila: *A Documented Chronology of Roumanian History* (Oxford, 1941).
Hart, Liddell: *History of the Second World War* (London, 1970).
Henderson, Sir Nevile: *Failure of a Mission* (London, 1940).
Hollingworth, Clare: *There's a German Just Behind Me* (London, 1942).
Household, Geoffrey: *Against the Wind* (London, 1942).
Howarth, Patrick: *Intelligence Chief Extraordinary* (London, 1986).
Ionescu, Ghita: *Communism in Rumania 1944–1962* (Oxford, 1964).
Jelavich, Barbara: *History of the Balkans* (Cambridge, 1983).
Kimball, Warren F.: *Churchill and Roosevelt, The Complete Correspondence* (Princeton, 1984).
Laqueur, Walter: *Terrorism* (London, 1977).
Macleod, Iain: *Neville Chamberlain* (London, 1961).
Manning, Olivia: *Fortunes of War* (London, 1981).
McJimsey, George: *Harry Hopkins* (Harvard, 1987).
Musat, Mircea: *La Signification de la Révolution . . . d'Aout 1944* (Bucharest, 1979).
Nanu, Frederick: *The First Soviet Double Cross* (Journal of Central European Affairs No. 12, 1952).
Pakula, Hannah: *The Last Romantic: A Biography of Queen Marie of Roumania* (London, 1984).
Pantazi, Ion: *Am Trecut Prin Iad* (Munich, 1987).
Pearton, Maurice: *British Policy towards Romania (1939–1941)* (Iaşi, 1986).
Pearton, Maurice: *Oil and the Romanian State* (Oxford, 1971).
Quinlan, Paul D.: *Clash over Romania* (Los Angeles, 1977).
Rich, Norman: *Hitler's War Aims* (London, 1974).
Rothwell, Victor: *Britain and the Cold War* (London, 1982).
Samuelli, Annie: *The Wall Between* (London, 1967).
Schmidt, Paul: *Hitler's Interpreter* (New York, 1951).
Seton-Watson, Hugh: *The New Imperialism* (London, 1961).
Seton-Watson, Hugh: *The East European Revolution* (London, 1950).
Seton-Watson, Hugh: *Eastern Europe between the Wars* (Cambridge, 1945).
Seton-Watson, R.W.: *A History of the Roumanians* (Oxford, 1934).
Shirer, William: *Berlin Diary* (London, 1941).
Shirer, William: *The Rise and Fall of the Third Reich* (London, 1960).
Sitwell, Sacheverell: *Roumanian Journey* (London, 1938).
Smiley, David: *Albanian Assignment* (London, 1984).
Stavrianos, L.S.: *The Balkans since 1453* (New York, 1958).
Strang, William: *Home and Abroad* (London, 1956).
Sweet-Escott, Bickham: *Baker Street Irregulars* (London, 1964).

Tappe, Eric: *Documents Concerning Rumanian History (1487–1601)* (London, The Hague, Paris, 1964).
Trevor-Roper, H.R.: *Hitler's War Directives* (London, 1966).
Vassiltchikov, Marie: *The Berlin Diaries* (London, 1985).
Walker, David: *Death at my Heels* (London, 1942).
Watts, Larry: *In Serviciul Mareşalului* (Munich, 1985).
Zinca, Haralamb: *Şi a fost 'Ora H'* (Bucureşt, 1971).

Index